REACHING THE AGED

Social Services in Forty-Four Countries

SOCIAL SERVICE DELIVERY SYSTEMS

An International Annual

Series Editors

MORTON I. TEICHER

DANIEL THURSZ

JOSEPH L. VIGILANTE

SOCIAL SERVICE DELIVERY SYSTEMS
An International Annual
Volume 4

REACHING THE AGED

Social Services
in Forty-Four Countries

Editors
MORTON I. TEICHER,
DANIEL THURSZ,
and
JOSEPH L. VIGILANTE

 **SAGE Publications**   Beverly Hills/London

For information address:

SAGE Publications, Inc.
275 South Beverly Drive
Beverly Hills, California 90212

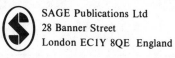

SAGE Publications Ltd
28 Banner Street
London EC1Y 8QE England

Printed in the United States of America

Library of Congress Cataloging in Publication Data
Main entry under title:

Reaching the aged.

   (Social service delivery systems ; v. 4)
   Includes bibliographies
   1. Aged—Services for—Addresses, essays, lectures.
2. Social work with the aged—Addresses, essays,
lectures. 3. Aged—Family relationships—Addresses,
essays, lectures. 4. Aged—Care and hygiene—Addresses,
essays, lectures. I. Teicher, Morton I. II. Thursz,
Daniel. III. Vigilante, Joseph L.
HV1451.R4   362.6   79-18525
ISBN 0-8039-1365-6
ISBN 0-8039-1366-4 pbk.

FIRST PRINTING

CONTENTS

Part III. AGING AND HEALTH

Part IV. COMPARATIVE PERSPECTIVES

PREFACE AND ACKNOWLEDGMENTS

This fourth volume of *Social Service Delivery Systems: An International Annual* welcomes a new editor, Dr. Morton I. Teicher, Dean of the School of Social Work at the University of North Carolina at Chapel Hill. Drs. Thursz and Vigilante wish to take this opportunity to acknowledge his help, which was most needed and satisfying.

Like the other volumes in this series, this one has enjoyed broad support. The editors are greatly indebted to the institutions with which they are primarily identified: Adelphi University, B'nai B'rith, and the University of North Carolina for providing the atmospheric, intellectual, and staff wherewithal to make parts of this volume possible.

In, or associated with, these institutions are many people without whose cooperation the work would not have been possible. At Adelphi University, Marc Arje, Joan Kleinerman, and Matthew Rosen, graduate assistants assigned to the dean's office, have made major contributions.

The editors would like to add a special note of appreciation to Marc Arje as the coordinator of the efforts among the graduate assistants and to specifically acknowledge him as a scholar.

The secretarial staff at the universities have been especially helpful. At Adelphi University, Angeline Kratunis and Marjorie Ryan and at North Carolina, Michelle Glover, secretaries to the deans, have been energetic and discreet in their work in recognizing the relative priorities of this project along with other university business.

The administrative coordination of the volume has been under the leadership and direction of Maria Elaine Georgiou, Administrative Assistant to the Dean of the School of Social Work at Adelphi. As usual, she made this book possible.

Finally, the editors wish to acknowledge the cooperation of the authors, many of whom we have reached over thousands of miles, for changes, modifications, adaptations. The effort has been cosmopolitan as well as international. We apologize to them if we have taken liberties about which they have question. And we, of course, assume all responsibility for errors in the text and the interpretation of the authors intent.

—M.I.T.
—D.T.
—J.L.V.

Adelphi University
Oak Street Campus
1979

INTRODUCTION

JOSEPH L. VIGILANTE

Perhaps because of Western society's emphasis on technological advance, a popular belief of the impact of an aging population upon the society has been that a social problem has resulted from great social advances, particularly in the technology of health care systems. Those who have worked as practitioners with the aged or as researchers of the aging process will recognize this ideation as a product of the coincidence of unprecedented data collection about the aged and growth of cybernetic processes during the past fifteen or twenty years, particularly in America. It is part of the concept that all new technological advances create their own problems which eventually lead to new solutions, a relatively optimistic view of the postindustrial society. However accurate that may be, it should be noted that this conception treats the aged and the aging process as a problem. We do not seem to be aware that for many aged people to be old is less a problem than they, or even the society, anticipated. As the reader will see in this volume, experiences from all parts of the globe suggest that many aged people are able to develop a dynamic, integrated, optimistic relationship to the social system. Indeed, their coping skills often appear to transcend those which they possessed during the dynamic middle years of career, family, and person building. Moreover, it seems apparent that the reality of an increasingly aged society has created, in many places, opportunities for new breakthroughs in social policy, not only for the aged but also for many other groups. The aged themselves have contributed.

Rapidly aging populations have varying impacts upon most modern nations, which emphasize the beauties and values of youth and, in some situations, actually denigrate the value of the aged. In the face of drastic technological change and ensuing changes in family patterns, those societies which for centuries have revered the aged have found it more difficult to deliver both the care and respect which tradition demands. Even for those countries which experienced this shocking phenomenon earlier, social structures for serving aged populations still are insufficient and unsatisfying for the aged themselves as well as for the majority of the population. The most advanced countries report disappointment in their means of dealing with aged populations. For developing countries, which traditionally have depended upon extended family models for providing services to all populations, particularly the aged, the shock of change is even more difficult today. Yet they unanimously recognize the inevitability of the need to provide social structures outside of the family for delivering this care.

In Tarek M. Shuman's "International Perspective," the first chapter of this volume, three or four significant factors in examining the aged from a demographic and international dimension are highlighted. First, the aging population will be increasing, worldwide, primarily because of technological factors in health care. Populations will be increasing more in underdeveloped countries because of the relatively rapid advancement of these countries and because of out-migration of youth. Nations have been and will be increasingly influenced by changing family patterns which permit less responsibility for the aged on the part of either the nuclear or extended family. And, fourth, the condition of the aging populations is receiving signal attention from most national governments throughout the world (and from the United Nations).

This volume brings to the reader a series of descriptive and analytic works regarding programs for the aging, including special program innovations identified by the editors. It has been built as a result of direct contact with authors in nine countries outside of the United States, who have written about problems and programs for the aging in approximately fourteen countries outside of the United States. In addition, eleven American writers have prepared analytic comparative work based upon their research in the United States and in twenty-six countries outside of the United States.

To facilitate the work of students and scholars, the volume has been divided into four parts. Part I, Chapters 2 through 4, offers innovations in organizing and delivering services for the aging. These include programs reported by the Community Service Society of New York, and Jeffrey R. Solomon and Fred D. Hirt's work, "Beyond Institutionalization: The Development of a Comprehensive Elderly Care System," describing the organization and development of an institutional care system in Miami, Florida.

Writers in three of the reporting countries, because of the nature of the family structure, have produced articles which deal especially with the relationship between family structure and problems of the aging. These chapters are from China, India, and Italy; they present one country in an early stage of economic and social development, another in a more advanced stage, and a third in an even more advanced stage. Together these make up Part II. The fact that Part II represents widely ranging and separate parts of the world is not without significance in light of Virginia Little's views about geography and differences in delivery systems discussed in Chapter 10 (Part IV).

The relationship between aging and health is mentioned in almost every article, but is highlighted in Part III. There, Chapter 8, by Gommers et al., provides an intensive comparison of aging and health in seven countries. Chapter 9 is principally devoted to health problems of the elderly and how they are dealt within Polish society.

Virginia Little's comparative perspective on aging in twenty-four different countries provides excellent background material for descriptions of aging programs and policies in six countries in Part IV. Some of the highlights of the chapters are the innovations which deal with the issues mentioned by Morton I. Teicher in his introductory comments preceding each section of the volume.

Little points out that assumptions seem to have been made that social changes (like urbanization and the increase in participation of women in the work force) tend to have a similar impact on all societies regardless of culture. Her point is well taken; namely, one cannot *assume* these results even where there has been significant social change. Although we have observed social impacts coincidental with social change at various levels of specific cultures, Little's work suggests the possibility that *geography* is an important variable in services to the aged, one in some ways even more important than national development or culture. For example, services to the aged in London, in certain local authorities, surpass services to the aged in rural England. In rural parts of the United States services to the aged may be surpassed by services in the major cities of less developed countries, like the Philippines. Little also shows that developed countries tend to view "traditional helping networks" with nostalgia. We have not been completely satisfied with the loss of the "caring quality" in the development of our highly institutionalized services. But she (using work in Western Samoa) cautions that the alternative of the extended family caring for its own members requires considerably more study. She does suggest a compromise between institutionally provided service and dependence on traditional helping networks, such as the extended family, which goes beyond service to the aged. She prefers a system of professional "backup" services to families which can carry fundamental self-help responsibilities. This point is also made by Henning Friis in his chapter on Denmark. Friis notes that well over half of the aged receive various kinds of assistance from their children and that the aged themselves assist their children to nearly the same extent. There is reason to expect that further expansion of the human services will diminish the extent of contact and assistance between children and parents. Aid from children will be more underpinned by the various professional services. This trend has become increasingly important as the work participation rate of women has grown, particularly in Denmark, during the past twenty years.

The use of natural helping systems is widely cited, partially for manpower reasons, partially because of the intrinsic advantages related to their proximity to service targets in the community. In the United States, the Community Service Society (CSS) of New York has developed an innovative program which it identifies as "a natural support program for services to the aged." As the title suggests, the program's purpose is to use natural helping systems in the community surrounding the aged to enhance the *caring process*. The project puts together a combination of family-centered casework services and group services to families linked to natural family and community support systems. Importantly, the CSS program is targeted at those individuals and groups caring for and concerned about their aging relatives, not at the aged themselves. Chapter 4 offers some suggestions about the use of the group as a medium for helping relatives of the aged.

Using the aged to help in the care of dependent children is becoming increasingly popular. In Yugoslavia (Chapter 10) there is a program for the placement of children deprived of parental care and children disturbed because of family conditions into institutions with the elderly. Chapter 11 also refers to the provision of social work services to aged with health care needs by the use of "village housekeeper services." The service utilizes local citizens as homemakers or housekeepers. This is a by-product of the organization of local community groups into clubs for the aged, day care centers, and the like.

The United States has not been without innovations in developing administrative models for home care. Little cites programs developed in Michigan and Minnesota and reported in *Social Casework* (1963) by Simpson and Farrow. She also refers to the Minneapolis Age and Opportunities Centers, Inc., which provides an innovative approach to the combination of volunteer service providers and professionals.

In their chapter, Solomon and Hirt provide a distinctive description of a decision which reflects the most advanced thinking about policy for the aged in the United States, namely, the use of institutions as a nucleus for community programs for the aged. Institutionalization and deinstitutionalization are emerging as highly sensitive problems. Institutions are increasingly offering a variety of services under central management, ranging from skilled nursing care and intermediate care (inpatient) to outpatient day care, home, health, homemaker service, and family counseling services. These policies have encountered considerable community resistance in many places.

The policy of differential benefits for the aged, based on race, which is put forth in the latter part of Chapter 15 on South Africa is perhaps the only place where the arguments on differential treatment of population groups based on race have been put into print for international consideration. The reader will find this piece of work to be particularly interesting, given the unprecedented social changes which are taking place in South Africa at this time and the focus of world opinion on this nation.

Drastic innovations in national policy are a response to changing needs, as reported by Yechiel Eran in "Innovations in Services for the Aged in Israel." Eran discusses the development of Eshel which is, for Israel, a new approach to the delivery of services for the aging. Early on, when aging was recognized as a growing problem for Israel, there developed a cooperative relationship between government and voluntary organizations. Out of this combination (voluntary agencies and government money) arose a new agency, Eshel, to develop demonstration and research projects. Under the jurisdiction of Eshel, a move toward decentralization of services resulted. The editors note that this is another example of a trend in decentralization of social service delivery systems, which has been reported in earlier volumes of this series. This change is particularly noteworthy since Israel is a small, compact country and has relied primarily on centralized services until now. Eshel operates as an "umbrella agency," plugging in a range of comprehensive services (including mobile services) where needed. The services are backed by large doses of community participation apparently striving for a nice balance between standardized national services projects tailored to meet local needs.

The Italian trend appears to be quite the opposite. In Chapter 6, Aurelia Florea notes that in Italy's Latium region, grants on a 75% matching basis are made to public agencies for services whereas grants on only a 50% matching basis are made for voluntary agencies.

An interesting innovation reported in Chapter 14, on Germany, is the use of public servants in assisting the elderly. Mailmen have been given an intensive two-day course at a geriatric center. Their chief function, in this respect, is to transmit the wishes and needs of older people along their route to the proper authorities. They can also report problems such as unemptied mailboxes or broken windows. They carry coupons for older clients permitting them to request nursing services or emergency food rations, counseling, or other public benefits. Louis Lowy, the author, also reports that in the city of Kassel there is a Senior Council of retired union members. More than 1,000 individuals participate in at least one major event each year, and 300 members meet twice a year in an "assembly" meeting. Thus, senior citizens have a strong opportunity to influence the union's decision-making process. One result of this has been the "seniorenrat." The seniorenrat has convinced the Kassel federation of trade unions that preretirement education is necessary for older workers. Continuing dialogue between older workers and retired persons is encouraged as part of preretirement education. Lowy reports on several methods that are used for educating workers for retirement. In Germany, self-help groups are involved in planning and monitoring services such as housing, continuing education, information and referral programs, and public transportation.

Perhaps the most persistent effort to resist community-institutional services for the aging is in the People's Republic of China, reported by Susan Kinoy in Chapter 5. In spite of major change in family life there, it appears that the revolutionary government, since 1949, has tried to maintain the responsibility of the family in caring for the aged. Although the extended family in China has undergone considerable change, family responsibility for the aged is mandated by law as well as supported through informal community structures. Kinoy's chapter clearly suggests that China's tenacious grip on the principles of agrarianism and the combination of socialism with agrarianism has permitted an approach to social services which relies greatly upon self-help principles and concepts at the community level. Whether or not this will continue now that the People's Republic is moving more directly into industrialism is a question raised by Kinoy's work.

Another interesting and innovative development is to be found in the area of housing for the aged. In several Asian countries, for example, government sponsorship of model homes for the aged, including a broad spectrum of services, provides opportunities for clinical internship for students in schools of social work to learn both direct services and policy in serving the aged. Further, in the United States, at Syracuse University in New York, there has been an effort undertaken to integrate aged persons with graduate students in university living facilities to encourage intergenerational interaction. These, of course, are a part of a series of activities which have been observed throughout the world representing an effort to avoid the isolation of an aged population.

There has been a development, in many places throughout the world, of classification of residential facilities for the aged under the supervision and general auspices of a variety of institutions like the Tokyo Metropolitan Institute of Gerontology or the Philadelphia Geriatric Institute. In both of these places, care for the aged is classified as hospital care, institutional care, or community living programs. At the Philadelphia Institute there is a specifically designed hospital and assessment unit supplemented by a separate building for supervised residents and a row of private homes, immediately across the street from the hospital, where older people live independently with the geriatric center providing services. Within these systems there is the expectation that an older person may move progressively from one level of care to another, depending upon need.

Experiments and innovations with respect to Health Care abound. In Western Samoa, for example, medical care is assumed primarily by the family and the use of home remedies is encouraged. There is, in each community, a women's committee which provides a back-up to home remedies with a supply of Western medications. Nearby is a district hospital which has a physician and some trained nurses for the seriously ill. When a person is admitted to the hospital as a patient, the family is used to provide a good deal of the care and personal attention. The family provides laundry, bedding, clothing, food preparation, companionship, and supervision. Not unusual is the emergence of postmedical services and paramedical services and post-hospital services for the aged. One example is the mobile unit for foot care in a city in New Jersey. This minimizes the need for travel. In some parts of Western Europe, an effort to counter the stereotype of aging as an inevitable decline in physical strength and mental capacity is being launched through a program of sports and physical exercise for the aged, including calisthenics, breathing exercises, and musical exercises. These activities are quite popular in both France and Denmark, and in these countries there are also newly developed programs of subsidized vacations for the aging.

In the area of work and income maintenance, various experiments and innovations with regard to flexible retirement programs depending upon cost of living changes and/or special needs of the aged have been reported. Little reports that in some developing countries such as Western Samoa, as well as in Israel, the provision of flexible retirement is being tested. In these countries, there have been experiments in reducing the work week to three days and then two days or to four days and then three days and then two days in preparation for retirement. This, connected with other efforts to prepare people for retirement, is accompanied in some situations by establishing sheltered workshops for aged people. The effort is to provide gradually diminishing work activities by shortening hours of work.

Of particular interest to the editors is the move in many countries in the world toward the organization of aged groups into a political force. This is highlighted in Chapter 12, Mikio Mori's chapter on Japan, as well as in references to programs in the United States and in Israel. Many writers have reported that as the aged become a political force they are able to influence government policy so that increasingly improved services appear to be a result. Indeed, the service delivery systems for the aged in many countries of the world seem to be directly dependent upon the political power, or potential political power, of aged citizens. Mori's analysis of the relationship between general social policy and policies for the aged is quite revealing. He refers, for example, to the Japanese housing policy which, because it favors younger families, has a long-range negative impact upon the aged. The cost of education as well as the cost of housing, analyzed within the context of the pension policies of Japan, makes it difficult for individuals and families to prepare for aging. His analysis of the educational standards in Japan (99% of the graduates from middle school enter high school and one-third of the graduates of high school go into the university) related to the cost of education suggests that the ability of the families to care for the aged is inhibited by the need to educate the younger population. "The younger generation frequently marry with heavy financial support from their parents. The adult in older middle age also has many financial expenses of his own. For example, there is a matter of a loan to pay for the construction of a home. With all of these financial responsibilities most people are unable to prepare adequately for later years." Mori provides the reader with an entrance into the tangled web of social policy demonstrating the mutually dependent systemic character of all social policies as they impact on a particular social group, in this case the aging in Japanese society. He also points out the efforts that are being made by the Japanese government to counteract some of these negative policy impacts. He cites subsidies for industry which postpone the retirement age or the establishment of special sections for the elderly in employment offices.

The editors would observe, in summary, that in all the countries reporting in this volume there is a clear and similar understanding with regard to the needs of the aged for health care of a specialized nature, for participation in community life, for social relationships with families, for involvement in the productive effort of the society, for special tax or income transfer benefits due to inability to work, and so forth. We believe that the similarity of programs and the similarity among innovations in various countries in the world where there has not been a great deal of direct communication is significant. We sense a similarity in values among the countries reporting in respect to the rights of the aged, as well as similarities among nations regarding an understanding of the needs of the aged not unlike those which we have reported in the three previous volumes. We also note that in many countries the information reported to us has come from legislation and administrative regulations. In some countries there is not much evidence of relationship between the intent of social policy and actual operations.

We observe, at the same time, a range of difference in the ability of countries to meet their own expectations for serving the aged. This often appears to be a result of bureaucratic difficulty. We think it is fair to say, with respect to serving the aging, that most countries seem to know what the goals should be but that many do not know how to achieve them. If this is the result of lack of experience with an aged population, it is clear that this particular limitation will not be for long.

1

AN INTERNATIONAL PERSPECTIVE

T A R E K   M.   S H U M A N

A recent United Nations' publication (1975a) suggested that in the twentieth century those of advanced age are increasing worldwide at a more rapid rate than are younger age groups. Although the changing aging structure of the population has been most pronounced for the more-developed regions of the world, with the sixty and over population increasing the most rapidly, it is in the less-developed regions of the world that such proportionate increases will be more pronounced in the immediate decades ahead. The less-developed regions of the world can anticipate a higher proportionate increase in their elderly population than can the more-developed regions. In addition, according to the United Nations (1975), the older age group will have the highest percentage increase of all main functional groups within the world's population between 1970 and 1980 and within both the more-developed and less-developed regions. Furthermore, the ratio of females to males is higher among those of advanced age, and, for the less-developed regions, particularly after 1985, there will be a slight increase of the proportion of females to males in the older age group.

United Nations' projections (1975a) indicate that in the developed areas of the world the population aged sixty years and over numbered nearly 154 million or 14.1% of the total population in 1970 and that this older population was projected to increase to 231 million or 15.9% of the total population by the year 2000. It is significant to note that for these regions the increase in the population as a whole will be 33% from 1970 to 2000, while those aged sixty years and over will increase by 50%. For the less-developed regions the proportionate increase of the older population is even more pronounced. In 1970, the population sixty years of age and over numbered 137 million or 5.4% of the total population. By the year 2000, this sector of the population is expected to increase to nearly 354 million or 7% of the total population. While a 98% increase is anticipated for the total population between 1970 and the year 2000, in these regions the increase of those sixty years and over will be approximately 158%.

As a result of the above-mentioned trends, many countries of the world are witnessing an "aging" of their population structures. In other words, the "aging of populations" process will increase the ratio of older adults to younger adults, a phenomenon that has never occurred to the human population before. In this respect it should be recognized that there is a distinct difference between the concepts of individual aging and the aging of human populations. While individual aging emphasizes the irreversible stages of the life span, the aging of human populations stresses the proportionate increase of older persons within a given society or the decline in fertility and birth rates. It should be noted, however, that although the birth rates may remain high, particularly in the developing countries, the control of infectious diseases will progressively postpone the age of death. This is one explanation why in these countries the proportions of the aged populations are low while their numbers are large and are increasing at a faster rate than is the population as a whole.

For the more-developed countries of the world which have experienced a decline in birth rate, the proportion and numbers of the older population have increased steadily over the past decades. It is in these highly industrialized societies that great attention has been given to social policies and practices with regard to the aging.

Furthermore, over the past century, an increase in life expectancy at birth has occurred. In the developed countries this has averaged about seventy years in the 1970s, while it reached only fifty in the less-developed countries during the same period of time. It should be noted here that the expectation of life at birth is higher for females than for males, particularly in the more-developed countries.

The trends in the aging of the world's populations and the changing age structures of the total populations are further impacted by two additional factors which have a bearing on aging throughout the world. These are the rapid urbanization which is occurring worldwide with increasing movement of people from rural to urban areas and the international migration or the "out-migration" of the young.

The consequences of these phenomena are multiple not only to the aging themselves but to society as a whole. They constitute a significant factor in economic, political, cultural, and social systems. Because of modernization and high living standards, norms, mores, and attitudes change, and, consequently, the organism, the personality, and the role of individuals within society change during their lifetime. Such changes have important implications for governmental policies and programmes, particularly for older people. Aging itself, as a life-span process, has begun to raise fundamental questions in regard to existing and needed social policies and practices in all regions of the world, developed and developing.

The issues and needs of the aging resulting from these changes, particularly from the demographic area, and the consequent role and responsibility of the society in meeting these needs require special consideration by governments of both developed and developing countries. The status and conditions of the aging, however, differ from country to country and tend to be influenced by many institutional factors. Among these are the binding kinship ties and extended family patterns. In the developing countries, ample evidence exists indicating the high esteem in which older people are held.[1] Many households still contain three or four generations which share a common life. Kinship is the most important integrative bond and, although property may be owned by the family as a whole, real economic power and degree of control over opportunities for the young often reside in the older head of the family. However, because of the increasing trends of industrialization and urbanization, the traditional concept of the place and relationship of the elderly in the family is undergoing major change.

THE AGED AND THE FAMILY

The family in the more-developed countries of the world is changing and moving from the three-generation family into a one-generation family. This phenomenon, coupled with the extension of the family in space through increasing migration within countries and between countries, has placed a strain on traditional integrational roles and responsibilities of family life, particularly in regard to older family members.

Although recent studies, particularly in developed countries, indicate continued interaction and contacts of adult children with elderly parents, there is little knowledge yet available about the strength of ties between them. In the developing countries of the world, although it appears to be a continuing view that the family takes care of its elder members, studies are needed to establish how and under what conditions younger children care for older family members. It may be a myth that traditional responsibilities are carried out in the present world of rapid technological and social change, thus, making it necessary and important to assess the impact of the aging population on traditional social institutions of society, with particular attention to the aging of the individual within the context of the family and its extension into four and five generations.

With the attempt to understand the changing age structures of societies and the increased numbers and proportions of older persons within a framework of knowledge about human and societal aging, governments are beginning to develop policies and programmes relating to the aging of their populations. There is increasing recognition of their role and responsibilities; consequently, there is the beginning of organized attention to services needed to assist older persons in their adjustment to major life changes associated with growing old.[2] Until very recently there was little recognition of the untapped reservoir of skill, talent, and knowledge in older persons or of the need to develop opportunities to permit older persons to retain and utilize such capacities and potentials. Now, however, in the developed countries, for example, there is increasing emphasis on specialized services, both for the individual and for groups of older persons. In some of these countries services are provided in a positive approach in assisting the aging to adjust to new roles and to the development of meaningful use of time which may not necessarily be related to economic productivity.

HEALTH NEEDS

A major area of concern to the elderly is related to their health needs. Increased longevity has resulted in making these needs one of the most serious problems for them. Most governments are providing health and medical care services to older people under a variety of plans, such as services for the chronically ill, long-term facilities, nursing homes, homes for the aged, and so on, including supportive programmes to older individuals confronted with death and dying through terminal illness or extreme infirmity. In some developing countries there is a beginning emphasis on the use of special institutions to care for the aged based upon the models of the more-developed countries.

One of the major impacts of aging on traditional health and medical services is the shift in morbidity patterns among aging populations. New approaches to understanding the health needs of this sector of the population are required. As long as the aging are viewed as sick, infirm, and incapacitated, rational planning for a programme of health care is impossible. Because of the perpetuation of these myths, there has been a severe lag in providing innovative and preventive health services. Some governments, however, in planning or providing health services to the aging, are emphasizing the following:

(1) sustaining the aged's independence and comfort in their own home and, when independence begins to wane, supporting the aging by all necessary means for as long as possible;

(2) offering alternative residential accommodations to those who, by reason of age, infirmity, lack of proper home, or other circumstances, are in need of care and attention; and

(3) providing hospital accommodations for those who, by reason of physical or mental ill health, are in need of skilled medical or nursing attention.

Governments seem to be recognizing that health programmes for the aging must, of necessity, be integrated, coordinated, and based on teamwork of all those disciplines concerned, with the purpose of achieving a comprehensive range of services that combines medical, public health, and social services.

NUTRITION

Nutrition is another important factor which affects health in later years. Poor nutrition usually affects mental and physical vigor, adds to the hazards of disease, and retards convalescence. Conversely, there is evidence that proper nutrition helps prevent illness. Some countries are taking concrete measures to assure that the aging are provided with the means to secure appropriate food and diet.

HOUSING

Another important area receiving increased attention by governments is the provision of adequate housing for the aging. Recent research has emphasized that housing is more than mere shelter. It has psychological, emotional, and social significance in addition to meeting physical needs. Suitable housing is even more important, however, to the retired or economically inactive elderly, whose homes are the centre of virtually all of their activities.

Substantial progress in providing services in the area of housing, however, is lacking in every region of the world. According to a recent United Nations' global housing survey (1975b), most developing countries showed a pattern in which overall housing conditions have been progressively deteriorating. Another United Nations' study (1977) analyzed the housing situation of the aging in slums and squatter settlements. This study noted that inflation affects the housing sector more adversely than most other sectors of the economy. The prevailing worldwide inflation has particularly hurt the housing market and the aging, who are often living on fixed or low incomes and are finding it harder than ever to purchase new or improved housing. Thus, although safe structural features and affordable housing could determine whether the aging live in insitutions or independently, their relatively poor physical and economic condition handicaps their acquisition of improved housing.

NEEDED SERVICES AND PLANNING

Evidence indicates that in establishing housing programmes and services for the aging, every effort should be made to ensure that housing be available for the aging and that this housing facilitate access to family, peers, and neighbours as well as to supporting health and social services, thus promoting the social integration of the aging in the community and society as a whole. Also, the establishment of a broad range of congregate and shelter care programmes is required. These may include: day care programmes for older persons; specialized housing and residences for older persons designed to support their social, psychological, and physiological functional capacities; substitute family care where older persons may reside in the households of unrelated individuals who would be reimbursed by and under the supervision of a community agency, either voluntary or governmental; temporary inpatient emergency shelter to enable older persons to have shelter, care, and protection at times of crises and yet assure their return to their previous living arrangements. It is impossible to define adequately the full range of possible facilities or services in this area of care of the aging. However, it is imperative to recognize the need for planning a wide range of alternatives in housing and living arrangements in concert with social, health, and recreational services in order that they may respond to the unique requirements of aging individuals.

Studies, (e.g., Butler and Lewis, 1973: 29) have revealed that loneliness, desolation, and isolation characterize the social lives of many of the aging, particularly in developed countries. Perhaps the most characteristic aspect of aging is that of loss, and the losses may occur simultaneously—loss of a marital partner, loss of elderly friends, colleagues, relatives; loss of status, prestige, and participation in society.

Yet, little organized attention has been given by any of the disciplines or professions with regard to the programmes and services needed to assist older persons in their adjustment to major life changes and the losses associated with growing old. Further, until very recently, there was little recognition of the untapped reservoir of skill, talent, and knowledge in older persons or of the need to develop opportunities to permit the older person to retain and utilize such capacities and potentials.

OLD-AGE PENSION SYSTEMS

The increasing economic vulnerability of older persons, especially through the erosion of their work roles, has resulted in the emergence of national old-age pension systems.

A United States Office of Health, Education, and Welfare study made in 1978 states that the majority of the countries of the world have created, by statute, some type of social security programme. By 1977, 114 of these countries had some type of old age, invalid, and survivor benefit programme.

All social security programmes are established by public statute. They usually provide for some form of cash payment to individuals to replace at least part of the loss of income caused by a long-term or a short-term risk, such as retirement from the labour force. Social security programmes may provide medical services to individuals or they may be concerned with the financing of such services, in addition to making cash payments.

Other income security programmes may include one or more of the following: social insurance, social assistance, public service programmes, publicly-operated provident funds, and special pension funds. In addition, some governments have developed innovative policy approaches to income security and retirement plans and included such measures as "time credits," periodic withdrawals from the labour force with pay, the reduction of hours of work, and the extension of vacation periods, particularly as one approached retirement.

With increasing industrialization and urbanization and the increasing numbers of wage earners, retirement is beginning to be perceived as worldwide in scope. For those who, through retirement, lose their work roles and for those whose children leave the household, the meaning and use of time becomes a new issue. There is need for recreational and leisure activities. Current recreational programmes include a variety of activities to meet the different needs of the aging. Some activities provide pleasurable experiences and self-renewal for the individual. Others, more therapeutic in nature, are concerned with the physical and mental restoration of the individual.

National and local policies and programmes are being developed to address the special recreational and leisure time needs of the aging.[3] Emphasis is being given, particularly in the developing world, to strengthening the traditional approaches to leisure through such activities as clubs, coffee houses, and informal family associations.

In the area of education for older people, there is growing recognition that all persons, regardless of age, should be guaranteed the right to education. Presently, however, most national education policies are geared towards the young, and are not designed for the life span. Consequently, many of the aging find that their skills are outmoded and/or obsolete, and thus better-paying jobs and opportunities are going to the young. Some countries, however, are including continuing education and adult education for those citizens in their middle and later years. Also, information on aging is being included in the basic curriculum for the young.

The United Nations Department for International Economic and Social Affairs as well as the more specialized agencies of the United Nations are much involved in services to the aged. These organizations provide for countries throughout the world information exchange, technical assistance to governments in developing policies and programs for the aging, the conducting of seminars, workshops, and specialized studies, and promotional activities. For example, the United Nations has published research studies on trends and policies in the field of the aging and on the conditions and needs of the elderly in slums and uncontrolled settlements. Currently, research is being conducted on the situation of the aging in rural areas and the special needs of older women. A United Nations Interregional Seminar on Aging was held in Kiev, USSR, in May 1979. With reference to information exchange, the United Nations issues semiannually a *Bulletin on Aging,* which summarizes the latest developments in this field.

The International Labour Organization (ILO) has long been concerned with aged workers, their retirement, social security, and pension schemes. The Food and Agriculture Organization (FAO) of the United Nations has been investigating conditions of the aged in rural areas. The World Health Organization (WHO) has devoted attention to various problems of the aged and has been concerned with geriatrics and the provision of health and social services for this sector of the population.

The general Assembly of the United Nations will convene a World Assembly on the Elderly in 1982. In conjunction with this meeting the United Nations systemwide activities will be instituted before and during the 1981-1982 calendar year.

NOTES

1. This information is based on unpublished United Nations' countries studies.
2. This has been reflected in the debates in the United National General Assembly.
3. This information is based on unpublished United Nations' countries studies.

REFERENCES

BUTLER, R. M. and M. I. LEWIS (1973) Aging and Mental Health: A Positive Psycho-social Approach. St. Louis: C. V. Mosby.

United Nations (1977) The Aging in Slums and Uncontrolled Settlements. United Nations Sales Publication Number E 77. IV. 2. New York: UN.

United Nations (1975a) The Aging: Trends and Policies. United Nations Sales Publication Number E. 75. IV. 3. New York: UN.

United Nations (1975b) World Housing Survey 1974. United Nations Sales Publications Number E. 75. IV. 8. New York: UN.

Part I

INNOVATIONS

INTRODUCTION

The new phenomenon with respect to aging persons is their universal increase in numbers. This change has not yet been matched by large-scale development of new programs of services to aging persons. Creative approaches to meeting the needs of the aging are urgently required.

One seedbed for innovation is recognition of need. The aphorism "necessity is the mother of invention" applies to the social as well as to the technological field. The Israeli situation reflects this understanding in that the new approach to meeting the needs of aging persons had to await acknowledgment by Israelis that the situation of the aging in Israel was indeed a social problem. Once this recognition took root, a new approach was devised. It is well described in the chapter by Yechiel Eran. The approach focused on creating a new partnership between government and the voluntary sector with the specific charge of bringing about changes in the way services to the aging are provided.

Decentralization of responsibility for serving the aging to local communities was for Israel a departure from previous practices. Insistence on board participation by a variety of local organizations was seen as a way of insuring the development of services which are appropriate to locally perceived needs. Similar insistence on cooperation among the various ministries concerned with the aging also represented a new approach to comprehensive planning.

Whether or not the Israeli innovation is applicable elsewhere must be determined by each country with its unique culture and set of social provisions.

Another effort to respond innovatively to the growing number of aging persons and to their growing needs is described by Jeffrey R. Solomon and Fred D. Hirt. Their approach is based on the concept that a continuum of care is required if the needs of the aging are to be addressed comprehensively. Institutions become vital parts of that continuum if they relate themselves to the community's entire support system. Through the rationalization of such a system, consideration can be given to the specific needs of a particular aging person and choices can be made from a variety of alternatives. Expanding the range of choices is an essential ingredient of a comprehensive system. When the choices are restricted, the individual has to fit the system rather than the preferable arrangement which adapts the system to the individual. In order to give reality to the concept of a care continuum, Solomon and Hirt argue effectively that the institution can be the "spine" for community support services such as an outpatient mental health center, a senior adult day center, community-based medical services, meals on wheels, a drug program, congregate housing, and some health services.

It is clear that a progressive institution can be imaginative in breaking down the wall of separation between it and the community. Solomon and Hirt describe well how this can be achieved.

The section on innovations concludes with a chapter by Iris Ellen Hudis and associates which focusses on strengthening the family as a natural support system for aging persons in the community. Their approach is based on recognition of the fact that the bulk of services for aging persons is provided not by the formal health and welfare system but by the family. In providing this care, the family is usually on its own. To counter this situation, the "Natural Supports Project" perceives the family rather than the aging person as the client. The family needs occasional respite as well as supportive counseling. Such assistance enhances the family's capacity to serve as caretakers. It recognizes the reliance on the family by most aging persons. By strengthening the family's ability to fulfill its role, the project helps to maintain the most crucial support system utilized by aging persons. Thus, family care, the most widely used method of caring for aging persons, becomes part of the community's support system and extends the range of available choices.

—M.I.T.

2

INNOVATIONS IN SERVICES
FOR THE AGED IN ISRAEL

YECHIEL ERAN

The network of social welfare services of a given society expresses that society's commitment and responsibility to the welfare of its members. This commitment is expressed in different forms by various societies, in accordance with the societal values, life style, concept of social reality, nature of needs, and ideal image. Each society thus maintains its welfare services in accordance with the above.

Israel is often considered a welfare state with a highly developed network of welfare services. The network of services for the aged, however, is only partially developed. Recent studies (e.g., Doron, 1976) have shown that it is lacking many important components, including a proper legal base, as well as being fragmented and scattered among many organizations. This discrepancy between different components of the social services system was bound to create tension in the system. As this tension increased to a degree that the system was unable to contain, modification of the system became necessary and, thus, we see several developments taking place in the seventies in regard to the services for the aged in Israel.

In order to understand these developments, one must examine the history of the social welfare system in Israel and the place of the aged as a client group in the framework of this system.

Most of the social welfare services in Israel, as in the majority of western countries, were originally initiated and developed by voluntary organizations. Many of these services were later turned over to government authorities or became heavily supported by them (Rouff, 1957; Kramer, 1973). Voluntary organizations traditionally serve as pioneers in identifying areas of need. They also conduct demonstration programs and gradually involve governmental authorities in the programs both conceptually and financially to various degrees. In a situation of scarce resources, politically based priorities, and bureaucratic inflexibility, voluntary organizations serve as one of the most important vehicles for social innovation and improvement.

The social welfare infrastructure in Israel was built by voluntary organizations before the establishment of the state in 1948. The special circumstances of the Jewish society in Israel, the Yishuv, before the establishment of the state, had a major impact on this development.

In its early stages, the young pioneering society of the Yishuv had no use for social welfare. Proclaiming the return to the soil and the sanctity of physical labour, it did not sympathize with nonproductive sections of the population. The General Federation of Labour, however, built up a network of social and medical insurance. Later on, several social services were established, mainly by the Jewish Agency and other voluntary organizations such as immigrant associations and Landsmanschafts. In 1949, AJCD (American Joint Distribution Committee), a Jewish philanthropic body, established Malton, a major voluntary agency to help in the absorption and care of new immigrants.

Within this infrastructure of social welfare services, there were few services for the aged. The Jewish society, before the establishment of the state and during the first two decades of its existence, was a "young society." The immigrant settlers were mainly young people who left their family, home, and tradition in order to materialize the Zionist vision of a new, improved society. Their central themes were: the desire for rebirth, renewal of national youth, creation, productivity, and future orientation. It is not surprising that in such a society the aged were a marginal section, both quantitatively (about 4% of the population) and qualitatively.

Even as the relative growth of the aged population increased with the waves of mass immigration to the country (in the years 1949-1965), the role of the aged in society did not change significantly. They were considered a marginal immigrant group, and as a result, a special network of services was developed for them. These services were carried out by voluntary organizations and not by the state.

RECENT CHANGES IN THE AGED POPULATION

In recent years, several phenomena have occurred which brought significant changes in this area:

(a) The aged population has been growing constantly. In 1976, they constituted about 9% of the total population. This growth may be attributed to several factors: the low birthrate of the Jewish population, longer life span, and high percentage of aged immigrants.

(b) The composition of the aged population has been changing as well. About two-thirds of the aged population are foreign-born who came to Israel in their later years. They were never fully integrated economically, socially, and politically; and they had a low socioeconomic status in the society. Recently, more and more cohorts of veterans have joined the aged population.

(c) Several studies conducted in the late sixties (Cohen, 1974; Lach, Techniczek, and Man, 1974; Weil, Natan, and Avner 1974) revealed the poor and distressing living conditions of the aged population in Israel.

These together with the development of gerontology as a professional area of activity in Israel has made Israeli society more aware of its aging population and its problems on the one hand and of the inadequacy of societal measures to cope with those issues and problems on the other hand. This situation has created an uneasiness, strain in Israeli society along with a strong social desire for changing and improving services for the aged.

A RESPONSE TO NEED

As Neugarten (1968) has noted, the issue of aging is a social problem in modern society not just because of the large numbers and their suffering but mainly because of the problems occurring in society because it is not prepared for the "sudden" appearance of large numbers of aged people.

Merton and Nisbet (1971) define a social problem as a situation in which there is a significant discrepancy between social standards and social reality. This discrepancy became visible in Israel in the late sixties.

The recognition of the situation of the aged in Israel as a social problem was a breakthrough in societal attitudes toward this issue. However, Israeli society found itself unprepared conceptually and organizationally to cope with the new challenge.

The government established several committees which looked into the conditions and the problems of the aged and presented recommendations for tasks to be done to improve the situation of the aged. The government was hesitant to carry out these recommendations since they called for major legal changes and a vast investment of scarce resources. Being reluctant to take over full responsibility for the welfare of the aged, the government sought a mechanism that would enable it to move ahead in this area at a gradual and not overly demanding rate, making possible experimentation and demonstration of several possible approaches of service delivery.

History may have its own rules and dynamics, but it is often shaped and molded by what Barry (1958) calls special events. The historical development of services for the aged in Israel was undoubtedly shaped significantly by the events that were taking place in one of the major voluntary organizations in Israel, JDC-Malben.

Founded by the United Jewish Appeal of the United States of America, JDC-Malben was involved both in direct and indirect services to immigrants who, because of illness, physical handicaps, or age, had difficulties in being absorbed into the new country. In the middle sixties, this organization went through a process of change, deciding to cease its direct services in order to make room for new ventures. JDC-Malben proposed to the government to hand over its direct services for the aged (mainly homes for the aged) and to create a joint organization that would provide the necessary "impetus" for the neglected area of services for the aged in the country. This proposal appeared very attractive to the government since it complied with their strategy of tackling the issue of service development for the aged.

After a period of negotiation, the government and JDC-Malben agreed in 1969 to create a new voluntary organization which would be supported on a matching basis. It was called Eshel: The Association for the Planning and Development of Services for the Aged in Israel.

ESHEL: A NEW MODEL OF
VOLUNTARY ORGANIZATION IN ISRAEL

It has been noted (Levin and White, 1960; Reid, 1964) that many necessary efforts of coordination and cooperative arrangement among agencies fail if the agencies do not have shared goals, possess complementary resources, and decide on efficient mechanisms for controlling the exchange among them. As it happened, both the government and JDC-Malben had before them the aims of improving the services for the aged in the country, and had complementary professional and financial resources. In order to facilitate the process of exchange between them, it was necessary to devise proper organizational structure that would efficiently serve their aims and interests.

Both parties wanted to join forces but, at the same time, to retain their independence. They decided to create a new joint organization—Eshel—built on a consensual basis. Eshel is governed by a voluntary board of directors, half high-ranking members of JDC-Malben and half governmental ministries (Health, Finance, and Welfare). The board is responsible for giving direction to, determining policy for, and making major decisions for Eshel. A small professional staff specializing in planning and development of services was recruited to work for Eshel, and they were assisted by a professional committee, again staffed voluntarily by professional members of JDC-Malben and the government.

Because of the complicated tasks and of the expected difficulties inherent in the ambitious endeavor to induce changes in the existing system, it was decided from the beginning that Eshel would not start its operation by formulating new policies and introducing major changes in the service delivery system. Eshel would initiate piecemeal demonstration projects; and based on their effectiveness, policies would be formulated and new modes of operation would be introduced.

Eshel has decided to focus its activities on three areas:

(a) Planning and developing institutional services (such as homes for the aged) in the areas where there is a shortage of beds, and incorporating geriatric wards in general hospitals, which were almost nonexistent in Israel at the time.

(b) Planning and developing demonstration projects of comprehensive community services in order to improve living conditions and enable the aged to continue to live and function in their family and community as long as possible.

(c) Planning and developing training programs to prepare professional manpower to staff the above-mentioned services.

Projects were chosen according to several criteria:

(a) Governmental priorities
(b) Diversity of types of communities (small, large, veteran, new, and so on).
(c) Commitment of the community to continue with the project beyond the initial stage of demonstration.

On the basis of its general policy and goals, Eshel made itself available to various organizations and communities to render its help in planning, developing, and participating in financing new services for the aged on the condition that these organizations and communities would continue to support and develop these services after the termination of Eshel's assistance. In this way, Eshel achieved two aims; first, creating innovative services, thus changing and enriching the services system; and, second, guaranteeing that these innovations would continue beyond the demonstration period and become integrated into the existing services system. Thus, JDC-Malben made sure that it would continue to play the role of pioneer and innovative agent and the government made sure that only those innovations that can be integrated into the system, both conceptually and financially, would take place. Since every project has to be approved by government representatives, government support was assured for its development and continuation.

Eshel also decided that the programs would have to be planned by members of the communities and organizations which would later run these programs. The assumption was that the local community would have a better knowledge of local needs and of the services that could best respond to these needs (Eran, 1971). Furthermore, the effectiveness of service programs depends, in part, on local motivation, mobilization of resources, and backing of the programs. For this purpose, the responsibility for implementing the programs was embodied in local associations for the aged made up of both professionals and lay people. Being aware of the limited capacity of many communities and organizations to carry out the planning, developing, and running of the services, Eshel made available to them various resources in the way of experts and planning aids. Eshel's small staff extended its help to the local interdisciplinary planning teams in preparing the proposals and to the local associations in running the programs. Thus, it was assured that the programs would be along the general guidelines of Eshel and, at the same time, suited to the specific needs, circumstances, and resources of each community.

The handing over of the responsibility for the planning of service to the local communities and the involvement of lay people in the process were quite new phenomena on the Israeli scene. Many of the communities were reluctant to accept this responsibility; thus a long and demanding process of reorientation, guidance, and assistance by the Eshel staff was required. The planning process took approximately ten months, during which time information about the aged population and their needs was compiled, the existing network of services was examined, goals and priorities were determined, alternatives were evaluated, and a proposal was formulated.

After approval of a proposal by Eshel's services committee, a local association, made up of lay people, professionals, and representatives of the aged of the community was created in order to give its auspices to the implementation of the project. Efforts were made to make the association as representative as possible of various sectors of the local community in order to promote the involvement of the community in caring for its aged and to ensure a wide local backing for the project. Eshel signed contracts with the local associations defining mutual rights and obligations. The local associations negotiated with various local service organizations for their facilities and professional manpower, keeping to themselves the functions of coordination and supervision.

The endowment of the local association with the responsibility of implementing the services program was again a new phenomenon. In a highly centralized country such as Israel, this required a shift in the power structure and the relationships between lay people and aged on the local and national levels and also between the local community and central authorities. This shift did not always go smoothly, and it required careful coaching and sometimes even manipulation by Eshel's staff. The control over the project budget provided the local association with the necessary motivation and authority needed to exercise its functions.

It may be assumed, even though not yet systematically investigated, that those communities which had the Eshel experience in the process of planning services for the aged and running these services via an umbrella organization, involving many sectors of the community, will be more competent in marshaling their local planning and executive resources when called upon to plan and carry out service programs in other areas.

POLICY PRINCIPLES OF ESHEL

On the basis of Eshel's service operations, several principles have emerged which were translated by the board of directors into formal policy.

(1) *Every project supported by Eshel should ensure a coordination and concentration of efforts and resources of all major organizations caring for the aged in the local community.* This is achieved in several fashions. All the organizations dealing with the aged are encouraged to become members in the local Association for the Aged which determines policy, initiates and implements programs, and determines the budget. This facilitates a pooling of all the local resources of the various organizations, financing, facilities, and manpower for use in a more effective and efficient way. Various existing services are integrated, or at least coordinated, and new services are developed with a client-centered rather than organization-centered orientation. For example, in every program, an interdisciplinary team is established to do the screening, to check up, to prepare the treatment plan, and to refer the aged to the proper services. This team is made up of employees of different agencies. The physician belongs to the Sick Fund, the public health nurse to the Ministry of Health, and the social worker to the Public Welfare Department.

(2) *The local community should be involved and play an active and responsible role in the planning and implementation of welfare services for its members.*

This is done through the establishment of local interdisciplinary and organizational planning teams, which are responsible for preparing the program proposal, and through the establishment of the local Association for the Aged, which gives auspices to the program. The associations are made up of lay people, specialists, representatives of the organizations, and representatives of the client-system, the aged. The associations are independent entities involved in initiating services, coordinating programs, recruiting and allocating resources, and in taking social action on behalf of the aged.

(3) *Every project is unique in itself, and though the guiding philosophy is general, the combination of the various components of the project and its*

delivery system is determined according to the specific conditions of each community. This takes into consideration the specific features of the local aged population and its needs and makes the best use of existing local services and facilities. This principle is less relevant to institutional services which are more uniform in nature. The homes for the aged planned by Eshel are usually regional and small, consisting of 100 to 150 beds. They include three categories: the physically well aged, the infirmed aged, and those aged needing nursing care. This enables patients to move from section to section as their needs dictate without removing them from their environment, and it permits continued mingling with other persons in other sections. The home also provides day care to the aged residing in the vicinity.

The geriatric wards are established within existing general hospitals making use of the specialized and sophisticated facilities and the skilled personnel of the hospital, and are designed for diagnosis, treatment, and rehabilitation. They, too, include a day hospital for the aged needing less intensive care.

The community services are comprehensive, trying to provide a variety of services to meet the special needs of the aged. They usually include such components as: preventive and curative health care, nutrition, laundry, employment, homemaking, home care, day care, basic household equipment, friendly visiting, social and cultural activities, and transportation. The way in which these services are organized and delivered may differ from one community to another according to the needs and local conditions. In places where the aged are a poor and deprived group, priority is placed on providing employment, household equipment, nutrition, and so on. In places where the aged are more well-to-do, more emphasis is put on planning social and cultural activities and finding new roles for the aged in the community. Efforts are made to concentrate the services in strategic locations easily accessible to the aged. Day care centers are established in various available facilities such as clubs, community centers, and homes for the aged. The various agencies outstation their workers in the centers so that the aged can receive a variety of services in one location. The public health nurse, the social worker, the occupational therapist, the counselor, all belonging to different organizations, come on a regular basis to the centers to provide their services.

For people with mobility handicaps, special transportation is arranged to enable them to use the centers, medical clinic, and other services. For those who are home-bound, services are extended to their homes.

In rural areas a special mobile unit has been created which enables the various professional workers to reach the villages on a regular basis once or twice a week. In some communities mobile repair units have been established for home repairs (plumbing, electricity, household equipment, and so on). An effort is made to recruit volunteers to assist with care of the aged through local volunteer agencies with an emphasis on involving the young both in fulfilling various tasks and in sharing social activities with the aged.

(4) *The key factor in promoting the development of the project is qualified skilled personnel.* For this purpose a condition was made by Eshel that each project have a project coordinator to guarantee proper professional supervision. Eshel is concerned both with the basic training of professional manpower and with conducting in-service training for people in the field. Eshel prepares, with the aid of specialists, courses, programs, and teaching aids to be incorporated into the curriculum of professional schools for social workers, physicians, nurses, occupational therapists, and physiotherapists. Eshel also provides scholarships for people who train for a career in gerontology.

For workers in the field, Eshel has designed several in-service training programs which are carried out either by Eshel staff or by various training institutions. These programs are designed as workshops to increase knowledge and improve skills. In some projects a special local training program is designed to promote interdisciplinary and interorganizational team work in order to facilitate the implementation of the programs along the concepts which underlie them.

ESHEL: PRESENT AND FUTURE

Eshel's mode of operation, specifically the principle that all decisions should be made on a consensus basis, has slowed its decision-making process, and has not allowed the materialization of all new ideas and innovations proposed. The fact that Eshel staff has to work through the existing network of welfare service bureaucracies without having any direct control does not always allow the desired pace for development of the projects.

The establishment of Eshel was accompanied by many doubts about its capacity and its chances of success. The novelty of its structure and mode of operation created many feelings of uncertainty. Everything was done to ensure that Eshel would be a temporary mechanism that would have to be tested carefully. The staff was hired on a short-term basis, no equipment was purchased, and plans were made for five years of operation. The first year was dedicated to thinking through and exploring avenues of operation. It was only in its second year that Eshel began to move gradually into actual planning and development of projects.

During the first five-year plan, Eshel assisted in the planning of the development of ten comprehensive community services programs, four homes for the aged, three geriatric wards in general hospitals, and five manpower training programs. As most of these programs began to materialize in the third and fourth years, it became clear that the five-year period would not suffice; so the board of directors of Eshel decided upon a second five-year plan. The second five-year plan would, in addition to continuing the program which had started late in the first five-year plan, encompass many other new programs.

In the second five-year plan, Eshel is assisting in the planning and development of seventeen new, comprehensive community service programs, ten special community services, six new homes for the aged, two geriatric wards in general hospitals, and a variety of training programs. Eshel has also decided to enter even newer areas: sheltered housing and research.

While the priority for the bulk of Eshel's resources is for developing basic needed services for the aged, an effort is constantly made to experiment with new kinds of services. Among these are: training of personnel managers in big organizations to conduct preretirement education for their employees; developing day care programs within existing homes for the aged for the benefit of the aged residing in the surrounding neighborhoods; preparing audio-visual aids to be used both by professionals and by the aged themselves; establishing sheltered and semi-sheltered housing for the aged based both on adapting existing apartments to the needs of the aged—through renovation, installment of daily living units, and providing proper maintenance—and building specially designed houses with auxiliary services such as homemaking, meals, and laundry.

These programs are now in various stages of development. The programs modeled on the types developed in the first five-year plan are proceeding at a rapid pace, whereas the new programs are still in the process of exploration. Careful thought is now being given to conducting evaluation research to provide Eshel with the necessary systematic and reliable feedback on its operations.

After eight years of operation, the many doubts that had accompanied the creation of Eshel have given way to the recognition of Eshel as one of the leading organizations in the area of services for the aged in Israel.

CONCLUSIONS

Eshel has provided probably the first forum for thinking about and planning services for the aged in Israel on the national level. Eshel guidelines were accepted by all the governmental ministries as a blueprint not only for Eshel operations but for the operations of each ministry as well. The government has also asked Eshel to serve as a clearing house for various private and public service programs for the aged requesting government support, and has handed over to Eshel the responsibility to plan and develop many projects not intended originally to be included in Eshel programs.

Most Eshel programs called for a new type of collaboration among the ministries which extended beyond the scope of Eshel programs. Some of Eshel's innovations, such as creating comprehensive programs, establishing local associations, introducing the role of project coordinators, were adopted by the ministries and local authorities and were applied in more and more communities. Eshel also prepared various planning and training aids in the way of manuals which were made available to many communities and organizations.

Today, Eshel is flooded by more requests than it can handle for professional and financial assistance from various communities and organizations, and serious thought is being given by Eshel's founders to looking into ways of broadening Eshel's activities.

It is clear that the mere fact that Eshel brought together three governmental ministries within a voluntary organization had an impact beyond the scope of Eshel operations. Local patriotism and vested interests, though never given up completely, tended to give way to a more comprehensive nonpartisan outlook and brought about new thinking about the responsibilities of the various ministries in regard to the needs of the aged and in regard to one another.

There is no doubt that Eshel has gone a long way in a relatively short time, far beyond the expectations of its founding fathers. The innovations that it has introduced in the area of services for the aged in Israel are there to stay. Moreover, Eshel's effect goes even further than that inasmuch as a similar national voluntary organization has been created for developing services for the retarded.

When looking into the factors that played a crucial role in the success of this kind of venture, one can conclude that a unique combination of demographic and organizational circumstances, combined with careful thinking and planning and skillful monitoring and handling, has proved again the rule that when luck joins forces with determination and skilled hard work, even the most far out vision can turn into reality.

REFERENCES

BARRY, M. (1958) Community Organization in Social Work Education for Better Services to the Aging. New York: Council on Social Work Education.

BERNARD, J. (1975) Social Problems at Mid-Century. New York: Dryden.

COHEN, S. (1974) New Immigrant Recipients of Old-Age Benefits. Survey No. 12. Jerusalem: National Insurance Institute.

DORON, A. (1976) Community Care of the Aged. Jerusalem: Department of Research, Planning and Training, State of Israel, Ministry of Social Welfare.

ERAN, Y. (1971) "Planning local welfare programs." Community Development Journal 8, 2.

――― and G. FRIEDHEIM (1976) Services for Older New Immigrants in Israel. Jerusalem: Brookdale Institute for Gerontology and Adult Human Development.

KRAMER, R. M. (1973) "Future of the voluntary Service Organization." Social Work 18, 6.

LACH, S. Y., D. TECHNICZEK, and B. MAN (1974) The Absorption Problems of Older Immigrants in Regard to Israeli Society: A Comparative Study of North American and East European Immigrants. Jerusalem: Henrietta Azeld Institute.

LEVIN, S., P. WHITE, and B. PAUL (1966) "Community interorganizational problems in providing medical care and social services," in R. L. Warren (ed.) Perspective on the American Community. Chicago: Rand McNally.

MERTON, R. K. and R. A. NISBET [eds.] (1971) Contemporary Social Problems. New York: Harcourt Brace Jovanovich.

NEUGARTEN, B. (1968) "The aged in American society," in H. S. Becker (ed.) Social Problems: A Modern Approach. New York: John Wiley.

REID, W. (1964) "Interagency coordination in delinquency prevention and control." Social Service Review 38, 4.

ROUFF, M. (1957) Voluntary Societies and Social Policy. London: Routledge and Kegan Paul.

WEIL, H., T. NATAN, and U. AVNER (1974) Investigation of the Family Life, Living Conditions and Needs of the Non-Institutionalized Urban Jewish Aged 65 in Israel. Jerusalem: Ministry of Social Welfare.

3

BEYOND INSTITUTIONALIZATION
The Development of a
Comprehensive Elderly Care System

JEFFREY R. SOLOMON
and FRED D. HIRT

A series of hurdles looms in the way of achieving gerontological service plans during the 1970s. The obstacles stem from the "too-little, too-late" syndrome present in all areas of service provision to our elderly population. The continuing growth of the geriatric community, both numerically and in proportion to the population at large, has outdistanced the adequacy of systems available to care for the agglomerate needs of the elderly. This developing gap grows wider daily, quite apart from the consistently neglected adequacy of services ranging from income maintenance to social services, from health care to transportation.

The authors of this chapter intend to define here one approach to helping the community identify, plan, and propose solutions in its attempt to meet the ongoing and accumulating needs of our elderly. It is one in which the long term care facility seeks to break down the walls that exist between it and the community it serves, one based on a recognition of the comprehensiveness of the elderly's needs. Progressive homes are making advances in the quality of care being delivered to institutional residents. Yet, in addition to these continued advances in the institutional environment, the authors believe that the institution could serve as a nucleus for community programs. They fully concur with the position statement of the National Association for Jewish Homes for the Aged (1974) stating:

> NAJHA affirms the conviction that older people have the inherent right to alternatives, choices appropriate to their style and functional capacities; therefore, there is an obligation to assure provision of quality solutions. These rights and needs should give impetus to the fullest

43

exploration and expansion of services and the development of new systems of delivery, staffing and financing. Jewish Homes should become the "CENTER" from which services for the aged emanate. A home must become a geriatric agency rather than an institutional service.

Marie Callendar (1973), former Department of Health, Education and Welfare Director of Long Term Care, says:

We see . . . an inevitable trend toward a long term care system which will offer a range of services under one central management, ranging from skilled nursing care and intermediate care on an inpatient basis to outpatient day care and home health and homemaker services without moving the patient from one overall management of care to another.

THE ELDERLY IN THE UNITED STATES

It is a common mistake to think of the elderly as a homogeneous group. Development and growth continue through the later years of life in spite of the changes in social, psychological, and physiological functioning which typically accompany aging. Aging adults have a variety of needs and levels of need; clearly, any effective program must address the uniqueness of the individual (Garrison and Howe, 1976; Kalish, 1977; Senate Standing Committee on Health and Rehabilitation Services, 1976).

Health is the most strongly related variable to subjective well-being (Larson, 1978). As a group, the elderly are more likely than younger people to suffer from multiple, chronic, often permanent conditions that may be disabling. Despite that, the majority are living active lives and are able to remain in their own households. However, persons over 65 are hospitalized at a rate greater than two and a half times that for younger persons. Further, the average length of stay for the over-65 patient is almost twice as long as that for younger persons (U.S. Department of HEW, 1977). In a recent study of the utilization of hospital inpatient services, Polliak and Shavitt (1977) indicated that the number of admission days was 1,717 days/1,000 persons 65 and over as compared with 570 days/1,000 persons under 65 years. They concluded that "about ¼ of all the hospital admissions might have been avoided by strengthening domicilliary and social services. It is . . . apparent that ambulatory, medical, nursing and social services will have to be expanded and coordinated so as to meet these needs and decrease hospitalization." It should be further noted that the prevalence of chronic diseases and impairments and the utilization of medical services which increase with age increase more rapidly beginning at about age 75 (Kimmel, 1974; U.S. Department of HEW, 1977).

Short-term disability is an important factor in assessing health. For the noninstitutionalized elderly, the average number of days of restricted activity for the elderly person in 1975 was 38, of which 13 were spent in bed. Approximately two-thirds of these days of restricted activity were accounted for by chronic conditions and one-third by acute illness or injury (U.S. Department of HEW, 1977). Persons who experience isolation and loneliness are documented as being at high risk for mental illness (Dade-Monroe Mental Health Board, 1976; Mental Health Program Office, 1977). For the elderly in general and for Miami Beach specifically, where over 47% of the population lives alone, this is an essential concern. It is not surprising that mental health problems and levels of dysfunction are indicated, in part, by high suicide rates for older adults. One-fourth of all suicides in the United States are committed by persons over 65. The highest rate in the nation is exhibited by males in their 80s (U.S. Senate, 1976).

This is demonstrated in Miami Beach, where the suicide rate for persons over 65 is 47.3/100,000 in contrast to the national average of 11.5/100,000 and the Florida statistic of 17.2/100,000. Yet, the elderly receive only a small proportion of all mental health services, e.g., less than 2.3% of outpatient care. This is due to a combination of the following factors: physical and/or emotional inability to avail themselves of services; inability to pay; too few services; inaccessible services, and prejudice of therapists (U.S. Senate, 1976).

For the elderly poor, living on a relatively fixed income creates problems which are of a more serious magnitude than for other age groups. Their purchasing power in terms of price inflation is drastically limited and greatly affected by the increased incidence of major health problems, increased cost of rent and food, and other unplanned expenses. Further, these fixed incomes place elderly citizens at a serious disadvantage in competing for the available goods and services needed for a dignified human existence (Senate Standing Committee on Health and Rehabilitation Services, 1976).

A number of studies (Garrison, 1976; Senate Standing Committee, 1976; Areawide Agency on Aging, 1977) cite transportation as a major concern for persons over 65. For many it determines whether the community is a useless facade or a dynamic social system. It is clear that services in the community can be useful only to the extent to which transportation is workable. Affordability, convenience, and accessibility are indicated as the principal problems.

Lack of leisure, recreational socialization activities, abuse by family, friends, or caretakers, and lack of alternatives for care are further documented as problems for persons over 65.

The disadvantages and tragedies of premature and inappropriate institutionalization have been extensively explored in the literature. Decreased quality of life as it relates to personal dignity, liberty, contentment, morale, cognitive stimulation, family and friendship relationships, society's lost productivity, and cost are cited as effects of overreliance on long-term care facilities (Kalish, 1977; Larson, 1978; Senate Standing Committee, 1976).

COMMUNITY-BASED PROGRAMS

The history of Jewish Homes' involvement with the community goes back many years. In the 1950s, a geriatric day care center was provided on the Miami Jewish Home and Hospital site. Other day centers which were developed early in the day care movement and based from a long-term care facility were the Handmaker Center, Tuscon, Arizona, in 1967, and the Levindale Hebrew Geriatric Center and Hospital, Baltimore, Maryland, in 1970 (Rathbone-McCuan and Elliot, 1976).

Formerly, quality homes provided a specialized geriatric counseling service to the general community through their social service departments. These and other concepts are now being revitalized in the 1970s as a part of the objective of designing alternatives to institutionalization.

Nevertheless, community-based services for the aging adult are both fragmented and duplicated. The system is aggravated by inconsistent eligibility criteria and significant service gaps. These factors combine to hinder provision of a continuum of care, and they handicap the system's ability to coordinate services into a rational, effective, and efficient system. Combined with the lack of uniform assessment criteria, these problems have led to the excessive and inappropriate use of institutionalization as the treatment of choice (State of Florida Office of Aging and Adult Services, 1978).

Recent publications serve to delineate the benefits of community-based care. Reichel (1978) suggests that "geriatricians aware of the harmful aspects of transplantation know that the vigorous opposition of patients and families to such transfers are rooted in reality. . . . Apart from patient and family wishes, there are good reasons for believing that a familiar environment such as the home, has significant advantages." The 1976 Florida Legislative Study on the Elderly (Senate Standing Committee, 1976) maintains that the advantages of community-based services include decreased length of stay in medical and rehabilitative institutions, significantly improved quality of life, and lower costs.

It must be noted that although the benefits of community based care are recognized, it is not currently an available alternative for the aging adult. As of July 1975, 30,000 aged Floridians were institutionalized in long-term care facilities. It is estimated (Senate Standing Committee, 1976) that 30% to 75% do not require this extensive and costly service but would be able to be maintained independently if alternative services were available. These estimates were corroborated in a 1977 Study on Long-Term Care Placement in New Jersey, which claimed that 35% of those currently institutionalized at an intermediate level of care could be discharged if appropriate levels of care were available in the community. Further, Kraus (1976) reported a study of 193 applicants to a long-term care facility wherein community-based care was determined to be the most suitable alternative for 34% of the applicants.

Experience in community-based care and home care programs extends to the program begun by Montefiore Hospital of New York in 1947. The program, emphasizing the long-term care of the chronically ill, paralleled the team approach in the hospital. The experience clearly indicated that home-bound patients with moderate incapacity due to terminal illness can be rewardingly cared for in the home, given appropriate circumstances such as the presence of a caring relative. Reichel (1978) suggests that many patients sick and incapacitated to the same degree as those in skilled nursing facilities, nursing homes, and chronic hospitals can be cared for in the home.

A recent modification of this concept has been developed in Norristown, Pennsylvania, where a geriatric psychiatric mobile team has been able to provide immediate, flexible intervention at the older person's place of residence. A significant decrease in admissions to the state mental hospital and increased utilization of family members for support was reported by Sherr et al. (1976).

It must be recognized that maintaining the individual in the community requires an integrated continuum of health and social services which focus on prevention and intervention.

Solomon (1974) states:

> The obvious concentration of planning efforts must be for the 95% of the elderly population that does not require institutionalization. These persons must be able to receive services aimed at assuring their personal self-fulfillment. . . . Opportunities for personal counselling must be available. One often forgets the severity of personal and family problems faced by the elderly. Grief from numerous losses of spouse, siblings and children often tends to facilitate degenerating processes. Often these emotional factors begin a final downward whirlpool in which the physical and psychological synergistically interact toward severe pathology.

THE SPINE PLAN FOR
SERVICES FOR THE ELDERLY

The critical theme which provides the "spine" for all gerontological planning and services is that in serving the community, the home can use its own resources in concert with other public and voluntary resources to develop an effective and efficient management of all services. Essentially, the departments of a well-managed institution can be readily adapted for community services without additional management overlay, which too often results in excessive cost for the same service.

For example, in developing a home health service, the nursing department of a home provides the obvious base from which to grow. A food service department can serve both meals on wheels and day care programs. The housekeeping and maintenance departments can assume key responsibilities in all of the community alternatives. The social service department of the home should reach out to the community to make its expertise available to persons in need. It is imperative that the institution be built to a level of strength which exceeds the demands placed upon it by its residential population. Once this has been accomplished, through the recruitment of competent personnel in all substantive areas, then the institution may face outward and offer the community a package of services which is both program-effective and cost-efficient.

In the spectrum of services required by the elderly, one can observe acute and chronic care hospitalization, long-term care and special residential programs, specialized day care, services in the home, recreational programs and other extramural programs. Utilizing the model developed at the Miami Jewish Home and Hospital for the Aged, one can track the development of these community programs from the institutional base. The important theme to maintain is the "spine" concept presented above.

An outpatient mental health center was opened in 1974 on the Miami Jewish Home and Hospital for the Aged site. As the first gerontological mental health center sponsored by a long-term care institution, this one has already proved its value to the community (Glasscote et al., 1977). Serving persons from ages 50 through 94, with the median age at 67.2, the program is designed to meet the mental health needs of the many area residents who have no place to turn or anyone to turn to. These patients, with a median income of under $4,000 a year, receive psychiatric and psychological evaluation, individual and group therapy, medications, occupational therapy, and other necessary services in a dignified and respectful manner, both at a Home-based main office and a satellite office located in South Miami Beach, a high density, poor, elderly neighborhood. The range of diagnoses in evidence at this program is quite varied. The five most common are: depressive disorders, organic brain syndrome, schizophrenia, personality disorders, and anxiety neuroses. A significant number of persons seen have alcohol problems. Medical evaluation also is uncovering a large number of serious geriatric drug misuse situations (Solomon, 1978). Here, the Home's administration, medical staff, supervisory social service staff, and education staff have been able to expand their purview to this program. It should be noted that this outpatient mental health program led to a planning grant in community mental health which, in turn, led to an approved comprehensive community mental health center. This exemplifies a ripple effect in the reaching out to the community from an institutional framework.

A second alternative is a senior adult day center. Through several funding sources, the Home provides the administrative and technical management for two such meaningful programs. As health-related day care centers, these programs offer some 275 elderly persons a dynamic diversion from a lonely existence. Most of the participants are able to maintain themselves in the community, living with their families or alone, but requiring day care. Of the first 25 participants, 14 came directly from nursing home waiting lists. Had they been admitted to those nursing homes, these 14 alone would have cost the community $100,800.00, a cost that is in excess of the total cost of this first alternative program. Here again, institutional departments, including administration, social service, nursing, food service, maintenance and house-keeping, are intimately integrated into the program.

Another area of reaching out into the community is through the provision of medical services. Specialized geriatric health services, delivered by a team of clinicians including physicians, geriatric nurse practitioners, laboratory and ancillary personnel, are most difficult to come by in many communities. A nursing home, through the cooperation of its medical staff, is able to offer community-based elderly the same kind of fine medical care it provides to the institutional residents.

Meals on wheels represents another expansion of the nucleus into the community. Through the combined efforts of cooperating agencies' food service and transportation departments, the Home is able to utilize its resources in the delivery of a critical service which, by itself, often makes the difference in maintaining persons in their own apartments rather than in a more expensive institutional facility.

Other programs which have been developed in Miami and which utilize the Home as a nucleus include an indigent drug program which opens the pharmacy to impoverished community residents, a senior citizen's update program which uses the mass media (radio and television) to keep the elderly informed as to issues of concern to them, and a geriatric clinical evaluator project which tends to objectify a multifunctional assessment of the elderly in the community. Other programs which are logical extensions currently in the planning stages at the Miami facility include a congregate housing project for dependent elderly based on a campus model which utilizes all aspects of the institutional program, and a home health service which utilizes medical and paramedical personnel in the delivery of health care services in an elderly

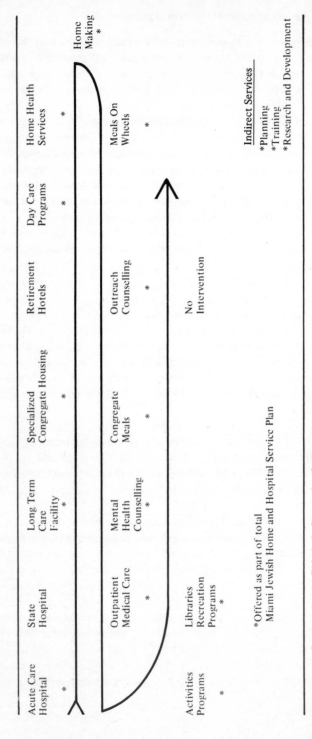

Figure 3.1: Services for the Elderly in Decreasing Order of Importance

person's home. Indirect services, including training and research, are important outgrowths ancillary to this system of service delivery. Figure 3.1 specifies an entire service system in greater detail.

CONCLUSION

It is our contention that as the eleemosynary institutional nucleus expands, the potential for the institution to serve as a catalyst and service provider in the community geometrically expands with it. It is our goal to help fulfill the demands placed in Recommendation XII of the Section on Planning of the 1971 White House Conference on Aging (1972):

> In the final analysis, planning in behalf of aging stems from the basic values of society. Those values are translated into goals, objectives and priorities. As planning for aging proceeds, it will be necessary to address these values on priorities. This should be accomplished through a re-ordering of priorities at all levels to increase the commitment of national resources to meet human needs.

REFERENCES

Areawide Agency on Aging and the Metropolitan Dade County Department of Human Resources (1977) The State of the Elderly, Dade County, Florida.

CALLENDAR, M. (1973) "The future of long term care." HEW-AMA Region X Seminar, March, Seattle. (mimeo)

Dade-Monroe Mental Health Board (1976) A Mental Health Plan for Dade County, Florida, 1976.

GARRISON, J. E. and J. HOWE (1976) "Community intervention with the elderly: a social network approach." Journal of the American Geriatrics Society 24: 329-333.

GLASSCOTE, R., J. E. GUDEMAN, and D. MILES (1977) Creative Mental Health Services for the Elderly. Washington, DC: Joint Information Service of the American Psychiatric Association and the Mental Health Association.

KALISH, R. A. (1977) The Later Years, Social Implications of Gerontology. Belmont, CA: Wadsworth.

KIMMEL, D. C. (1974) Adulthood and Aging. New York: John Wiley.

KRAUS, A. S., R. A. SPASOFF, E. J. BEATTIE, E. W. HOLDEN, J. S. LAWSON, M. RODENBURG, and G. M. WOODCOCK (1976) "Elderly applicants to long-term care institutions. II: The application process; placement and care needs." Journal of the American Geriatrics Society 24: 117-125.

LARSON, R. (1978) "Thirty years of research on the subjective well-being of older Americans." Journal of Gerontology 33: 109-125.

Mental Health Program Office (1977) State Mental Health Plan 1977. Tallahassee, FL: Senate Standing Committee on Health and Rehabilitative Services.

National Association of Jewish Homes for the Aged (1974) "Position Statement." Dallas: NAJH. (mimeo)

POLLIAK, M. R. and N. SHAVITT (1977) "Utilization of hospital in-patient services by the elderly." Journal of the American Geriatrics Society 25: 364-367.

RATHBONE-McCUAN, E. and M. W. ELLIOT (1976) "Geriatric day care in theory and practice." Social Work in Health Care 2 (Winter).

REICHEL, W. [ed.] (1978) Clinical Aspects of Aging. Baltimore: Williams and Wilkins.

Senate Standing Committee on Health and Rehabilitation Services (1976) The Elderly in Florida: A Legislative Study (April).

SHERR, V. T., O. C. ESKRIDGE, and S. LEWIS (1976) "A mobile, mental-hospital-based team for geropsychiatric service in the community. Journal of the American Geriatrics Society 24: 362-365.

SOLOMON, J. R. (1978) "The chemical time bomb: drug misuse in the elderly." Contemporary Drug Problems 6: 231-243.

——— (1974) "Considerations in planning services for the elderly." Journal of Jewish Communal Services 11, 1: 90-94.

State of Florida (1978) Community Care for the Elderly. Concept Paper. Tallahassee, FL: Office of Aging and Adult Services. (mimeo)

——— (1976) Florida Vital Statistics. Tallahassee: Department of Health, Education and Welfare.

U.S. Department of Health, Education and Welfare (1977) PHS National Center for Health Statistics HRS 77-1232. Elderly People: The Population 65 Years and Over. Washington, DC: Government Printing Office.

U.S. Senate (1976) Joint Hearing Before the Subcommittee on Long-Term Care and the Subcommittee on Aging, First Session. Mental Health and the Elderly. Washington, DC: Government Printing Office.

White House Conference on Aging (1972) Toward a National Policy on Aging: Final Report. Vol. 2. Washington, DC: Government Printing Office.

4

STRENGTHENING NATURAL SUPPORTS
A Group Program for Families of the Aging

IRIS ELLEN HUDIS
ANNA H. ZIMMER
JANET S. SAINER
CELESTINE FULCHON

In an effort to develop new strategies and services that would support the elderly in the community, the Community Service Society of New York[1] initiated the Natural Supports Program in October 1976. Its objectives are to explore the nature and extent of care provided to the elderly by their "natural supports" and to determine what services might be designed to recognize, enhance, and prolong this care. The program utilizes two different service modalities, one is family-centered casework to individual care-giving families, providing services and benefits to strengthen the supportive role of the family. The other modality, which this paper addresses, is the development and implementation of group services as a possible strategy for strengthening the natural support systems of caring by concerned relatives of the aging.

THE GROUP PROGRAM

The first year of the group component of the Natural Supports Program was seen as an exploratory phase with the following objectives:

(1) to develop guidelines for a group program that would meet the needs of a diverse population in order to strengthen the supportive role of those caring or concerned about their aging relatives;
(2) to develop group programs in different types of communities to provide a broad population base for the collection of data;
(3) to identify characteristics of the client populations attending the group programs including the nature of the caring relationships;

(4) to determine the nature and variety of service needs and requests; and
(5) to locate cases for individual services as appropriate.

This paper presents data gathered at four community meetings and also reports on fifteen small discussion groups that were an integral part of the community meetings. Information was obtained from 126 questionnaires filled out by the attendees and from the narrative reports of the discussion groups. Approximately 40 caring relatives attended each meeting as well as a number of agency professionals who were interested in the program. The data presented are from the client questionnaires only.

The two communities in which these programs were organized were Jamaica and Staten Island, New York. In both locations, Community Service Society has existing programs serving the aged, but neither had worked with or identified·the family care-giving populations in a formal or structured way. Community social service task forces were the local mechanisms through which these meetings were planned. This paper does not include a description of the planning process and the outreach techniques used, but it is important to note that the audience sought was those caring for and concerned about their aging relatives, not the aged themselves.

The exploratory meetings were developed as a two-part evening series in each community with a one-week or two-week interval between sessions. There was no preregistration, and admission was free. The first sessions of the series consisted of a presentation for the entire group by an expert on aging followed by five concurrent discussion groups of no more than twelve persons. Each of the small groups had a leader, a resource person, and a recorder. The discussion groups were designed to provide a forum for sharing experiences and concerns, for expressing needs and interests as well as service requests, and for conveying some general information about the aging process and entitlements.

The format of the second sessions focused on small discussion groups and a display of specialized community resources with agency representatives available to explain their programs and to accept individual referrals where appropriate. The questionnaires were filled out by client attendees at the end of each evening session.

Data About Attendees

The ages of the attendees (n = 126) indicates that 60% were in the 40-59 year-old age group with 28% in the 40-49 year-old category and 32% in the 50-59 year-old category. Twenty-one percent were in the 20-39 year-old age group with 13% between 20-29 years and 9% between 30-39 years. Fourteen

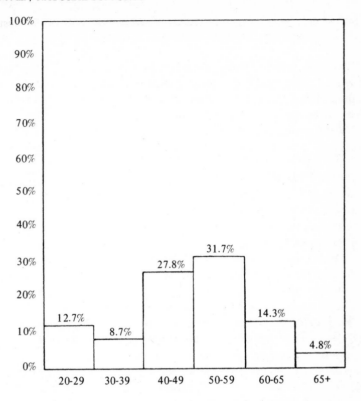

Figure 4.1:   Age Distribution of Meeting Attendees

percent of the attendees were in the 60-65 year-old age range, and 5% were over 65. (See Figure 4.1.)

The racial composition for the four meetings consisted of 84% white, 13% black, and 2% other. The religious affiliations were 39% Jewish, 32% Protestant, 23% Catholic; 2% of the respondents listed other affiliations or none at all.

The income distribution indicates that 63% of the respondents were members of families earning at least $15,000 a year: 39% were in the group whose family income exceeded $20,000 a year, and 24% were in the range of $15,000-$20,000 a year. Twenty-one percent had family incomes below $15,000 a year with 9% ranging from $10,000-$15,000 a year, 8% comprising the $5,000-$10,000 a year group and 4% reporting an overall family income of $5,000 or less a year. Almost 17% of those who completed questionnaires did not report any income figure. (See Figure 4.2.)

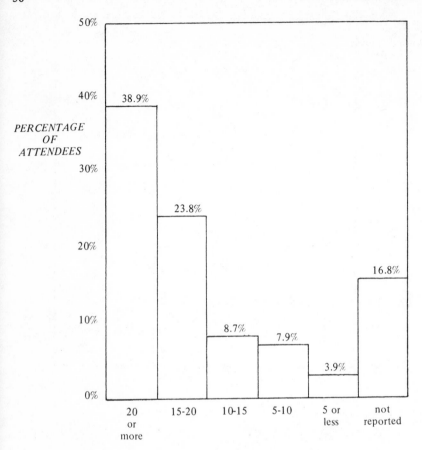

INCOME IN THOUSANDS OF DOLLARS

Figure 4.2:   Income Distribution of Attendees

Data About the Older Relative of Concern

The attendees (n = 97) indicated the following ages of the older person of concern. Ten percent were between the ages of 60-69; 29% were between 70-79 years of age; 45% were between 80-89 and 4% indicated relatives of 90 years or more (see Figure 4.3). Twelve percent indicated ages of more than one relative of concern, and these ages were not recorded.

As to living arrangements (n = 89), 37% indicated that their older relative was living alone and 52% that the relative was not living alone; 11% of the respondents indicated that their older relative was living in a nursing home.

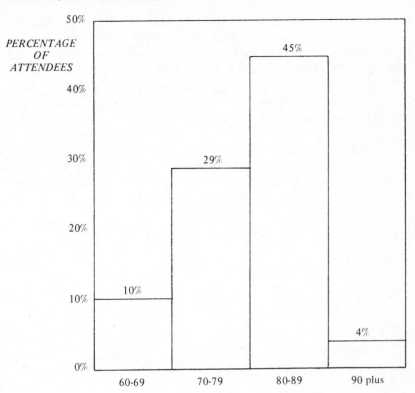

YEARS OF AGE OF ATTENDEES' RELATIVES

Figure 4.3:   Age of Older Relative

Sixty-three percent said that there were no friends or neighbors involved in the care of the older person.

Characteristics of the Caring Networks

The data reveal that 68% of the attendees (n = 121) were actively involved in caring for an older relative and that 32% were not. The definition of active involvement was left to the judgment of the respondent.

Of all those who reported (n = 126), 66% indicated involvement with a relative with impairments and 4% indicated no impairments. (Thirty percent did not respond.) Of the population (n = 108) who defined themselves as

active care givers, 43% indicated that their older relative had multiple functional disabilities such as problems with bladder control, bowel control,
speech and hearing, vision, mobility, confusion, and use of hands and arms.
This indicates that the most significant involvement is in dealing with older
people who have multiple functional disabilities.

Attendees (n = 60) were asked to indicate how many additional family
members were part of the support network. Fifty-two percent noted no
additional family members, 21% noted one additional family member, 14%
indicated two additional family members, and 13% reported three or more
additional members in the support constellation. The data illustrate that the
majority of the people responding see themselves as the only support that
their older relative has to call upon. (See Figure 4.4.)

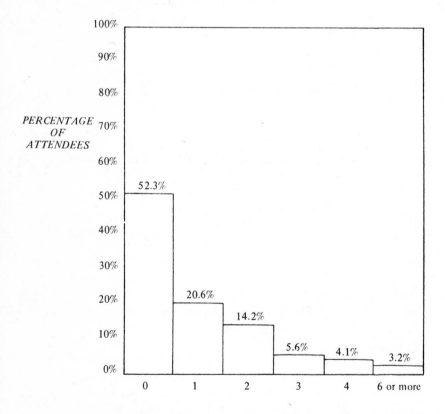

NUMBER OF ADDITIONAL MEMBERS IN SUPPORT NETWORK

Figure 4.4:   Additional Members in Support Network

Reasons for Attending Meetings

Attendees (n = 126) were asked to choose their primary reason for attending the meeting from five suggested categories. Seventeen percent indicated that they came to share experiences with others; 14% came to learn about home services, and 13% to learn about illnesses and disabilities of aging; 11% expressed interest in professional counseling and 6% in learning about public benefits; 36% indicated more than one of the choices; and 3% chose other reasons. (See Table 4.1.)

Table 4.1: Primary Reason for Attending Meeting (n = 123)

Reason for Attending	Affirmative Response
To learn about disabilities/illnesses of aging	12.7%
To learn about home services	13.5%
To learn about public benefits	5.6%
To share your feelings with other families	17.5%
To obtain professional counseling	11.1%
Multiple reasons recorded	35.7%
Other	2.9%
Total	100%

NOTE: Discrepancy caused by rounding

Topics Indicated for Subsequent Meetings

Eighty-four percent of the attendees (n = 105) expressed interest in having future meetings. Attendees were presented with an open-ended free-response item on the questionnaire where they could indicate topics they would be interested in for subsequent meetings. Data from those who requested more meetings indicate that 28% wanted more information about the aging process, including the psychological/physical/social issues related to aging; 26% requested information identifying available resources for support; 16% requested information related to institutionalization; 13% requested help relating to problems experienced by individual family members that result from having an aging relative in the home; 10% requested help with interactional problems in the family that related to the aging relative; and 6% requested support groups for families who were caring for older relatives. Public policy and political action considerations in addition to special problems such as the situation of the only child or children with absent relatives each made up 5% of the additional service requests. Obviously, some persons recommend more than one topic.

Table 4.2:   Topics Recommended for Subsequent Meetings
(n = 105)

Topics	Percentage of Agreement on Each Topic
Psychological/Physical/Social Issues Related to Aging	28.4
Identification of Resources Available for Help and Support	26.3
Interactional Problems in Family Related to Aging Relative Living in the Home	10.5
Problems of Individual Family Member Related to Aging Relative Living in the Home	12.6
Public Policy/Political Action Consideration	5.3
Support Groups for Families Requested	6.3
Special Problems	5.3
Problems Related to Institutionalization of Relatives	15.8

Clearly, the participants indicated a need for more sessions that would provide an opportunity to understand the stresses on the family, to develop better skills for coping, and to share their experiences with other families in similar situations.

OBSERVATIONS OF THE RECORDER-OBSERVERS

In addition to the data collected from the individual attendees, there were recorder-observers in the small group sessions who were asked to focus on the group composition, basic identifying information about the group, the general tone of the group, the kinds of interchanges occurring, the content of the group discussion, ways in which the group coped with problems, and the reactions of the group members to the meeting. Included here are the most frequently reported observations from all the sessions. They are grouped into four categories that relate to (1) the caring role, (2) coping with feelings about the role, (3) requests for resources, and (4) the tone or interactional quality of the meetings.

The Caring Role

Participants indicated that they were finding the caring role difficult, often not knowing what needed to be done. Some were anticipating increased demands, and made requests for ways of preparing themselves for assuming a more demanding role in relation to their older relative.

Another problem presented was the issue of defining limits and managing the delicate balance between meeting one's own needs, family needs, and the needs of the aging relative.

Several of the group members in different sessions expressed feelings of being pressured by a strong sense of responsibility to provide care for their aging relatives. These were sometimes expressed as feelings of being trapped between their older relative and the rest of the family, between agencies and the older person, and between "right and wrong."

One problem expressed frequently in the groups was how appropriately to assume the caring role in relationship to an older relative who lives in a distant location. For those who had an older relative in a nursing home, the families were experiencing difficulty defining an appropriate role with which they could be comfortable.

Coping with Feelings

Another concern presented by the attendees during the group meetings was the difficulty that people had in managing their guilt feelings. What seemed to be reflected was a cycle of guilt and anger in which they were trapped. Feelings of frustration and hopelessness existed in relation to the inability to adapt their relationships to the changes in the older person. People discussed anticipation of crises and were seeking ways of preventing them from occurring.

The participants also expressed feelings of fear related to the increasing dependency needs of their older relatives. They noted that low frustration-tolerance levels, frequently ending in conflict, were the result of trying to adjust to the limited functioning of a confused or depressed older relative.

Requests for Resources and Services

Another characteristic of the exploratory meetings was requests for services that could help to provide relief for the caring relatives. Many people stated that they had difficulty locating appropriate resources or did not know what was available in the way of assistance, especially in relation to legal and financial problems. Requests were made for information about places where the elderly who suffer from some functional impairments could be sent for vacations. Also indicated was a need for relief, as was evidenced by the significant number of suggestions for someone to come in once a week so that the care givers could have some respite from the caring role. Many of the participants felt that their ability to cope would be enhanced by this kind of relief.

Comments on the Tone of the Meeting

Many of the participants were very informed and articulate about what they were experiencing and feeling. With few exceptions, the need for more opportunities to share experiences and obtain information was prevalent. There was a great deal of listening, peer support, and sharing of problems and solutions. Suggestions for possible ways to cope with problems were offered by participants. Ways to involve other relatives in the caring network so that the burden of caring could be shared were offered, and advice and information that reflected people's experiences in dealing with agencies providing services to the elderly were exchanged. The desire for an ongoing group for peer support was strongly expressed.

There was an important caution noted by several of the recorder-observers. In some groups, people were so intent and emotionally involved in their own problems and their need to share their experiences that they were unable to respond to others. Thus, great skill is needed on the part of the group leader to be sure that single individuals do not dominate group sessions.

Comments by Workshop Participants

Many of the comments which were expressed by the recorder-observers were reiterated and emphasized by the participants on the "comments" section of the questionnaire. There were repeated references to the usefulness of the meetings and the desire for more discussion groups. The need for follow-up groups and a support network for the caring relatives was clearly articulated.

The comments made references to both the need for information about the availability of resources and the need for a group setting in which people could share their feelings about the role they were assuming in relation to their aging relatives. Requests for information about nursing homes and placement, vacation places, feedback from the meetings, and other matters—both specialized and general—also characterized the comments that appeared on the questionnaire.

IMPLICATIONS AND CONCLUSIONS

From the data collected and the narrative reports, the interest in the continued development of a group program for families of the aging is clearly indicated. What has emerged are suggestions for the focus and content of such a program which can serve as guidelines for those interested in expanding the group approach for strengthening natural supports. The nature of this program should take into account the several areas.

Program Content

For many persons, moving into the caring role creates stress, since it requires the learning of new skills and the changing of perceptions. The findings clearly demonstrate interest in subsequent meetings to help relieve stresses. The content of these meetings should include:

(1) information for increased understanding of the aging process;
(2) strategies to help caring relatives cope with increasing disabilities and confusion of their older relatives;
(3) skills for care and maintenance of a multiply disabled older person;
(4) techniques for handling interactional family problems; and
(5) focused information about resources, entitlements, home services, and institutionalization.

Group Interaction

The group modality offers the unique opportunity for participants to share their concerns with others, engage in a process of mutual aid, develop skills for problem solving and coping, facilitate problem definitions, and clarify values and roles. These group experiences become the enabling mechanisms for the development of peer support groups, and together they provide the potential for the evolvement of self-help groups.

A group modality also offers an efficient way of disseminating services and information to many people at one time and provides an additional option for strengthening natural supports.

Differential Populations

The findings have indicated several important groups that need to be addressed. Of particular importance are:

(1) those who are anticipating the caring role;
(2) those who are already caring for an older relative;
(3) those whose older relatives live far away; and
(4) those whose relatives live in institutions.

Differential Age Groupings

Intergenerational responsibilities and obligations may have a significant influence on the stresses felt by caring relatives. Therefore, the ages of those in the caring network should be considered. Since most attendees were in their middle years, special attention should be focused on this group. The care-giving characteristics of the younger generations require further exploration. In addition, there is a need for increased focus on the needs of the older generation of care givers.

Other Factors to be Considered

Socioeconomic, cultural, and ethnic factors should be considered as to how they affect filial responsibilities and the types of services required. Cultural expectations and certain social pressures are also likely to influence responsibilities and stresses. The size of the caring network and the extent of disability of the older person require further exploration as to their effect on the nature of the caring relationships.

Our findings confirm the belief that there is a great potential for strengthening natural supports through a group approach. Such an approach makes it possible to reach those who are already caring for an older relative and can benefit from group services. Also, others can be helped to prepare for their caring role in the future, a role that many of us may face at some point in our lives.

NOTE

1. Community Service Society is one of the oldest and largest nonprofit, nonsectarian social agencies in the United States.

Part II

FAMILY AND AGING

INTRODUCTION

The family is a universal social institution, and, universally, caring for the aged is a concern of the family. There is no known society in which the bond between people and their families is totally cut off as individuals age. The bonds may become weaker, but kinship ties universally differentiate relatives from nonrelatives and result in obligations and responsibilities.

For the most part, families attempt to meet their obligations and responsibilities to aged family members. Failure to do so evokes a sense of guilt. In those few societies where families kill the aged, they do so as a way of meeting obligations and responsibilities. It is either a way of insuring an intact soul for life in the hereafter, or it is rationalized on the basis of a belief in reincarnation.

As cultures come increasingly to be influenced by Western patterns, the traditional ways of regarding the aged in the family are changed. Nowhere is this more dramatically illustrated than in China, as described by Susan K. Kinoy. In pre-Communist China, the peasant family included several generations who had a strong sense of family solidarity. The grandfather or great-grandfather was the head of the family and was treated with great respect. Indeed, the sons worked the fields under his direction and revered him. His wife was also a dominant person because she had daughters-in-law who took orders from her. The critical place in the culture of family lineage guaranteed esteem for the aged and continuing concern with their well-being.

Kinoy describes the shift in contemporary China from a system in which family loyalty predominated to one where loyalty to the collective is paramount. Nevertheless, there has continued to be concern, now shared by the collective and, to some extent, by the state. Retirement pay and free or very inexpensive medical care are new features of the system which have a profound effect on the care of the aged, easing the burden on the family. Still another feature of contemporary China that affects the aged is the expectation that everyone will work, even those who have supposedly retired. Kinoy states that even in one of the few institutional facilities for the aged "planned work schedules are a part of their program."

The tradition of respect for the aged has apparently been sustained with the family now being aided by the collective in expressing that respect by broadened responsibility for meeting the needs of the aged.

In India, as described by M. M. Desai, changes are also taking place in the traditional family. Industrialization and urbanization have tended to undermine the patriarchial pattern, lessening the authority of the senior male member of the family. Although the sense of family obligation to the aged persists, according to Desai, there are destitute aged and their social status is declining. The situation of the aged widow is particularly precarious. The lack of a comprehensive social security system in India heightens the burden on the family. There is little relief from this burden through institutional care since the number of institutions is totally insufficient.

Aurelia Florea describes the situation of the aging in Italy almost wholly in terms of public provision—a contrast to the emphasis on how families meet their obligations and responsibilities as they are changing in China and India. Growing awareness of the need for services is based in part on the considerable increase in the number of aged persons in the population. There has also been a significant increase in the percentage of aged persons in Italy. These facts highlight the need for services.

The universality of the family in social organization highlights the need to recognize and to strengthen the family as a prime source of support for aging persons.

—M.I.T.

5

SERVICES TO THE AGING IN THE PEOPLE'S REPUBLIC OF CHINA

SUSAN K. KINOY
with the assistance of
ELSIE HELLER

THE ROLE OF THE AGING IN THE FAMILY—
PRE- AND POST-LIBERATION CHINA

Pre-Liberation

The average person's life expectancy in China in 1935 was, according to Horn (1971), 28 years. With the exception of a few old people in the landlord class, there was very little aging population prior to "Liberation." In some provinces during 1927-1928, more than 75% of the population starved to death. In 1941-1943, over one million people died in a famine. The average life span was also shortened by wars. Thousands of persons were killed who had been forceably recruited for defense by landlords, or who were recruited by the "Red Army" to fight both against the so-called "War Lords" and against the foreign invasion of China. The result of these three factors left the average person with inadequate food, no disaster relief, and virtually no

AUTHORS' NOTE: *Susan K. Kinoy traveled in China for three and one-half weeks in May 1975. She was one of a group of eight professionals from various disciplines who were invited to visit. The group included a teacher, attorney, family counselor, psychologist, physician, and businessman. Ms. Kinoy was the only social worker. Elsie Heller visited mainland China in August 1974. She traveled with a group of twenty educators sponsored by the* Guardian *newspaper. One-third of the group taught at the university level, one-third at the secondary level, and one-third at the elementary and nursery school levels. Ms. Heller was included because she had been on the faculty at the School of Social Work at New York University.*

medical care. Illiteracy was rampant. Where families could farm, children could not be spared to go to school.

In the prerevolutionary Chinese society, the family with its complex kinship structure was the major influence which governed an individual's life, attitudes, education, career, social associations, and financial security. The father, the oldest and most experienced family member, had major authority. He was revered. The relationship between father and son took precedence over the husband-wife relationship. A family organizational scheme existed which assigned each person to a specific place in the hierarchy. A woman was first supposed to obey her father, then her husband, and then her son. The marriage was arranged. She was not consulted. Age as the key factor in family status and authority was constantly emphasized. Both chronological age and generational status provided authority. The kinship patterns were further formalized by a nomenclature system. Absolute obedience was demanded. The authority of age was absolute. This rigid family design also became a basis for the political life as embodied in the feudal landlord structure.

Starting in 1911, at the beginning of the revolt against the feudal society, youth began to obtain Western knowledge. As young people learned to read and acquired scientific education and knowledge, they were placed in political positions of authority. They pushed the aging aside and seized more and more leadership. Frequently they had little consideration for the aged. The aged were often neglected. The aging craftsmen were unemployed as industrialization began. The great wars against the Japanese and the internal social upheaval gave more and more power to youth.

Post-Liberation

After Liberation in 1949, the new society had to reformulate its attitudes toward the family. The conditions of industrial work in China favored the growth of a collective spirit and encouraged the development of loyalty to the collective or the working group. Loyalty to the family ceased to be the only allegiance that society demanded of the individual. Family loyalties were not destroyed, however. It is significant that the first national legislation to be promulgated by the People's Republic, on May 1, 1950, was the marriage law, which included the following: "Parents have the duty to rear and educate their children, the children have the duty to support and assist their parents. Neither the parents nor their children shall maltreat nor desert one another." This is also the law which abolished the feudal marriage system, based on male dominance, and asserted that the equality of men and women in marriage is the cornerstone of women's emancipation in China.

But a new law needs to be obeyed. The aging were cared for begrudgingly at the start of the new society. Young men and women chose marriage partners, wished to raise children in new ways, and took over family leadership. Painful family adjustments had to be made until a new balance in family relationships was created. In order to destroy the abusive patriarchal system, it was also necessary to destroy the family as the sole economic unit. In a few instances, old parents sued children for protection under the new marriage laws. During the long campaigns to involve and educate every person about the new society and his or her role in it, the techniques of "criticism and self-criticism" were used. People analyzed their actions, argued about the redistribution of land and property as well as about how each family member was to participate in the new society. Gradually, social pressure was placed on children who failed to aid parents and grandparents. Elders also "proved themselves" by participating in major campaigns for eradication of pests, mass inoculations, the fight for literacy and for higher food production. Finally, the aged often were called on to care for grandchildren when parents were away at work. Gradually, the new balance in relationships began to occur. The aging began to win a new type of respect based on their past and present contributions to the family. Today families are small. Leadership stems from the young parents. To visitors, young parents frequently talk with open respect and admiration for the grandparents' present activities and express horror about their "bitter past."

Cooperative and collective farming has become the major economic pattern, instead of patriarch-dominated family holdings in a feudal, landlord-dominated society. Strong efforts are being made to establish equality of the sexes. Marriage partners are supposed to select one another on the basis of mutual admiration and love, without consideration of property and status. The children are not the private property of the parents. Children of all ages have rights.

Family leadership usually rests in the young parents. However, it must be noted that the "Production Team" which is the basic and smallest unit of farm life is composed of families. Thus, family structure of new kind is basic to the society.

Successful literacy programs have had great impact in making possible the active and knowledgeable participation of citizens at all age levels. The changing role of women, young and old, has strengthened their position, giving them independent rights and a dignity that was unknown in the past. It strains the imagination to think of the change for old women in today's China who fewer than fifty years ago were treated as chattel and who now are respected because they survived the "bitter past," contributed to the revolution, or presently are active farmers or are playing other vital roles in their family or community.

DEFINITION OF SERVICES TO THE AGING

It is not possible to review services for the aging in China today unless one first attempts to observe and understand the political and theoretical framework within which these services take place. Services provided by and for the aging are an integral part of, and cannot be divorced from, the political, economic, and social structure of contemporary China—a country that underwent a fundamental revolution 29 years ago.

Services to the aging in the People's Republic of China will be interpreted broadly in this paper. Services will include both traditional and novel patterns relating to health and welfare. Secondly, since the provision of retirement income and the availability of food, clothing, and shelter to the aging are considered by the Chinese government to be a part of the service pattern, the distribution of such income and facilities will also be noted. Finally, since China today views as a service both to the aging and to the country the active involvement and participation of retirees in many aspects of government and production, this too will be included.

Every unit of government and every institution establish yearly goals for production, construction, creation of new equipment, housing, and so forth. In order to achieve these goals, an ongoing process of group participation and discussion takes place. Within these discussions, human and technical resources are matched against production goals and the responsibility to serve the needs of the vast population of approximately 900,000,000. All persons currently are needed to contribute their best efforts. This involves each community's evaluation of the physical strengths, weaknesses, and needs of so-called "retirees," and its determination of how best to meet their needs and maximize their limited contributions. All able persons, are expected to participate at some level and to some degree in extended group discussions. Out of these discussions, decisions are made concerning services for or performed by older people.

The most important aspects of life for China's aging today are: (1) that unless or until they are extremely infirm or fragile, the old (to the extent of their ability) are expected and continue to be functioning, respected, and productive members of society and to participate in the social and governmental patterns of the community; (2) that all have financial security based on retirement benefits and that all have adequate, though not elaborate, food, clothing, and shelter; (3) that all are provided with comprehensive health care—free of charge or at minimal cost; (4) that the tightly knit, interdependent society is organized in such a manner that the family and community provide ongoing and consistent intervention and care for the aging when they are ill or homebound, usually in the persons' home, but also, if required, in institutions.

China's goals today, are: that material benefits are considered to be appropriate and effective only if they are provided on an egalitarian basis; that social and economic development for one group of citizens is not considered to be effective unless everyone rises together; that no one is to be "left behind" either economically or culturally. This pervasive attitude has tremendous and direct impact on the care and role of the elderly in China. No one is "expendable." Work assignments and useful contributions to society as well as protection, education, and care are the right and responsibility of every citizen, regardless of age.

In each small community in China, there is an extraordinary interrelatedness of people. It is still a struggling frontier society. In a sense, no one is a stranger to anyone else. Men and women are attempting to create a society that is inspired by such maxims as "serve the people," "hard work," and "self-reliance." These new thrusts are reflected in the everyday world of China's aging.

Perhaps the most difficult concept for some outsiders to understand about China is the deep respect given to people who work with their hands—in the countryside and in the factories. A major ideal of the postrevolutionary society is that every man and woman has worth because of his or her creative contribution to social change. Furthermore, it is a goal of that society that every person who labors physically can also achieve intellectually.

LIFE AND SERVICES FOR
THE AGING IN CHINA TODAY

The basic "five guarantees" to the people have been carried out: "enough food, enough clothes, enough fuel, an honorable funeral and education for children." By Western standards, China's people, including her aging, live frugally, almost austerely, with few frills or amenities. However, there is no unemployment or inflation. The yuan, equivalent to U.S. 50¢, has not changed in value in thirty years. There are few older people in China today who have more than a few sets of clothing, often owning only one quilted jacket which is refilled and refluffed every year. Every person is housed adequately, but modestly, by our standards. However, most people have one or two rooms. Even in new housing, a person is provided with approximately 35 square feet. Food is adequate, meeting essential needs. It is varied, but not elaborate. On the other hand, there are not aging persons who must beg on the streets, neglect medical care for lack of funds, go hungry, or wear rags.

"OLD" AGING AND "NEW" AGING

In reviewing the services to and the functioning of old people, it is necessary to distinguish between the "old aging" and the "new aging." There are relatively few persons who were middle-aged (age 45 to 60) at the time of the revolution or "Liberation" in 1949. Those people now are aged 75 to 90—the survivors of the floods, famines, and wars of the old regime. Large numbers of persons who were 25—participants in the process of social change—now are beginning to retire. Retirement age for women is 55; for men, 60. The experiences of these two groups, the "old aging" and the "new aging," are very different.

Demographic statistics are relatively unavailable. It is estimated that the total population of the People's Republic of China is close to 900,000,000. Because of the dramatic change in the total society during the past 29 years, "the new aging" may soon be a highly significant portion of the population.

According to Yong-Luo Liu (1974), in a rural commune near Shanghai, of a total of 27,250 persons, 8.1% were aged 60 or older—706 men and 1,305 women. In one Brigade visited, the aging were 6.3% of the population. Of 1,902 people, 72 were women 60 and over and 47 were men 60 and over. In one urban district in Peking, of 51,000 persons, 5,000 (9.7%) were 60 years of age or older. As reported by Hsinhua (1978), Fankua Lane, formerly a major slum in Shanghai, now is a residential quarter consisting of 35 blocks of five-story buildings. It consists of 1,000 two- and three-room apartments. Each apartment houses 3 to 7 persons, the majority of them workers. Currently the Lane also houses 285 retired workers. Approximately 20 or more workers will retire during each of the next several years. Half of the projected retirees are women.

HOUSING

Housing for most retirees is adequate, often modest. A retiree living in a city in a two- or three-room apartment with his or her children frequently shares a room with a grandchild. Many families now have individual bathrooms and kitchens. In some instances, two families share these facilities. Some housing still consists of rooms or suites of rooms which previously had been part of large compounds owned by wealthy families.

Housing in rural communities is varied since the country is so vast. Usually, families (including aging grandparents) live in their own homes. The number of rooms and square footage is often related to availability of fuel for heating. In some new rural areas, apartments in two- or three-story buildings house much of the population. Here patterns are similar to those in urban housing.

In many areas, social (human) services are provided by paraprofessionals or nonprofessionals who are a part of the basic factory, farming, and housing structure of the urban or rural community. Although there are no formally trained social workers, men and women do receive considerable on-the-job training and some formal preparation if they are working in homes for the aging or in neighborhood clinics. Trained people work in hospitals and psychiatric clinics, always assisted by and, in turn, learning from large numbers of paraprofessionals. The sensitivity and intimate daily under-standing of the patient or client by the paraprofessional is highly regarded and acted upon by the more highly trained personnel. It is difficult to explain to a Westerner, the pride and excitement generated and constantly reinforced by the twin practices of (a) self-reliance (on behalf of both the client and worker) and (b) support of one person for another, leading to a group approach to solving a problem. A typical example follows.

A hospital chief reported to us that an older man with mechanical skills went to a clinic for acupuncture. While there, he made suggestions for and later helped to reorganize the outpatient clinics's electrical system, thus permitting a greater utilization of the facilities.

RETIREMENT

A man may retire at age 60; a woman, at age 55. Retirement benefits average 70% to 80% of earnings. Anyone who has worked less than 15 years retires with a minimum of 50% of salary. Most persons receive 60%. Yong-Luo Liu (1974) has noted that men working 20 years and women working 15 years obtain 70% of salary. It is assumed that since almost everyone works, the retirement benefits of a worker cease upon his or her death. However, factory committees reported to us that if a retiree dies and the spouse does not have adequate funds, the situation is discussed by that person's factory or block committee, and frequently some welfare funds are made available. Every person receives retirement funds. It is our understanding that these arrangements are not formalized. There is no national public welfare or retirement system.[1]

If a person has been physically or mentally impaired all of his/her life and unable to earn, the local commune or urban structure (with additional central government funds) continues to assume responsibility for care after age sixty.

Some older experienced scholars, artisans, or skilled workers are asked to continue to work past retirement age.

PAYMENT FOR HEALTH CARE

There are no private social or medical services in China today. Medical care is either free or very inexpensive. There are several types of payment systems. If a family or an individual is unable to pay a required fee, medical care is always provided.

Health care is available to all. It is free to persons who have retired from state farms or from state-run units relating to production, e.g., factories, mines, communication units. Free medical care is also provided to retirees from all government jobs (administrative, organizational, economic, medical, and educational) as well as to disabled veterans. Retired dependents of working persons pay some or all of a total medical fee, depending on specific contracts. Retirees from nongovernment occupations may also pay no medical fee or a minimal amount, depending on the contract at the work site from which the person has retired.

Workers are covered by the National Labor Insurance Regulations.

More than 70% of all Production Brigades in the countryside have established cooperative medical care systems. Persons pay an average of 1 or 2 yuan (a yuan equals 50¢) a year. The Brigade supplements this payment. It pays for care at a local health clinic and in a hospital, if needed. The central government adds funds to rural health plans to supplement payment for equipment and staff.

Patients pay a very small registration fee and the cost of meals while in the hospital. The registration fee for a hospital visit is one chiao (5¢). Lab tests are one or two chiao. Daily hospitalization is usually less than one yuan. Operations cost from 5 to 15 yuan. (Experimentation with cooperative plans are being undertaken to cover these costs where they are not provided for already by medical care systems.)

Although people pay for medicines, the cost has been going down radically. All vaccinations and other forms of immunization are free. Programs for control of endemic disease, such as snail fever, are totally community- and government-sponsored and supported.

RURAL ORGANIZATION AND SERVICES

The vast majority of all persons, including the elderly, live in rural areas. This is the traditional pattern of life for most Chinese. The economic, social, and political structure which governs all farm and nonurban activity is the Commune. The Commune, in some respects, is like a small town community.

The Commune is responsible for the overall planning and supervision of farm and small industrial production and the distribution of those goods, as well as for health and social services, education, housing, and social or cultural activities.

In China, as in most agricultural societies, it is frequently possible for a person of retirement age to remain a part of the functioning society. This is especially true in a society where farming is not yet highly mechanized. Old people (both men and women) are expected by their families and by the Production Team (organized work group) to perform many tasks, depending on their physical stamina. In some areas, "the respected aging" are permitted or encouraged by the Team to retire from work. Repeatedly, however, the authors were told of aging people who theoretically had "retired" but who "volunteered" to participate at critical times in the farm cycle, such as picking when crops needed harvesting or hoeing during a dry spell. It was reported to us that if neighbors felt that the old person was being overworked or exploited, or if he or she was shirking responsibility, they could inform the local committee or team.

Rural Health Care

In Volume I of *Social Service Delivery Systems*, Ruth Sidel (1976) succinctly reviews health care in China. It would be repetitious to go into detail in another volume. Therefore, we will merely summarize this most important and perhaps most formalized aspect of the human services system.

The Commune usually maintains and staffs a hospital which it has built. The most highly trained doctors and medical personnel are supplied to the Commune hospital by country or city hospital centers or medical schools. The rest of the personnel (at all levels of skill and training) live in the Commune.

In addition, most Production Brigades (composed of Production Teams) have built and staffed small clinics. These are used as centers for immunization, for first aid in emergencies, and for rough diagnoses which will determine whether the patient should be provided with more intense care in a hospital or visits at home. At these decentralized local health centers aging people with chronic illnesses are seen regularly to check blood pressure, urine, eyesight; to conduct posthospital check-ups; to provide and check on medication; and to administer acupuncture or physical therapy. Health care in the home of the older person is another basic element of this community system. Bringing all levels of medical care to the old person and helping the family and the neighbors to understand his/her problems, and how to assist, is seen as a medical responsibility.

These local clinics built and organized by Production Brigades, and the activities both inside and outside of the clinic walls, are often undertaken by "barefoot doctors." Barefoot doctors are agricultural workers who receive a

short, intensive course of training and then combine their agricultural responsibilities with health care. In addition to preventive and first aid work, they
train and supervise "health workers" who are members of the Production
Teams. In many respects, the health worker is the untrained social worker.

OLD AGE HOMES

In some instances, where they have no family or cannot find their families
because they were sold as children, aging people elect to live in Old Age
Homes or Homes for the Respected Aged. Old people may also move into
such a home if they wish to remain in a certain community and their family is
transferred to another part of the country. It is not believed that large
numbers of such insitutions are in existence.

One of the authors had an opportunity to visit a Home for the Respected
Aged, part of a Commune, outside of Peking. The home was a modest but
adequate structure which housed about 75 persons. It was an integral part of
the Commune, with its programs and activities very much coordinated. The
general atmosphere was one of comfort, relaxation, and involvement. Residents were almost euphoric in their praise of the home. They proudly showed
us their comfortable private quarters; each had a single room containing the
usual family pictures and few personal possessions. Most of the residents were
in their early 70s, but a few were octogenarians. By and large they were
ambulatory and physically quite intact. Some we noticed had mild disabilities
but nevertheless still functioned as an active part of the group. There was a
clinic attached to the home, with ongoing medical services available, largely
through the local barefoot doctor. More serious medical problems were
referred on to the next level of care and on up to an elaborately equipped
provincial hospital.

Planned work schedules are a part of the homes' program. All contribute
to the home according to their abilities. They work in extensive flower and
vegetable gardens, the products of which are used by the residents. In some
homes for the elderly, contracts are worked out with local factories whereby
residents make small parts for machines or assemble simple mechanisms.
Work here is similar to our "sheltered workshops," but with the difference
that the residents (with the assistance of staff) organize, plan, and carry out
the·program.

A 1978 feature news story (Hsinhua, 1978) describes an old worker's
home for retired miners near Fushun. There are 37 members of the staff. The
average age of the 79 residents is 75. The oldest is 91. Some have lived there
for 25 years. All retirees receive 70% or 80% of their original pay. Their

pension checks are brought to them monthly by miners from mining units where they used to work. In addition, the State spends 10,000 yuan on management and 4,000 yuan yearly on medical care.

URBAN ORGANIZATION AND SERVICES

About 20% of China's 900 million people live in cities. The urban society is organized through a series of Revolutionary Committees. The hierarchy starts with the Residents' Revolutionary Committee, which reports to the Neighborhood Revolutionary Committee, which in turn reports to the District Revolutionary Committee, and from there to the City, or County, then National structure. Most of these committees consist of from ten to twenty members.

The District Committee sends representatives to city government. In Peking, for example, the city, including its suburbs, is composed of more than 7,000,000 persons, and within this area there are nine districts.

Services organized through this structure include:

- municipal affairs, such as drainage and street lights
- political education
- education of children (including school supervision)
- education of adults
- health education
- care of preschool children
- children's lunches when parents work
- health care
- care of homebound
- "street factories"
- individual counseling and settling disputes between family members
- transportation to institutions.

Services to the aging are provided at all levels of government. Once again, it must be noted that care for retirees is included as an integral part of all community planning. For example, separate campaigns to inoculate the aging are not conducted. Instead, all persons based in the community (differentiated from persons based in their factories) are included in all disease prevention programs.

Urban Social Services and Health Care

The points of contact for social services and health care for retirees and older persons is the Residents' or Lane Committee or the Factory Committees. There are no social workers. Members of a committee intervene in personal problems. Some persons, as in all societies, need help, for example, in preparing for retirement. Responsibility for this is sometimes given to a member of a Factory Committee.

In China, in spite of its structure and its philosophy, some elderly face deep emotions in terminating useful and highly structured work careers. At times, friction develops between older men and women and their sons- or daughters-in-law. This is a problem area in many societies. However, in China this situation may be especially acute because roles of the aging have changed so radically in one or two generations. We were told of one instance where neighbors overheard repeated arguments and tearful discussions among several family members. A representative of the Lane Committee was sent in to discuss the problem with the family. The family had not asked for help.

It is difficult for a Westerner to understand that the local Committees will insert themselves into such a conflict situation because of a request for help or even without being asked. Although such intervention may be a difficult experience for the family, it is accepted and understood as part of the total political structure. The underlying social and political concept is that every individual and family wishes to and must be helped to participate in all levels of activity, and that, therefore, the problems of one family are the problems of the whole community. They must be resolved in order for the individuals and for the community to function more adequately. This type of "social work" or "social intervention" is common. Frequently, if a solution to a problem cannot be worked out at the local level, it goes to members of the Neighborhood Committee.

Within urban communities, health care is provided on a daily basis by "Red Medical Workers," urban counterparts of the rural "Barefoot Doctors." They usually are based in small clinics. These simple clinics are furnished with one or two beds in which ill people sleep on a short-term basis, or which serve as examining tables. All neighborhood preventive health services, first aid, home care, posthospitalization, care of chronically ill aging, and many types of social intervention are carried out by these Red Medical Workers. These neighborhood workers receive limited training. They function closely with physicians assigned by local hospitals and with local governing committees. Because these workers live in and are a part of each community, there is an intimacy and trust which flows between them and the residents.

Home care for chronically ill aging persons in a Lane would consist of the efforts of a team of neighbors. One family might cook and bring the food over, another might add the older worker's clothes to his laundry, students might perform light housecleaning, and the local health worker would bring medical services to the home and/or escort the patient to a hospital. Periodically, the "case" of this neighbor would be discussed, and reviewed at community meetings.

Although formal responsibilities for home care, "friendly visiting," help with activities of daily living are given to various community members, the neighbors along with the formal structure function as a therapeutic community. Obviously, these patterns of community behavior are successful to varying degrees. What must be understood is the political nature of community work. The neglect of a homebound or sick person (as well as of a child) is interpreted as a serious failure of an entire community.

HOSPITALS

Hospitals exist in nearly all neighborhoods. In addition, there are large teaching hospitals at the district level. Psychiatric institutions are also available for inpatient treatment. In hospitals, as in neighborhood health centers, a combination of Eastern and Western medicines and medical techniques are used.

While visiting in a busy clinic in a housing project in Shanghai, we noted that many old people chose the herbal medications rather than the newer synthetic medicines. Acupuncture is used extensively. In one hospital, we observed older people receiving acupuncture on an outpatient basis to assist in motor functioning following stroke, to improve hearing, to help alleviate headaches, to help to correct insomnia, and so on.

Within the hospitals themselves, patients help one another, when possible. During periods of recuperation, patients participate in the maintenance of the hospital: cleaning, rolling bandages, and doing small needed factory jobs. A group of American psychiatrists and psychiatric social workers who visited such hospitals ascertained that aging patients suffer from the same types of psychiatric illnesses as are reported in hospitals in the United States—e.g., senile psychosis and schizophrenia. However, the visiting psychiatrists observed few old people in the hospitals. Not only were there fewer "older" aging people in general, but it appeared that old people who were senile, who "wandered" or who exhibited childlike behavior were frequently cared for in their communities, at home, or as outpatients. Not only is a close tie between the community and a general hospital or psychiatric hospital maintained, but the entire community is alerted and mobilized to give special care to someone coming back from a hospital or institution. Since regular follow-up outpatient care is stressed, either at a local clinic or hospital, the local medical workers make arrangements for old people to be escorted to medical care. Sometimes students or neighbors, after working hours, take "respected elders" to the clinics.

It is a political and economic necessity, say the Chinese, for persons old and young to maintain their health and to live harmoniously in order to function productively and at optimal capacity for themselves, their families, the community, and for the country and its new social order.

STREET FACTORIES

One form of postretirement involvement of the aging, especially women, has been participation in the creation of and continued employment in "street factories." (Young women with small children at home also participate.) These small production enterprises, sometimes using scrap materials, often manufacture small items too miniscule for inclusion in a major plant. Minimal payment supplements retirement benefits. Some street factories bring women together to embroider and knit. Work usually is part-time and tailored to the needs of women and retirees. As an integral part of their activity, most street factories engage the workers in classes in literacy, literature, current events, and political economy.

CONCLUSION

This chapter is based on visits to the People's Republic of China, as well as on perusal of the literature. It attempts to describe present services to the aging. The chapter tries to describe these services within an understanding of the country's need and drive for a rapidly expanding economic system which calls for maximum utilization of the skills of all people, including the aging. Serious emphasis, therefore, is placed on the continued involvement of the aging in the economy. Many retirees continue to work, some very hard for long hours as farmers, many for shorter hours in street factories or as baby-sitters. The paper notes that aging are also involved as leaders or participants in community services or governmental affairs. "Retirees" assume a variety of types of community responsibilities. Based on a tradition of respect, in honor of their "bitter past" as well as in appreciation of their present labors, old people today are usually valued. Life for the aging, and for most of the population, is stark and very hard. For most aging, China today, because of its tight, community-based economic and political structure, is a therapeutic community. It is a society where, in contrast to earlier generations, the aging feel secure economically and one where they are guaranteed comprehensive health care. Because of this security plus the reality of feeling needed, it appears that this society has, in many instances, succeeded in alleviating some of the fears of the aging—lack of involvement, isolation, feelings of uselessness, and fear of neglect when ill.

The authors are left with many questions. Will it be possible for a future, possibly more economically prosperous, industrialized China, to continue its present patterns of service delivery to the aging and continue to involve the elderly in the life of the society? Will future generations of aging continue to be guaranteed a wide range of social and health services delivered by many willing community hands, and continue to feel useful, involved, needed, and respected. Can the "caring quality" observed until now survive industrialism?

NOTE

1. Monthly income (while working) per individual ranges from 35-100 yuan a month. Usually, several family members work. Rent averages 3-5 yuan a month. For some, retirement funds are supplemented by earnings from "street factories" (discussed later).

REFERENCES

HORN, J. (1971) Away with All Pests. New York: Monthly Review Press.
Hsinhua (1978) "Chinese miners enjoy happy old age." Chinese Government Press Release (042819). April 28 (Shenyang).
SIDEL, R. (1976) "People serving people: human services in the People's Republic of China." Meeting Human Needs 2: Additional Perspectives from Thirteen Countries. Beverly Hills: Sage.
YONG-LUO LIU (1974) "Old people in new China." Perspective in Aging (May-June).

6

SERVICES TO THE AGED
IN ITALY

AURELIA FLOREA

The problem of the care for the aged has been felt very strongly in Italy in the last few years. On the one hand, the problem has become more serious because of the increase in the numbers of old people and the backwardness of social services. On the other hand, Italian society has been acquiring a greater awareness of social problems, and particularly of those concerning the emargination or possible emargination of particular groups of people. As a result, new trends have appeared both in the practice of existing social services and in the attempts to create new services which, from the beginning, would be different from the previous ones. They have as their main objective to avoid the institutionalization of old people.

The turning point of social policy legislation in Italy has been the legislation produced by the regional governments since 1970 and the parliamentary debates on the issues of the reform of the health and welfare systems. The different strategies chosen by regional governments are inspired by the first reform projects still in discussion at the national level. These indicate the objective of offering to old people a range of services, alternative to residential care, characterized by domiciliary delivery, including capillary health and welfare services (such as outpatient clinics and rehabilitation centers) decentralized as much as possible. The reorganization of health and social services should be accompanied by a continual revision of social security benefits, on the basis of a "minimum guaranteed standard."

THE DEMOGRAPHIC SITUATION

The Italian population has undergone a constant process of aging during the last century. While the age group 0-15 has moved from 34.2% in 1861 to

24.4% in 1971, and the age group 15-35 from 33% in 1861 to 28.3% in 1971, the proportion of Italian citizens age 60 and over has stepped from 6.4% in 1861 to 10.8% in 1931 to 16.7% in 1971. In 1971, there were in Italy 8,925, 288 persons over the age of 60, in a population of about 54 million.

In the percentage growth of the aged population, there has been a considerable increase also in the growth of the more aged groups. Persons over 65 have increased more than 7% in the last century (from 4.0% in 1861 to the present 11.3%) while persons over 60 have increased from 2% to 7% in the same period.

Statistical projections for the year 2000 indicate that almost 20% of the total population will be over 60 years of age, with a large proportion being 65 years old or older. A greater longevity is anticipated for women than men.

HISTORY AND ORGANIZATION OF PENSION SYSTEM

As in many other European countries, in Italy the first insurance and protection of workers for illness, disability, and old age was the establishment of Friendly Societies. In 1860 there were in Italy about 240 such organizations.

The first category of workers to benefit from an old age insurance in Italy was that of state and local employees (both in the civil and military services) according to the law of April 14, 1864, n. 1731.

Voluntary insurance become possible with the law of July 17, 1898, n. 350, which instituted a National Insurance Fund for disability and old-age pensions for workers. This was an autonomous fund, under the supervision of the Ministry for Agriculture, Industry and Commerce.

Compulsory insurance for disability and old age was established by the law of April 24, 1919, n. 60, which became operative in July 1920. It concerned all citizens (men and women) between 15 and 65 years of age employed in commerce, agriculture, public service, fishing, and so on. The pension obtainable at the age of 65 was proportionate to the contributions paid by the employee during his working life.

This insurance system was administered by the National Fund for Social Security (Cassa Nazionale per le Assicurazioni Sociali), which in 1933 became the National Institute for Social Security (Istituto Nazionale di Previdenza Sociale) and which is still the agency administering these benefits.

At present, several principles control the system of benefits: there is no sex discrimination between men and women workers as far as the amount of the pension is concerned; there is an automatic increase in pensions, linking the annual increase of benefits to the cost of living index; there is a minimum benefit standard rate for salaried workers, which links the pension to a

33.33% of the average salary of industrial workers; and finally there is a linking of pensions to salaries for all public employees (law of April 29, 1976, n. 177). The introduction of the principle of linking pensions to salaries establishes a close relationship between the condition of workers and that of old-age pensioners.

There is a major problem of reorganizing what is generally known in Italy as the "pensions jungle." The present system provides for a large number of different pensions—old age, disability, widow, and survivor's—which can be drawn concurrently and to which one can become entitled at different ages. In order to improve the pension system, several measures are now under study, including a general reorganization of the agency INPS; a transformation and unification of pensions for all workers both salaried and self-employed.

With the law of April 30, 1969, n. 153, the so-called "social pension" was established, i.e., a noncontributory pension for all persons of 65 and over whose income is below a minimum level specified by the law. The number of people drawing this type of pension in 1973 was 846,514, of which 87.9% were women. The minimum social pension today is Lit. 53.600 a month, whereas the minimum for employees and self-employed is Lit. 66.950 per month. It is reckoned that about 75-80% of the pensioner population in Italy draws only the minimum pensions.

THE OLD SYSTEM: RESIDENTIAL HOMES AND PUBLIC ASSISTANCE

Before the introduction of the "social pension" and the services established by regional government legislation, a large percentage of the people receiving assistance were in fact old people. This assistance could be in cash, or it could be given in the form of residential care. The cash benefits were discretionary as to amount; they generally consisted of paltry sums of money, administered by the Public Assistance Agency (Ente Comunale di Assistenze). This agency existed in every municipality and was an autonomous body under the supervision of the local Council. It was also responsible for organizing and running the old people's homes. The Welfare Reform Bill provides for the suppression of all such agencies (ECA), transferring all their responsibilities to the Local Units of Social Services, to be established in each municipality or group of municipalities. As far as placement in old people's homes, there is a law (Testo Unico di Pubblica Sicurezza) dating back to 1931, which is no longer enforced, requiring people unable to work and destitute, having no family, be placed in institutions supported by public assistance. In 1934, the law concerning local authorities established in Article

8 that people placed in charitable institutions as well as those financially dependent on ECA subsidies or those placed in local authority homes could not be eligible to public appointments. Being destitute carried the stigma of moral disapprobation.

There are no reliable data regarding residence of old people. Some studies (e.g. Florea, 1977) using relatively small samples, however, indicate that 50% of old people live either alone or with an aged spouse, about 40% live in household with relatives, and the remaining 10% live in various types of residential placements for old people (homes, hospitals, psychiatric hospitals, and even jails).

According to the Statistical Yearbook of Social Security and Public Assistance for 1976, there were 1,919 old people's homes with 135,138 residents. Of these institutions 1,327 are administered by public agencies and 472 are private institutions.

Public institutions serve approximately 90,000 old persons, whereas private ones have approximately 45,000. Among public institutions there is a difference between those which are managed by local authorities (Institutioni Publiche di Assistenza e Beneficenza) and those managed by national agencies of a public character such as the National Agency for Pensioners (Opera Nazionale Pensionati d'Italia) or by agencies supervised by local authorities (such as ECA, which I have already mentioned). Among the voluntary agencies there are some that are managed by private voluntary associations, and some by religious bodies. Among the latter, some have a special status, defined by the agreement between the Italian state and the Holy See.

According to recent estimates, there are now in Italy some 2,000 old people's homes with a total of 140,000 beds. The percentage of people over 65 in homes is estimated at 3%.

Although some changes have been taking place, both in attitudes and in the actual reorganization of the services, many of these old people's homes are in fact "closed" institutions. They often are located in old buildings (sometimes former convents, not suitable for the purpose and rarely converted), or are situated out of the town center, in far away suburbs, or even in the country. But they are "closed," particularly in the sense that the quality of life of the inmates is poor, with rigid timetables, with a lack of recreational resources and suitable occupations within the home, and with little or no contact with the outside world.

Even though the 40 "Case Serene" (Restful Homes) of the ONPI are much better from an architectural point of view and can also offer better services (food, social work staff), they too can be criticized for their isolation from the community.

Even worse is the situation of long-term nursing homes for sick old people; they are not, properly speaking, long-term hospitals, and they lack suitable facilities and staff to care properly for patients who really need specific medical care. According to some 1970 data (Florea, 1976), the staff/patient ratio was 1/100 for doctors, and about 1/50 for nursing staff. It is particularly difficult to find trained staff prepared to work in long-term nursing homes, since the salaries offered are lower than those in ordinary hospitals.

THE NEW SYSTEM OF HEALTH AND
SOCIAL SERVICES FOR OLD PEOPLE

The new organization of health and social services in Italy is a consequence of the political, cultural, and technical debate which has been going on for some years. The main principles of reorganization are integration of health and social services with the emphasis on prevention and rehabilitation. Services for old people should be a part of the general services for the population of a given geographical area (Local Unit of Health and Social Services). The Local Unit should be self-managed and controlled by the users and by the representatives of the local social organizations. There should be a minimum of separate services, e.g., specialized geriatric consultants. Old people should avail themselves of the same services offered to citizens in general. Emargination from family and community life should be avoided, as can be the case with institutionalization.

There still is not a framework of a national law concerning all aspects of the reform of the health and social services. Some of the regional governments have made laws concerning the regional territory in areas and subareas or districts for reorganization of services in new Local Units of Health and Social Services. The laws concerning special categories (day nurseries, family welfare clinics, services for old people) have been thought out in the reference to future Units. More than half of the regional governments have issued laws concerning old people's financial assistance and have established services for the rehabilitation and socialization of older citizens.

There are many contradictions and gaps in these laws. A major drawback is the system of financing the regional governments for the services they intend to provide. Often these are inadequate; most of them are in the form of grants towards expenses which have been borne by the municipalities. Since most municipalities are very small in size and their budgets are already very strained, very few are able to allocate funds sufficiently to qualify for the regional grant. The services, therefore, tend to concentrate in the richer municipalities, whose problems are less acute. Beyond these limitations and others that we shall examine, it cannot be denied that a tremendous effort has been made by legislators to begin to design a new system of social services, which should avoid, or at least delay, the need for placement in a home and provide a greater choice of alternatives.

Housing

The housing problem is one of the most pressing and urgent, not only for old people also but for much larger social groups. At present in Italy about one-half of the needed dwellings every year are not being built. The situation is particularly serious in regard to cheap housing, where public action has been practically absent. In the last few years the amount of public expenditure for subsidized housing has gone down to 2% of all investments. The housing market is therefore characterized by a massive presence of private initiative and lodging at very high prices.

The problem of housing for old people must be considered as part of this general situation. Very often, old people are found to be living in old, unsanitary dwellings which are unsuitable for them because they are too large or too cold or on the top floor of buildings. Old people have not been the subject of special consideration. On the contrary, a policy favoring demographic increase tended to give priority to large families in the lists for subsidized housing. Not until 1972 in the housing reform law was some interest shown in the condition of old people. This law provided that special housing for the aged be provided (such as hotel-housing or small flats with communal facilities and a resident matron). However, the funds allocated for this type of housing were very limited and so are the results.

Regional interventions in this sector have been of two sorts: the provision of residential facilities of a more traditional type (homes, service flats with residential matron, flats housing groups of old people leading independent lives) and the "open" provision of housing in the planning of dwellings through subsidies (reserving some flats for the use of older people) or through grants for the repairs of old buildings, grants toward the payment of rent, and so forth.

The legislation, such as it is, is generally characterized by these features: very small flats meant for individuals or couples; centralized services of the hotel type; absence of specific social or health services; locations in the center of towns which are often used by different groups besides old people (e.g. handicapped people). Some regional governments (Lombardy, Latium) make it a condition for their grant for "hotel-houses," homes, and other residential facilities that the institution include provisions for the participation of the guests and other external social organizations.

A form of intervention which takes care at the same time of housing and welfare needs is the provision of residential facilities, indistinguishable from ordinary lodgings. These are called "communal lodgings." According to the

Latium law, they are protected communities of a family type, capable of receiving from eight to ten persons. They are, in general, ordinary flats in ordinary buildings in a residential area, and they are not provided with special health or welfare services. For this reason, the link with local services must be constant and close; the "communal lodgings" must be authorized by the municipalities or group of municipalities.

A parallel solution is that of the multifunctional lodgings, planned by the regional government of Emilia-Romagna; these are, however, offered to any citizen in need and not just to old people. They may receive disabled people, self-sufficient old people, handicapped people, young people who have left children's homes, and so on.

Together with these solutions, the old "home" still survives, but attempts are being made to restructure it both in terms of the number of guests and in terms of qualified service. The law recently approved by the regional government of Latium, for example, established that new homes should not be built for more than 50 to 60 guests and the old ones must be restructured to limit their guests to the same number. A law of the Bolzano province prescribes that the staff/resident ratio should be 1:6 for care personnel. As an alternative to residential solutions, various regions have planned interventions aimed at maintaining the old persons in their own homes.

In some cases, grants are offered toward the buying of the home; more often toward improvements of old and unsanitary buildings, or for the supply of particular services (recent legislation in the region of Liguria, for example, provides for the installation and use of telephone) and toward the payment of rent.

The Lombardy regional government has decided to offer to old people lodgings in residential property owned by the local authorities or other local welfare agencies at a subsidized rent. Some regions have planned to include in the regulations for subsidized housing the provision that a proportion of the flats should be reserved for old people and, in many cases, that these flats should be built according to criteria that would suit this particular class of tenants.

Domiciliary Services

In connection with housing and with services aimed at the general population in need, several regional governments are establishing or are considering domiciliary services. These services are considered essential in the new welfare policies, and they usually are given a high priority in most plans. Not all the regional laws describe, in detail, the structure of domiciliary services. In any case, there seem to be three types of services: (1) a home help service given to facilitate personal and home life of old people—personal cleanliness, house cleaning, errands, and shopping; (2) home nursing, given by qualified health visitors, professional or registered nurses, physiotherapists, or other rehabilitation personnel under the guidance of the general practitioner in charge of the case; and (3) social work care, in the sense of casework treament, and organization and coordination of the various services. In general, all the types of domiciliary care described are aimed at all people in need, although, in practice, they are used mainly by old people.

Economic Assistance

Some regional laws consider financial assistance a special form of domiciliary care; others have a separate service administering it; others only give financial assistance in relation to housing needs (improvement grants or contribution towards rent). Financial assistance is usually given as a personal or as a family benefit which can supplement other types of pension in cases where other types of care would not meet the need. Financial assistance in the Province of Bolzano is needed in order to prevent change in the normal living conditions of the old person when such change is due to finances. The law of the Latium region states that financial assistance can be given "where it would encourage the start or the continuation of productive and social activities enabling the old person to continue playing a role in the life of the community."

Day Centers

The day centers are even more general than the ones for other services. A first distinction can be made between the laws that consider the day centers also as health centers and those that limit the functions of day centers to social and cultural activities. The law passed by the regional government of Trentino-Alto Adige (Province of Bolzano), for example, mentions explicitly the fact that the day center can house both social and health services.

According to most laws, the day centers must offer in a given geographical area (municipality or town area) services related to basic needs (subsidized canteens, cheaper meals, baths, showers, hairdressing and chiropodist services) as well as services involving the use of leisure time activities or other activities of a social nature giving the aged practical possibilities for an independent life. Although the day centers give priority to the needs of the aged, they are however always meant to cater to the needs of all types of users. In this sense, the law of the Lombardy region states that day centers constitute "the first nucleus of socio-educational centers serving the whole community and offering services to all the residents in the community and special services to particular groups in need." The problem of establishing connections between the day centers and other health and social services is particularly felt among local party or trade union branches, other neighboring centers, and public parks with areas reserved for the young or aged for sport or recreational activities.

Perhaps the legislators of the regional governments have provided only very general directions for day centers because they realize the importance of coordinating the new structures and services with existing facilities and services. Indeed, it is practically impossible to fix precise standards in terms of dimensions, location, and range of services to be offered. Day centers should be viewed as flexible services which can be adjusted to a variety of local conditions.

Day Hospitals

Since the function of hospital planning has been delegated to the regional governments, the day hospital has become part of the Italian health and social services. The day hospital is in fact a key element of the new program of hospital care, since it can be the link between outpatient services and proper hospital care. Day hospitals have not been conceived as a service for only the aged, though it seems quite likely that the aged will be the principal users. It is a great advantage, in psychological terms, particularly for patients who need only a few hours of treatment or care every day, to avoid the experience of entering a hospital, which carries the implicit risk of emargination. The hospital plan of the Emilia Romagna region highlights the multifunctional and rehabilitation aspects of the day hospital. It must be considered not as part of the general hospital but rather as an outpatient facility serving a population much smaller in numbers than the one served by the Local Unit of Health and Welfare Services. The link with the local general hospitals is contemplated for only a few cases. In its role as a multifunctional out-patient clinic and rehabilitation center, the day hospital must be considered as a separate and self-sufficient structure. However, the day hospital in Italy is still in a very experimental stage.

Financing

Regional governments, in general, have chosen, as a criterion for allocating funds, to have funds allocated proportionally to the numbers of persons served, with a ceiling expenditure for a single individual. The region Friuli-Venezia Giulia, for example, has a ceiling of 100.00 lire per person, whereas the region Tuscany has a ceiling of 150.00, and Veneto, a ceiling of 180.00 for each household.

Other regions allocate funds using different criteria, such as the quality of the services offered, the professional qualifications of the personnel, or the number of hours per person of domiciliary services. Clearly, these latter criteria tend to encourage the local authorities who are capable of organizing better services. The Piedmont region, for instance, provides special grants to the municipalities or groups of municipalities or "mountain communities" that have established professional social services.

A common trend in all the regional laws is, in any case, the tendency to give priority to public interventions rather than to voluntary agencies. For example, the Latium region gives 100% grants to the municipalities or group of municipalities that have established, and are operating, some services, whereas it gives 75% grants to other public agencies and only 50% grants to similar services and initiatives undertaken by private or voluntary agencies.

As mentioned above, one of the greatest dangers lies in the mechanism of grants given as "a contribution toward the expenditure" for different services. Such mechanisms favor those municipalities or agencies that are in a better financial position, whereas the ones which are worse off and whose needs may be greater are left unaided. The Piedmont laws have tried to avoid this risk by taking into consideration other priority criteria for grants, such as the number of people who would benefit from the service in proportion to the total population, the index of aging in the resident population, the size of the total population. However, even this law limits the regional grant to 60% of the cost for the personnel employed in the services (i.e., social workers, home help, and nurses). As far as day centers are concerned, the trend in current legislation is to give a grant toward the building costs (or the improvement costs), leaving the operation costs to the local authority. The only exception is the Piedmont region, where the grant provides only operating costs.

Again, with regard to financing, several smaller municipalities and agencies are finding it a serious problem. Some regional governments have clearly fixed the terms of the grant, but there are some that do not give adequate guidelines for the distribution and allocation of funds. This can create serious embarrassment for poorer municipalities that often have to incur expenditures without knowing the extent to which they will be reimbursed.

ADMINISTRATION AND PERSONNEL
OF DOMICILIARY SERVICES

On the basis of current experiences, we can recognize three types of administration of these new services.

First, services are offered and administered by the Public Assistance Agency, existing in each municipality (Ente Comunale di Assistenze, ECA). These agencies are attempting in this way to find a new legitimate reason for their own survival, since there is now a strong effort to dissolve them. In this case, ECA employs the personnel directly, and in turn the agency can benefit from the regional grants for these services, according to the mechanisms we have just described.

Another type of administration consists in the municipality promoting the new services and being responsible for them from a political-administrative point of view but subcontracting the actual running of the service to other agencies already existing in that geographical area.

In the third situation, it is the municipality which establishes and directly administers the services. In this case, the personnel are local authority personnel; the medical or paramedical personnel who come under the responsibility of the Medical Officer, or the organizer of the midwifery services; and the social work personnel, who are the same as the municipality social service. This last system of organization and administration of services is possible only in municipalities in a better economic situation. One of the problems most commonly met by the organizers of domiciliary services is the choice of criteria of eligibility to the service. It would be unthinkable, in the present economic conditions of the country, to offer a free service to all. In general, two solutions have been adopted. One is to have the service available to only citizens with low income, in which case the service becomes a welfare service. This solution is usually adopted where the service is run by ECA type agencies. The other solution is to have the service available to all citizens with a fee proportionate to the income of the household.

Other problems in operating these services concern the manpower. The basic team consists of a social worker, a nurse, and home help. Among the home help there is a high turnover, even after short periods of work, and in general a high rate of absenteeism. This is probably caused by an inadequate retribution scale, job insecurity, and the fact that the various roles are not yet clearly defined and understood by all. Home help needs better training than that provided at present. Quite often, regional laws provide for the utilization of volunteers who help those in situations where there is a lack of qualified personnel. In some cases, these laws permit volunteers to join courses of qualification run by the regional educational authorities.

EXPERIENCES IN SOME MUNICIPALITIES

Services for the Aged in Bologna

Since 1971, the municipality of Bologna has been establishing social services for the aged, aimed at helping them with three of their major problems: low income, due to the low social security benefits; housing problems; and the lack of an adequate health care. The municipality grants a supplementary benefit to a ceiling of 45.000 lire a month to supplement the pension already received by the old person; this sum does not include financial help toward rent, which can also be obtained. Other forms of financial support are a laundry service, coal or wood for heating, and free passes for transport on public conveyances. The problem of dwellings has been met in two separate ways. First, the aged have been offered flats owned by the municipality at a token rent (about 150 flats have been utilized so far). Second, flats for the aged have been reserved in all subsidized housing estates as well as in the new buildings by cooperative building societies erected on land owned by the municipality. Another important initiative was the improvement of the buildings in the historical center of town where 40% of the residents are old people.

To ascertain the actual needs in the health and social sector, each town area keeps a health register of the aged resident. A team of workers sorts out the applications for "rest homes," or hospitals, requests for home nursing, home rehabilitation treatment, and after care of aged discharged from hospitals. The team is made up of a nurse, a social worker, a chiropodist, and the local medical officer.

The Day Hospital in Monza

The day hospital in Monza was established in 1970 by the initiative of the local geriatric hospital. It takes care of about 90 old persons. The population consists mostly of patients from geriatric and psychiatric hospitals, and home bound elderly. They are all people who need rehabilitative physiotherapy or psychotherapy but do not need permanent hospitalization. The team is composed of a geriatrician, two physicians specialized in the field, one neuropsychiatrist, one social worker, and professional nurses and rehabilitation therapists.

The patients are picked up and dropped off at home by bus. They spend a full day at the hospital receiving the necessary treatments and care, including lunch. And in the afternoon they are encouraged to take part in other activities. The patients often have visits to museums and other excursions, and they produce a small newspaper. The results can be considered quite positive since none of the patients has needed to be hospitalized again.

The "Meeting Centers" of Valle Pellice

Valle Pellice is a depressed area partly because of geographical isolation, partly because of depopulation due to migration. The meeting centers result from a practical attempt to reconstitute the community. In order to prevent any form of segregation, the centers are not specifically aimed at one category of the population, such as the aged. The old and young meet there to discuss the general problems of the community, including the problems of the aged themselves. Young and old people jointly organize meetings, discussion groups, and activities of a recreational and cultural nature. The effort is made to overcome the isolation so typical of old age so that the meeting center is a real alternative to the solitary drink in the "osteria."

Meeting centers often contain facilities open to the general population of residents, such as a cafeteria, public baths and showers, and some rooms for temporary emergency shelter. They are surrounded by a garden, and often land that can be cultivated jointly as vegetable gardens. Each center has a social worker responsible for the various activities and general functioning of the center. All the domiciliary services of the Valle Pellice are linked with the centers.

CONCLUSIONS

The new regional legislation represents a step forward from the way in which social services were once thought of in Italy. Unquestionably, there are still many gaps with some interventions only partially put into practice. Italy still lacks a national law dealing with the reform of social services. A bill for this reform has been waiting in Parliament for years. There is a further delay at present because of the need to coordinate some of the provisions with those contemplated in the National Health Service Bill. Until these two bills become laws of the country, the picture will be incomplete.

Regional governments have tried to stimulate the national government. They offer the first examples of "open" services from which it will be possible to draw some conclusions based on experience. We must underline two characteristics of basic importance for this type of service, without which it would be meaningless to speak of reform. There is a definite attempt to start a democratic participation in the service management, both on the part of the users and one the part of other social groups. There is a definite awareness of the importance of involving the users in the service delivery. The regulations established by the Lombardy region for residential homes are exemplary, as are the provision of the Umbria region, where the users can benefit either by the service directly or by an equivalent amount of money.

Another area where regional governments have shown the way is in adjusting the architectural features of buildings to the needs of the aged and handicapped. The design of service centers can be seen as examples.

There is still a long way to go before we can say that Italy has a satisfactory social service system, but at least we can see at present its necessary beginnings.

REFERENCES

Annuario Statistico dell'Assistenze e della Previdenza Sociale (1976) Istituto Centrale di Statistica, Vol. XX Roma.

FLOREA, A. (1977). Anziani e societa industriale. Napoli: Liguori Editore.

FLOREA, A. (1976). "Isolamento e solitudine della donna anziana" in La Rivista di Servizio Sociale, I part #4/1975, II parte #2/1976.

7

INTERVENTION STRATEGIES FOR THE AGED IN INDIA

M. M. DESAI
and M. D. KHETANI

In traditional Indian society, old age is considered a "storehouse" of knowledge and wisdom. The aged in India are looked upon with respect and reverence, whereas in a "future-oriented" western society, the aged tend to be considered as a "spent force." Yet, depending upon sub-cultural differences within India, aging has different implications. In rural communities, with a strong agricultural base, aging may not pose as serious a problem as it does in urban, industrialized communities. Furthermore, aging to a man and woman has different meaning in terms of status, roles, and expectations.

The family as an institution is passing through revolutionary changes in most parts of the world. The Indian family of the future is likely to be nuclear in structure, consisting of parents and their children. The larger family network consisting of the nuclear family, grandparents, unmarried adult children, aunts, uncles, and so on is likely to disappear as urbanization gathers momentum (Singer and Cohn, 1968: 340). Further, given the increasing tempo of social change, even in simple societies, the gap between the values and attitudes of the old and the young will widen (Desai and Bhalla, 1978: 40). According to some scholars, even preindustrial societies are not exempt from these inevitabilities.

In Indian society the problem of the aged has not yet assumed significant proportions. It is still a problem of the future, but one which demands our attention now. Planned intervention at this stage, therefore, would help to conserve the human and material resources to meet the needs of the aged. While considering the intervention strategies for the aged in India, it is essential to take into account their status and roles in relation to various socioeconomic groups within rural and urban communities and to base the intervention on the integration of traditional values and structures with modern concepts of organized service systems.

This chapter focuses on the social situation of the aged in India, in the context of traditional backgrounds, social change, and current demographic characteristics of the aging population. Their needs are then considered against this background, and the existing intervention strategies, informal and formal, are analyzed.

SOCIAL SITUATION OF THE AGED IN INDIA

Background

Indian society is broadly influenced by norms, values, and traditions basic to Hindu religion, though the individualities of other religions are maintained and the religions influence one another. According to the ancient laws of social organization, the life span of an individual is divided into four ashrams, or stages: (1) Brahmacheryashrama, or the stage of a celibate learner, (2) Grihastashrama, or the stage of work for the world as a householder, (3) Vanaprasthashrama, or a stage of gradual disengagement from worldly duties and loosening of social bonds, and (4) Sannyashrama, or the stage of complete disengagement leading to renunciation for achievement of spiritual freedom. Life is viewed as a pilgrimage of the human soul to eternal communion with the Supreme through evolving stages.

During the first stage, the growing child, through training and discipline of body and mind, is moulded to a life of duty. During the second stage, he, as a youth, is expected to lead the life of a householder or a grihasta. India knew for centuries that repressed desires are more corrupting in their effects than those exposed openly and freely. Marriage is considered necessary for the total personality development through a full life and the performance of social responsibilities. The family is considered to be a partnership, not only among the living but also between the living and the dead (Radhakrishnan, 1926: 84). During the third stage, an individual is expected to end his affiliations and associations with various social groups. It is a stage of gradual social disengagement, a life of inquiry and meditation leading to self-realization. As Radhakrishnan explains, man's social efficiency is not the measure of his spiritual strength, nor can a complete involvement in the family, the nation, and the world satisfy man's soul. At this stage, he should be a disinterested and detached individual, his life dedicated to the pursuit of the welfare of the community (Bhagvan Das, 1910: Kapadia, 1959). The aim of the fourth stage is to attain a state of complete spiritual freedom, which characterizes the life of an ascetic. It is a period of complete disengagement from all worldly connections. "These free men are solitary souls who have no personal attachments or private ambitions, but embody in their own spirit the freedom of the world" (Radhakrishnan, 1926: 91).

Hindu religion thus encourages the individual, through his life-span, to move toward attainment of inner peace and tranquility. This ancient concept has lost much of its original impact because of changing social conditions and personal goals. However, its significance is not entirely lost. The aged in India still pursue religious activities. Some are even preoccupied with voluntary welfare services to the community. Consideration of intervention services for the aged, to be realistic and meaningful, should, therefore, be based upon a synthesis of relevant concepts of the past with the present.

Understanding of traditional Hindu family is important, although the family is changing slowly. The traditional concept of life span remains closely related to the traditional family pattern and the role and status of an individual in the family. A typical traditional Hindu joint family is patri- carchal in nature: the senior male member is the head, holding the position of authority. It emphasizes a system of relationship between male copartners and their dependents. The age of the individual determines his status and role in the hierarchy. In such a family system the aged are respected and their advice is sought in the handling of intrafamily affairs. Further, the joint family, by providing social security through mutuality of relationships, helps and encourages interdependence. The aged along with other dependent groups are provided for within the family, in part because of moral obliga- tion. The benefits are often extended to a larger kinship network and even beyond. The aged can find a sense of fulfilment in being with grandchildren and playing vital roles in their socialization. According to Ross (1961: 70), in the Hindu system of family obligations, the sons are expected to look after their parents in old age and illness. If there are no sons, it is the duty of the daughters. After daughters, obligations fall on brothers, uncles, and, finally, other relatives. The traditional Indian social structure thus has a built-in arrangement for the care of the aged. But this traditional arrangement is undergoing slow but steady change.

Changes

Modernization tends to lead the change of a total society from a relatively rural way of life based on manpower, limited technology, and comparatively parochial and traditional values to a predominantly urban phenomena charac- terized by inanimate power, highly developed scientific technology, and differentiated institutions leading to segmented individual roles with emphasis on efficiency (Desai and Bhalla, 1978).

In analyzing family patterns in the changing social situation in India, it is important to know not only whether the family is "joint" or "nuclear" but whether it has begun to show a change of direction. For example, individuals may live in joint households and yet have conceptions of their roles, responsibilities, and expectations akin to those in nuclear family system, or other individuals may live in nuclear households and yet follow the norms of a joint family system. In most social situations, Hindu kinship patterns provide for the latter (Gore, 1968: 39). The 1971 Census of India gives the total population of India as 547.4 million, of which 108.8 million (20%) are urban. Statistically, the process of industrialization and urbanization in India is slow. Its significance is, therefore, likely to be underestimated. In addition, the growth rate of the urban population is greater than the growth rate of the rural population. However, even this level of change has great impact considering that a major part of it has been achieved within a comparatively short time since independence. Industrial economy has created new occupations for which the old person with highly crystalized attitudes and habit-patterns is usually unsuitable. Young people, either with training for new occupations or with the plasticity of youth and with years before them for molding, are preferred. Mass migration of the young and better-educated segments of rural population to industrial centers for jobs is increasingly evident. The older persons are usually left behind in rural areas. They, with those young left behind, carry the traditional task of agriculture and other rural occupations. The urbanization of Indian society is at the cost of the traditional joint family system. Several studies suggest that at present a majority of adults in Indian society do not live in joint families and that a majority of the rural people live in either a joint or supplemented nuclear family (a nuclear family including one or more unmarried, separated or widowed relations of the parents and/or married children; Singer and Cohn, 1968: 390). When families do not live in a joint household, close interrelationships are still maintained with the larger kinship groups. Most families continue to take care of their aged. Yet the aged without spouse, the childless aged, or those not having interrelationships with children often become destitute. When the aged parents stay with their sons in the cities, they may be consulted in socio-religious matters, but the employed sons, particularly if educated, tend to head the family. Further, the aged who could be gainfully self-employed in an agrarian society may find themselves unoccupied in an industrial society. Thus, in a work-oriented and youth-oriented environment of cities, the status between the generations is often inverted.

The traditional behavior pattern is often diffused with concepts of individualism and self-assertion. This change is generally observed among the educated middle class adults in service. However, in rich families involved in business and certain other occupations, the elders exercise a great deal of authority because of their experience and high social status. These social changes are observed largely in urban areas, but because of improved means of transport and communication they are also permeating the rural communities. According to Desai and Bhalla (1978) the status of the aged in rural areas is on the decline. Thus, studies of Burail village of Punjab in 1962, of Ratan Garh in 1963, and of Shamirpet village in South Central India in 1955 have shown that in preindustrialized agricultural Indian communities the aged occupy a precarious position. According to one study, two-thirds of the aged are in families where the head of the family is the son. One half reported that their absence would not disrupt the family's functioning. It was also observed that a majority of aged women have status primarily if their spouse is alive, while they are physically able to perform some beneficial functions in the family, or if they have valuable material in their possession.

Employment

Job opportunities in Indian society have not kept pace with the increasing population. The youth work force is increasing. Hence, the statutory retirement age for employment has been introduced in certain organized industrial sectors, such as factories, plantations, and mines. However, a sudden arrest of work and gross reduction of earnings irrespective of the person's physical fitness and efficiency on retirement have created problems. In India, 55 to 58 years is the usual age of retirement. However, as the Indian economy is still predominantly agricultural, retirement is gradual and voluntary for most. The working force participation among the aged decreased considerably from 1961 to 1971. As urbanization increases, a lower proportion of the older people in the working force is to be expected. Such an increase in the nonproductive consumer group will have significant effects on the economy of the country. The pressure of maintaining dependents will increase.

Demographic Characteristics

An important consequence of industrialization is the improvement in health and medical services, leading to a decline in the death rate and an increase in life expectancy. The death rate in India has fallen faster than the birth rate, resulting in rapid growth in the population on the whole and an increase in the population of those above 60 years of age.

The population of the aged in India has increased every decade in the twentieth century. Although the number of aged is increasing, their proportion to total population has not increased significantly. This may be due to high birth rate and reduction in infant mortality.

Increasing longevity, particularly when combined with malnutrition and undernutrition, contributes to an increase in nonproductive consumers, the extension of the family into more generations, an increase in the number of chronically ill and disabled requiring comprehensive delivery of health, medical, and social services. The majority of the aged in India are poor in health and usually indifferent to health care. However, only around 5 to 8% are invalid and in need of a helper (Desai and Bhalla, 1978).

In 1961, 46.4% of the aged were married with the spouse alive and 51.41% were widowed. However, in 1971, 53% were married with the spouse alive and about 45% were widowed. Fewer than 2% were never married, and fewer than 1% were divorced or separated. Further, it is significant to note that among the married aged there are more males than females whereas among the widowed there are more females than males. The aged who never married are mainly males.

About 50% of the aged live alone, mainly because of the death of the spouse, and in a few cases because of being unmarried, separated, or divorced. A majority of these staying alone are females. In Indian society, widows usually do not remarry whereas widowers do.

The aged woman in ancient India served as a "doorkeeper" to the past traditions, customs, and values. Her role has changed. In contemporary Indian society when a married son lives with his widowed mother, he is the formal head of the household. However, until the son becomes adult, the mother plays an important role in the household. The condition of the widows without children is particularly miserable. Few widows are independent; a majority live a life of economic and social dependence and, at times, one of total destitution.

Despite some new legislation, most Indian women are still economically dependent, educationally ill equipped, and socially tradition bound. For example, according to the Hindu Succession Act, women are legally coparceners with children in the inheritance of family property.

In general, life of the aged woman in India is bound to the home and family. She has limited interest in the world outside of her family. Her life centers around the care of her house and/or the grandchildren, going to temples or on pilgrimages, visits to relatives and neighbors, and the like.

ASSESSING THE NEEDS OF THE AGED IN INDIA

Health and Medical Needs

In India, the majority of the aged tend to take sickness for granted and depend on indigenous medicine. There are insufficient and inadequate medical facilities, particularly in the rural areas. Even when available, the cost of medical care is beyond the means of most. Hence, the health needs of the majority of the aged are unattended. Their primary needs are for (a) audio-visual aids and dentures, (b) accessible medical dispensaries, (c) visiting nurses, and (d) care in hospitals or institutions.

Need for Economic Security

About 4,500,000 aged males and 14,000,000 females in India are not working. Recent studies on the problems of retired people and civil pensioners conducted by the Indian Institute of Public Administration, composed of primary school teachers, clerical workers and gazetted officers in Bombay city, (Desai, 1975), on the problems of aging in India (Soodan 1975), on the problems of the aged in Delhi (Delhi School of Social Work, 1973), and a few others reveal the following common findings: (1) an inadequacy of pension in relation to current living conditions, (2) a lack of savings to meet the liability of marriage, house, children's education, and so on, (3) very little savings to depend upon in crisis situations, (4) a positive correlation between adjustment level and per capita income, (5) a majority belonging to a lower-income group, (6) a lack of planning for life adjustment after retirement, (7) some working out of habit, (8) a direct correlation between the status of the old person and his economic status, and (9) the younger generation's giving of lip service to the tradition of old persons still being the "heads," though in reality such is not the case. Further, it is noted that a small proportion leave their jobs because they want to, whereas a large proportion retire because they are compelled to by statutory or private rules. A majority work out of financial necessity as long as they can, if they are fortunate enough to get jobs. For those in agriculture and other self-employing occupations, retirement is gradual and may not cause sharp decline in income, loss of social status, or unscheduled leisure time.

Need for Planned Leisure Time Activities

Increased participation in religious activities among 44% of the women is observed by Soodan (1975). At the same time, a decrease in religious faith is reported for an equal number. Aged women also spend part of their time in taking care of grandchildren, visiting relations, attending social festivals, and so on. The aged men may take to increased domestic activities like marketing or caring for grandchildren. Organized recreation is possible for a very few, since the needed facilities are extremely inadequate and costly. A study of Saraswati Mishra in 1976 indicates that the aged who are active members of

Part III

AGING AND HEALTH

INTRODUCTION

In the following essays, particular, but not exclusive attention, is given to the health problems of aging persons. Material is presented from eight different countries. There is growing recognition of the need for specialized attention to the health and medical care needs of the aged. One set of issues deriving from this recognition has to do with whether or not these needs are best met as part of a total plan designed to meet the health and medical care needs of the entire population. Within such a plan, how are the needs of the aged singled out for special consideration? Should they be singled out?

A second set of issues has to do with the integration of health, medical, and social services. Preoccupation with meeting the health and medical care needs might conceivably deemphasize the importance of meeting social needs. Moreover, it could be argued that concern with meeting these needs must yield to priority concern with meeting the economic needs of the aged.

A review of provisions for meeting health and medical care needs points up the requirement for comprehensive and coordinated attention to all the needs of aging persons. Since public services are provided through governmental bureaucracies, there is inevitable fragmentation that coincides with the territorial boundaries of each governmental department or ministry. There is no simple, neat solution to this dilemma. Perhaps the most that one can hope for is that those responsible for meeting the health and medical care needs of the aging will keep in the foreground the knowledge that the aging person—like all other persons—is a whole human being with a variety of needs. Tunnel vision which focuses on only one set of these needs—important as that set may be—does a disservice to the aging person as a bio-psycho-socio-cultural-spiritual being.

—M.I.T.

8

HELP STRUCTURES FOR THE AGED SICK
Experiences in Seven Countries

ADRIENE GOMMERS,
BERNADETTE HANKENNE,
and BEATRICE ROGOWSKI

The seven countries studied in this report, the United States of America, Canada, the Netherlands, Denmark, Norway, France, and Belgium, were selected on the basis of two main considerations: (1) their population comprises a high proportion of elderly persons, and (2) their health policies and structures correspond to the type called "liberal." Thus, we automatically excluded all socialist republics and those with a very structured national health service, like Great Britain.

The studies, necessarily succinct for each country, were based on bibliographic research and personal visits to officials and institutions. The latter activity helped us realize the enormous gap that exists between that which is planned, proposed, or reported and that which is realized.

Since our main concern is the sick elderly, the report reviews the old age policies for each country under consideration within the larger framework of its national health and social security programs. The report makes an inventory of health services, including those open to all comers and those catering to the sick elderly in particular. Also studied are the structure, organization, and functioning of alternative medical, social, and domiciliary services that allow an older person to remain at home though frail or infirm.

AUTHORS' NOTE: *The following is a synthesis of a survey report sponsored by the Committee on the Challenges of Modern Society of NATO. In its original form, it is 140 pages and its title is "Structures d'aide aux personnes agees malades, analyse des realisations dans sept pays occidentaux." The report was prepared by the Center for Gerontological Studies of the University of Louvain, Belgium, in 1977.*

THE NETHERLANDS

The situation of the elderly in the Netherlands appears privileged when compared to that of neighboring countries.

All persons over 65 receive a pension, independent of any financial help they can obtain from relatives. Pensions are adjusted to the national wage index. Eighty percent of the elderly are covered by social security and sickness insurance programs. The remaining 20% have recourse to private health insurance schemes. The National Sickness Insurance, with a limited duration of one year, covers practically all hospital, medical, and paramedical costs. The Special Sickness Insurance Act (*Algemene Wet Bijzondera Ziektekosten*—AWBZ), established in 1968, assists all patients, young and old, physically or mentally sick, who are in need of long-term medical assistance.

The planning and administration of matters concerning the elderly depend on four ministries: Health, Social Affairs, Culture, and Housing. This results in bureaucratic entanglements, as seen in the management of institutions for the aged which have both sections for the sick (Ministry of Health) and a residential section (Ministries of Housing and Culture). In typical Dutch pragmatic fashion, these matters are usually resolved without letting red tape affect the well-being or needs of residents. However, these four ministries are all represented in a coordinating body that establishes the main guidelines for old age planning and policy.

In 1970 their main emphasis focused on the well-being and housing of the elderly, with a general effort toward deinstitutionalization and home care. In 1975 the integration of the elderly within their community was accentuated by the decision to reduce the rate of institutionalized persons from 10% to 7% via the construction of more adapted lodgings to meet the special needs of the elderly, and increasing extramural and domiciliary services.

Help Structures

The general practitioner and the district nurse are the first line contacts for the elderly. There is no geriatric specialization, and doctors' fees are paid on a per capita basis.

Institutions

General Hospital. This is the point of entry of the sick person into the health system. In the Netherlands, as in most of the countries studied, about 25% of all acute beds are occupied by the elderly. Given the view that the general hospital can cope with any pathology presented by the aged, the official policy is to avoid the development of geriatric hospitals. Nevertheless, certain private, charitable foundations have established institutions reserved for the elderly. Certain general hospitals have opened geriatric wards which function as research centers and act as training facilities for medical and nursing personnel working with the elderly.

Nursing Homes (Verpleegtehuizen). Often the elderly person presenting chronic disease or disability when seen at polyclinics or by family physicians is referred directly to a nursing home. These are usually owned by charitable institutions and are oriented toward rehabilitation. Terminal care is also provided. Such facilities are open to all age groups; however, 85% of their population is 65 years old and over. There are about 33,000 beds in these institutions which service three types of patient populations: (1) physically disabled, (2) mentally disturbed, and (3) those needing mixed facilities.

The Netherlands is the one country discussed in this report that faces squarely the problem of the mentally sick elderly and provides specialized facilities for their care. Again, in typical fashion the Dutch are reluctant to segregate this category of patients and consequently favor the mixed facility solution where transfers from one section to another are not traumatic and the personnel and facilities are generalized rather than specialized. Nursing homes for the physically and mentally impaired concentrate on active treatment. This factor was the foremost impression gained during our visits in Holland, where beds and wards were usually empty, with patients shopping, visiting, or busy at various therapeutic activities.

Though nursing homes are mostly privately owned, they are subsidized, and the cost to the patients is taken over by the Special Sickness Insurance (AWBZ) entirely.

Day Hospitals. This service does not operate from general hospitals. Instead, most nursing homes are expected to offer day hospital care. As a result the turnover of patients is accelerated, since the elderly can leave earlier and continue to be looked after in an extramural fashion. This form of treatment is also fully paid for by the Special Sickness Insurance (AWBZ).

Old People's Homes (Verzorgingshuizen). These are public or private institutions that house invalid and semiinvalid elderly. They are supervised by the Ministry of Culture, which controls the licensing and overall planning for building, services, and tariffs. The core personnel of these institutions is comprised of assistant nurses specifically trained to look after the elderly. About 10% of the aged in Holland live in these institutions; since 1970 this population has not increased, due to specific government policy to stabilize or reduce the number of institutionalized elderly.

Medicosocial Services

Apart from adapted housing for the old and the handicapped (87,000 units) and service flats, which are small flats with centralized nursing and home-help services (15,000 units), special mention must be made of the service centers (*Dienst Central*). These are institutions peculiar to the Netherlands which provide medical and social services to the aged and the handicapped of all ages living alone. Each service center is responsible for at least 1,000 persons. They offer hot meals at home or in restaurants, home help, social work services, leisure activities, medical consultation, and a variety of paramedical services such as physiotherapy, ergotherapy, and chiropody. In 1974 there were 180 such centers.

There are also health centers (Gezondheidscentra), whose two main functions are coordinating the medical and medicosocial services available and emphasizing prevention (medical check-ups; hygienic, legal, nursing, and administrative counseling).

Besides nursing aides trained to help the sick and disabled old people, there is a category of personnel, also found in Belgium, called *Bejaardenhelpsters*. These home helpers for the aged work in old people's homes and in the community with the main emphasis now being on community and domiciliary care. The lack of trained personnel (nurses, nursing aides, social workers) is one of the main obstacles to the application of government programs. As in the past, voluntary workers are called in to help bridge the gap between what is intended and what can be put into application.

Conclusions

The Netherlands offers a great variety of services and institutions that seem to respond to the needs of the aged sick. Long-term planning and coordination underlie present efforts. Emphasis is on keeping the elderly in their own environment. Lack of personnel is a major obstacle for the fulfillment of this policy. Noteworthy in the Netherlands is the significant amount of active participation by the elderly at all decision-making levels and consistent efforts to integrate old people into larger social networks.

DENMARK

In Denmark the Social Affairs Ministry has a special bureau designed to deal with matters pertaining to the elderly. All requests on their behalf, whether coming from the family doctor or members of the family, are examined by an official from the ministry in order to find the best solution. It should be pointed out that this is never done without taking into consideration the wishes of the aged person. This centralization appears to be beneficial, and it contributes to the maintenance of the elderly in their own homes.

Social legislation and the total coverage by sickness insurance schemes help the Danes face their old age without any major financial fears.

Doctors are paid a per capita fee, which, as is the case in the Netherlands, diminishes after 1,500 patients in order to limit the number of patients and preserve a workable and therapeutic doctor-patient ratio. Hospitalization and medical consultations are free, though the patient must contribute 25% of the cost of prescribed medication.

In Denmark, a long tradition makes collaboration between government and private organizations (homes for the elderly, geriatric clinics, adapted lodings, and so on) easy, permanent, and beneficial for the elderly.

Help Structures

Institutions

General Hospitals. The elderly are first seen in the general wards, where a complete diagnosis is made. At the next phase of care they are either treated in the acute section or referred directly to long-term or geriactic wards. Here the emphasis is upon rehabilitation before placement in a nursing home or return to private domicile.

Day Hospitals. These exist for the elderly who are still in need of treatment but can spend the night at home. Medical, psychological, and social factors are attended to with the goal of the elderly maintaining their own homes as long as possible.

Nursing Homes. There is very little difference in the functioning or resident population of nursing homes and old people's homes with a nursing wing. Consequently, they shall be addressed simultaneously.

Nursing homes are generally small, about 50 to 70 beds; the average age of residents is 80 years; many are not sick but merely lonely and frail. These homes are under the supervision of long-term wards in general hospitals. Hence, purely social cases are not admitted. These homes are administered either by government or private auspices. A personnel-patient ratio of 1:1 necessitates considerable subsidization.

In Denmark nursing homes are not associated with general hospitals but are attached to adapted lodgings for the elderly and to day centers. Also typical of Denmark are the day nursing homes, where medical and social aspects are emphasized; this is the basic difference from a day center, where mainly social and leisure activities are dealt with.

The adapted housing solution, flats specially designed for frail or handicapped old people, an original effort, is highly in demand by the elderly and their families and positively encouraged by the authorities. These adapted flats are built in conjunction with a nursing home and a day center so that all medical and social aspects can be attended to. Such linkages enable transfers to occur promptly and smoothly. One of the best examples of this typically Danish alternative is the Peter Lykke Center in Copenhagen comprising 240 flats of this kind.

Medicosocial Services

About 25% of persons over 70 years are estimated to be in need of home-help services, and 2% are in need of nursing care at home. These needs are generally covered by existing organizations: the "Home Nursing System" and the "Home Help System." In order to avoid institutionalization, there is an extension of financial help to relatives (other than spouses) of the elderly who spend more than 16 hours a week caring for them.

Day Centers exist for social purposes, though they can also provide some nursing care.

Measures against institutionalization of the elderly also include meals on wheels, subsidized restaurants, daily telephone calls to check on needs or well-being, and subsidies for the creation of suitable housing conditions (ramps, wide doors, light switches, adapted toilets, and bathrooms).

Conclusions

State control and the encouragement and financing of private initiatives make a happy combination that benefits the elderly in Denmark. Here more than anywhere else in this study, the freedom of the individual is maintained. He keeps his dignity and his independence to the end, thanks to a variety of solutions and alternatives offered to him, by far the most attractive being that of the adapted lodging combined with nursing home and day centers, which seems to cover most of his needs. Here as in the other countries, the supply lags behind demand and need, both in equipment and in personnel.

NORWAY

The sick elderly are the responsibility of two ministries in Norway: the Ministry of Health and the Ministry of Social Affairs.

There is a National Council for the Care of the Aged, which coordinates different actions in favor of the elderly; the two Ministries mentioned, local authorities, research bodies, the elderly themselves, and organizations are represented therein. Doctors are the first contact the elderly have with the health system. They operate with great independence and are paid by the patient who is later reimbursed. Doctors refer the elderly to hospitals and nursing homes or give instructions for the intervention of a home nursing service where needed.

The government has a number of Medical District Officers, who are in charge of prevention and epidemiological studies and also have special responsibility for the health of the elderly.

Help Structures

Institutions

General Hospitals. The sick elderly are first treated or at least diagnosed at a general hospital before being directed to specific treatment services, including nursing homes. Very few hospitals in Norway have geriatric wards or long-term treatment units. Likewise, very few day hospitals exist.

Nursing Homes. Most nursing homes are run by local authorities, but some are in private hands. Some of them specialize in the care of the mentally sick. They operate as long-term care units, providing all medical and nursing care required. The patients are free to appeal to their family doctor for treatment.

Nursing homes have been included, since 1970, in the Joint Health Plan of each county; therefore, they are not only supervised and controlled but also subsidized (up to 75% of costs are covered by the National Insurance Scheme). There are long waiting lists; estimates indicate that only about half of the present need for nursing home beds is being covered. One factor in this high demand may well be the fact that nursing homes come under the Hospital Act. Thus, the cost of inpatient care in a nursing home is considerably lower than the cost in an old people's home.

Old Age Homes. These homes cater to the ambulatory elderly. As in Denmark and the Netherlands, many municipalities in Norway have "combined homes," with one section being an old age home and the other a nursing home. The shortage of beds in nursing homes obliges the old age homes to accept the sick elderly as well.

Medicosocial Services

It is estimated that because of the lack of sufficient domiciliary services about 13% of the elderly still in their homes will have to be institutionalized.

The Health and Welfare Center. Each center has the responsibility of serving about 3,000 disabled or elderly persons who remain in their homes.

There are 76 centers in Norway, 16 of which are in Oslo. They offer a variety of aids, ranging from home help, meals on wheels, chiropody, hairdressing, baths, social activities, and, above all, the services of social workers who advise the aged and put them in touch with necessary medical or nursing services when these are called for.

Home Nursing Service. Every town has a home nursing service supervised by a chief nurse. These services are given free to the elderly, who, nevertheless, must pay for prescribed medicines, bandages, and other materials.

To compensate for a great shortage of visiting nurses, Norwegians have created a nursing supplement whereby financial compensation is paid to neighbors or relatives who look after a sick old person. This measure allows a working person to stay home and tend to the needs of a sick friend or family member. Even if the person is not qualified, a very humane means of nursing is facilitated. Nursing aids and equipment are lent to patients at home from 2,000 centers operating all over the country and run by voluntary organizations.

Home-Help Service. The health and welfare services mentioned above assess the need for and assign home helpers to disabled elderly. They are paid according to the income of the elderly person. In 1971, 11% of the population were assisted by home-helpers. The number of hours assigned to each person is determined by the district social worker who appraises need. In this sector, too, there is an acute shortage of personnel. Relatives or neighbors are given financial payment for home help care they provide the elderly.

Conclusions

In Norway, as in Denmark, the government encourages and subsidizes a variety of private institutions and individuals who assist the elderly. Nonetheless, the government retains decision-making power in the appraisal of needs and assignment of resources. As in the Netherlands and Denmark, the "mixed solution" which combines residential and health institutions for the elderly seems to gain more and more favor in the municipalities of Norway.

One must point out the apparent shortage of nursing home beds, of adapted lodgings, home-nursing and home-helping personnel.

But, as a palliative and positive approach, the development of financial help to families and friends who give nursing or home help to the sick elderly must be praised.

In Norway, Denmark, and the Netherlands, the elderly can be considered as privileged in the range of opportunities offered them and in the financial assistance provided by the state, which ensures that at no point will a sick old person not have access to an adequate service because of lack of financial means.

THE UNITED STATES OF AMERICA

In the United States, more than in any other country considered in this report, the principles of individual freedom and nonintervention of the state in private matters are predominant and have delayed until quite recently many social legislation measures existent in other countries and a general sickness insurance coverage. The Medicare Program has existed since 1966 and provides hospitalization and medical insurance financed by general tax funds and monthly contributions by individuals. It covers exclusively persons 65 years old and over.

To help the aged and the poor of all ages, a Medicaid system was set up parallel to Medicare. It operates like a welfare fund and covers health costs up to a certain amount.

Medicare is not a total coverage system; prescription drugs, orthopedic aids, hearing-aids, and glasses are not included. It has been estimated that in 1973 Medicare only covered 47% of all health costs to the elderly.

Apart from the Social Security Act and Medicare, there are very few directives from the different states or the federal government concerning the elderly. A White House Conference on Aging has put forward a number of proposals, including the total coverage of prescribed medication and, above all, the setting up of a comprehensive health system with acute and long-term facilities, home care, day hospitals, and home help. Realizations remain scattered, and they are mainly created by private initiatives.

Help Structures

Institutions

General Hospitals. There are about 1,000,000 hospital beds, 30% of which are occupied by older people. Medical practitioners make few home calls and have a traditional tendency to hospitalize their patients; this leads to an increase of acute beds to the detriment of medium- and long-term facilities.

Day Hospitals. Apart from the pioneering efforts of Montefiori Hospital in New York beginning in 1972, there is little reference in the literature studied to other institutions of this kind in the United States. (In Great Britain, for example, day hospitals are much more numerous.)

Intermediate Care Facilities. These have appeared specifically in the state of New York. Slightly handicapped people are lodged and are able to use medical and paramedical facilities at a Nursing Home to which the facilities are usually annexed.

Nursing Homes. The recent proliferation of nursing homes is such that the expression "Nursing Home Industry" has been used. Seventy percent of them are in private hands, and their costs have escalated to such an extent that most residents must have recourse to Medicaid. They offer various degrees of care: (a) skilled nursing facilities, 33%; (b) limited nursing care, 42%; (c) personal care, 25%.

Transfers to and from hospitals remain one of the major bottlenecks in the health care system in the States. Another factor worth noting is the increased number of old people with mental disturbances who arrive at nursing homes as a direct result of the closing of or transfers from psychiatric facilities.

Although there are controls regarding hygiene and medical and nursing quality, conditions vary greatly in the United States (as in the other places studied, with the possible exception of the Scandinavian countries), going from excellent to appalling. The inordinate growth of nursing homes reflects a tendency, already discarded in some European countries, to institutionalize the elderly.

Medicosocial Services

According to the National Health Survey by Shanos (1971), about 15% of older people are homebound because of disabilities or frailties. Only 0.5% receive any kind of domiciliary help. It is precisely the medicosocial services which are most lacking in the United States. This can be attributed to traditional medical practices and the tendency to hospitalize.

Home Care. A Home Care Service was started in 1948 at New York's Montefiori Hospital. Despite its obvious success, only about 100 similar organizations exist today.

Home Nursing. There are about 2,160 certified home health agencies. They provide varied services such as physiotherapy, ergotherapy, speech therapy, nursing, and nutrition guidance. They are organized independent of hospitals and are run by private, voluntary, or government agencies.

Day Centers. Usually attached to nursing homes, day centers provide nursing help, rehabilitation assistance, and nutrition advice.

Conclusions

The main trend at present in the United States is the emphasis on institutionalization of the elderly, as is suggested by the extensive utilization of hospital beds and the proliferation of nursing homes. This occurs to the detriment of community health services and home health care facilities which would allow the elderly to remain at home at a lower cost to the community and to their greater satisfaction.

A significant development in the United States has been the creation of the geriatric nurse practitioner, a registered nurse with special training and extended responsibilities touching on medical acts. Such workers are called to play an ever-increasing health role with the geriatric population.

CANADA

General health planning and policies in Canada were based for a long time on the principle of the individual's freedom of choice of physician or favored health institution. Each provincial government also had its own health programs and financing schemes.

The Federal Medical Act of 1968 gives only partial medical insurance coverage. Old persons in need are assisted, but the amount varies greatly from province to province.

This independence of the provinces in their programming and allocation of resources produces great disparity in geriatric services. This is a major difficulty when trying to present a picture of Canadian help structures for the aged sick.

Help Structures

Physicians operate on a fee-for-service system, rarely making domiciliary calls. The sick person will frequently use emergency hospital services, though new services like the family medical practice located in the hospitals and the community health centers are being created.

Institutions

General Hospitals. These institutions can treat acute or chronic diseases. The aged sick occupy a large proportion of beds, 22% in acute and 76% in chronic wards. Because of the lack of more adequate structures, physicians tend to hospitalize the handicapped, whose real place is not in an acute bed. A tendency exists which compels acute hospitals to keep a certain amount of chronic sick. From the patient's point of view, it is preferable to be admitted and stay in a hospital, where his costs are totally covered, than to be treated on an outpatient or home care basis, which requires the elderly person to cover part of the cost. Since neither the individual, the physician, nor the hospital have any financial incentive to use them, this policy leads to the neglect of lower level facilities, outpatient clinics, and nursing homes.

Rehabilitation Hospitals. These institutions concentrate on reeducation therapies. Length of stay is of an average three months. They are excellent hospitals; however, because they are open to all categories of patients of all ages, the elderly tend not to receive very specific attention. Consequently, their stay here is less beneficial than a stay in a similar institution in the Netherlands.

Long-Term Care Centers. These centers for patients needing prolonged and heavy nursing can be paralleled to similar institutions found in many other countries. The patient must transfer from another hospital. Despite severe admission criteria, waiting lists are very long.

Specialized Structures for the Aged. These can be boarding houses, homes for the aged, or nursing homes. Sixty percent are run by private organizations. In all these institutions one finds frail or sick elderly. The level of nursing and admission criteria and the denomination vary from province to province. Adequate services such as rehabilitation, physiotherapy, or ergotherapy are not always provided.

Day Hospitals. Not exclusively reserved for the elderly, these facilities provide medical and nursing treatment as well as physiotherapy.

Lodgings with Services. Many construction programs are under way, and the waiting lists are very long. The main accent is put on quality-price ratio rather than on services. In 60% of these lodgings neither home help nor meals are provided.

Medicosocial Services

Day Centers. These give certain light treatments such as chiropody and basic nursing care.

Home Nursing and Home Care. These programs have existed for a long time in the various Canadian provinces. The hospital usually signals that a patient could continue his treatment at home. Then a liaison nurse contacts the hospital nurse, and, in conjunction with the physician, they decide if home conditions allow for home care. No isolated patient is ever admitted to this form of treatment. The nurses are instructed to spend sufficient time in training the patient and his family in elementary nursing techniques and hygiene, principal concerns of the home care program. This employment is highly appreciated by nurses and much in demand. Home care organizations are usually privately run although completely subsidized by the government. Treatment is totally free because this modality of care helps reduce the number of hospital beds in line with the present policy in Canada. The

11,000 patients who are under home care in Quebec would require a 100-bed hospital facility.

Home Help. This service provides hygienic assistance including baths, house cleaning, and the preparation of meals. Because of the limited numbers of home helpers, this service is reserved exclusively for the sick elderly.

The handicapped and the fragile will thus eventually find their way to the hospital because of the lack of minor domestic aid within the community which might have helped prevent institutionalization. New programs such as "Home Living Assistance Project" will help provide a remedy for this situation.

Community Health Centers. An original Canadian innovation, the community health centers program is still in an experimental stage. All ages are eligible, the guiding thought being that health is the business of everybody. The basic concept is to aid the individual in his own locality. These centers provide home help and home health care on a local basis and following local initiatives, for areas of up to 30,000 people. Their main emphasis is on social, psychosocial, and leisure activities. In theory this should allow the fitting of medicosocial programs to specific local needs; in reality there has developed a large controversy about the soundness of this alternative as far as geriatric problems are concerned. In fact, since they are oriented towards the whole community and act on requests coming from the community, a situation tends to develop where it is the more vocal groups, the young or the minorities, who receive the most attention, not the elderly. Also, their activities are more oriented towards the social and psychosocial end of the spectrum to the detriment of medical and domiciliary help, which is what concerns the elderly the most.

Conclusions

The different terminology and the recent implementation of geriatric programs make a clear assessment of the Canadian situation very difficult. A main trait in Canada is the spreading of decision-making powers to the different provinces, but an admirable corollary of this is the concern with placing health projects at community level where they can best respond to local needs. Equally remarkable in Canada is the way in which "health" is conceived; psychosocial aspects so often neglected in other countries seem to predominate over purely medical needs. Neither is prevention neglected, as is indicated by the concept of "frail elderly" and the programs being started for their benefit.

FRANCE

Among the countries studied, France and Belgium have the highest proportions of aged people. Even though 14% of France's population is aged, official interest and policy making in favor of the elderly are of fairly recent date.

A National Sickness Insurance Scheme covers 98% of the population. This provides for reimbursements to the patient for all types of medical, hospitalization, and drug expenses. This reimbursement is limited; usually the patient must pay part of the cost. Total gratuity is accorded to people with low or no income. Two ministries, Health and Social Security, are concerned with matters relating to the elderly sick. There is a National Old Age Insurance Fund (Caisse Nationale d'Assurance Vieillesse) that complements the state subsidies in the geriatric field. This fund, operating within the Social Security Organization, helps finance long-term care medical establishments, adapted lodgings, day centers, and the modernization of old age homes.

The sixth Five Year Health Plan, covering the years 1971-1975, had as one of its principal objectives the maintenance of the elderly in their own homes and the modernization of existing institutions. Measures were envisaged such as home helpers, home care, meals on wheels, day centers, adapted lodgings, and subsidized restaurant and activity centers. To achieve these goals, 19% of the health budget for the period 1971-1975 was allocated to geriatric programs. Of this, 30% was to create medium- and long-term wards in general hospitals, 40% was to establish specialized health centers, and 30% was to modernize old age homes. Thus, the basic plan has been made, but realizations fall far behind the desiderata of the policy makers.

Help Structures

Institutions

General Hospitals. The elderly usually enter the hospital on the recommendation of their personal physician or a doctor seen at a polyclinic. Eighty percent of hospital costs are reimbursed, the patient paying the difference. If the patient cannot afford it, Social Security covers the remaining cost. Treatment of some diseases such as tuberculosis and cancer is totally free of cost to patients. Many elderly sick are found in hospitals; sometimes they occupy up to 50% of the acute beds. Many are disabled or restricted to bed and do not receive appropriate rehabilitation treatment.

Medium- and Long-Term Care Units. The planners have conceived the medium-term care units as hospital departments where rehabilitation and return to the patient's own home are the main aims. The long-term care units are envisaged to care for the elderly who, after a stay in an acute and medium-term section, are still not fully recovered or ambulant. Here they can continue their treatment for a longer period, the final aim being return to the home. In 1975 there were four of these units under construction.

Regional Geriatric Center. The idea of a regional geriatric center is put forward in the Health Plan but not yet put into effect. The geriatric center will be a health complex comprised of acute beds, long-term wards, a polyclinic, day hospitals, a day center, and old age homes both for somatic and psychiatric patients. It should be noted here that there is a controversy between those wishing for "specialized" geriatric facilities and those preferring health services open to all comers regardless of age or physical impairment. The question of choice between the integration or segregation of the elderly which will be discussed in the general conclusions is very acute and hotly debated in France today.

Day Hospitals. These facilities have begun to operate in France, namely, in Grenoble, Nancy, and Ivry. Previous hospitalization is not required, and the costs are reimbursed by Social Security.

Old Age Homes. The nursing home such as is found in Great Britain, the United States, or the Scandinavian countries does not exist in France. Not long ago many old people's homes corresponded to the classical asylums for the old and poor—overcrowded dormitories lacking privacy, adequate facilities, and qualified personnel.

Many of these homes date from the last century. Because of the lack of alternative adequate health structures, more and more sick and disabled elderly are placed in these institutions. Hence, a major objective of recent health plans has been the modernization of these homes. The French express it in terms of "medicalization," which would have the effect of converting them into a mixture of nursing home and old age home. This would expand the health facilities and aim at rehabilitation. The cost to the patient in this new type of institution will be split into two categories: one covering the board and lodgings, to be paid by the patient from his pension; and the other, the medical and nursing costs, to be covered by Social Security.

Adapted lodgings. These (*foyer-logement*) are small flats with communal services (nursing, meals, house cleaning, social activities) for isolated or frail old persons who need not be in a hospital or nursing home. There are at present about 75,000 of them. The government is overly optimistic in estimating that 110,000 more units should be built by 1980. Despite the attractiveness of this solution in Denmark, the aged in France seem more reticent to adopt it, feeling that it isolates them from a more mixed environment and the general population. They see it as a step toward the segregation of the elderly.

Medicosocial Services

Home Help. There are 2,000 home-help associations in France, most of them privately organized. Home helpers have been receiving training since 1973. There is no specialized home help for the elderly as in Belgium (*aide-senior*) or in the Netherlands (*bejaardenhelpsters*). In 1973, 100,000 persons benefited from home help; the authorities estimate the need at 700,000 persons in 1975. This home help can be given in kind or in monetary equivalent.

Medical Services at Home. These include both home care and home nursing. Home care provides health acts comparable with those received in a long-term unit at a hospital. Costs are covered in the same manner as hospital costs. The home care team is not organized by a hospital; instead, it is run by an independent home-care association that operates in conjunction with hospitals. In 1974 there were 13 such home-care organizations (*hospitalisation à domicile*) in France, 3 of them are in Paris.

Day Centers. These were to be among the main innovations greatly contributing toward the maintenance of the elderly in their homes. Unfortunately, of the 100 day centers programmed to be in operation by 1975, only 11 existed in 1977. A day center in France is not merely a social center. It provides medical and nursing services, rehabilitation, ergotherapy, psychotherapy, and it can be the base of domiciliary health and domestic services. These centers are reserved exclusively for the elderly.

The main difficulties encountered in the creation of day centers have been the financing of building and running costs by the different government and official bodies. The main difficulty in the operation of existing day centers is explained by the resistance of doctors and social workers to utilize the facilities and services offered by these centers.

Conclusions

A fairly recent global project in favor of the elderly has been conceived by the government in France. Its basic principle is that of the avoidance of institutionalization by creating a series of medicosocial services that will facilitate the maintenance of the elderly in their own homes. Parallel to this is a vast project to modernize antiquated old age homes and to transform them eventually into nursing homes. Geriatric wards and long-term treatment units are being created to look after the chronic sick who need specialized care. There is a manifest gap between the coherent and geographically extensive planning at the governmental level and the actual realization of these programs. One of the main obstacles is the multitude of official bodies that are involved. Another is the lack of coordination that exists among all the new projects. A major objection is that most of the present projects increase the segregation of the elderly. Those concerned with the welfare of the elderly are conscious of this risk, and debates aimed at reaching an optimal solution to this very real dilemma continue.

BELGIUM

A Social Security System established in Belgium after the last World War covers all categories of the population. There is no uniform national pension, different professional categories having their own pension schemes. However, there are guaranteed minimum incomes and pensions.

Medical and hospital costs are paid by the patient, who the National Sickness Insurance reimburses for part or most of the costs. Widows, invalids, pensioners, and orphans with limited revenues receive medical care at no cost to them. A characteristic of the Belgium medical system is the total freedom to build and manage hospitals and other health facilities. Recently a National Hospital Plan has regulated their geographic distribution and established norms and number of beds for particular kinds of afflictions. There is actually a surplus of acute hospitals beds and not enough beds for chronic diseases.

The family doctor is the first recourse of the elderly sick. In Belgium, physicians still attend to the patient at his own home by day or night. The bulk of the clientele of the family doctor is made up of old persons. Despite this fact, there are no gerontology courses during medical studies, and there is no geriatric specialization, but this is, in Belgium as in other countries, a debated point.

Help Structures

Institutions

General Hospitals. After consultation with the family doctor or the physician in a polyclinic, the elderly sick go next to the general hospital in search of diagnosis and treatment. Though justified in case of acute episodes (cardiovascular accident, diabetic coma, fractures), many elderly occupy acute beds (from 30% to 50%) without medical justification. Some are kept there while waiting for transfer to more appropriate facilities. Others are there because of social circumstances, perhaps because their families want them placed in an old age institution and refuse to take them back.

Geriatric and Rehabilitation Units. These were created in 1963 in response to the situation described above. They are oriented toward rehabilitation of the elderly and a prompt return to their homes. They usually are specialized departments within a general hospital, but can also be autonomous hospitals where all necessary diagnostic and therapeutic equipment and personnel must be available. Of the 4,800 beds programmed for 1980, only 1,500 are actually in operation. The limited success of this type of institution may be attributed to a series of factors: the reimbursable part of the daily cost is inferior to that obtained in an acute or surgical ward; the quality of personnel and equipment is inferior; the physiotherapist cost is excluded from reimbursement; and manifest lack of interest is shown by doctors.

Long-Term Treatment Units. In view of the fact that treatment in the geriatric units did not always lead to a quick return to their own homes, in 1965 the government created long-term treatment units. Patients admitted to these units have already been in an acute or rehabilitation unit and are still in need of prolonged treatment. (This and the previously described institution closely ressemble those being planned in France.)

The long-term units are not exclusively reserved for the elderly, but research has shown that the average age of patients is 70 years, notwithstanding a certain number of younger persons suffering from cancer, epilepsy, multiple sclerosis, or other chronic afflictions. Of the 11,000 programmed beds only 4,600 exist at present. Reimbursement is often low, but it varies; and upon presentation of certain medical certificates, a patient can be reimbursed as if he were in a regular hospital. Since the stay is partly or fully paid by sickness insurance and the individual can keep his whole pension, a major consequence is the indefinite stay of the elderly person. This will be modified when the patient has to contribute to the costs after a stay of 40 days. Many other questions are raised in connection with these units, principally relating to their eventual autonomy or their liaison with a general hospital, geriatric service, or old age home.

Old Age Homes. In Belgium old age homes are legally defined as residences for the ambulatory elderly. They are licensed and supervised by the Ministry of Health and the Family. They can be government, nonprofit, or privately owned. The original subsidies accorded for building and basic equipment are not adequate to cope with the increased number of sick and handicapped elderly inmates. Consequently, these institutions are forced to operate as clandestine hospitals without any subsidies for personnel or specialized equipment. Hence, they subsist on the pensions of the elderly, which sometimes do not even cover the cost of their stay.

In response to this situation a new category of homes will be created, a nursing home with residential facilities, like that in France. At present, the National Council for the Aged in conjunction with the relevant ministries are working out the details and conditions for the establishment of this necessary type of institution, a missing link in the chain of structures for the care of the aged sick.

Day Hospitals. Though their need is recognized, day hospitals do not exist. One of the main obstacles to their creation is the fact that Belgium legislation only recognizes as hospitalization a hospital stay where the patient is lodged.

Adapted Lodgings. These are beginning to be created, although at present only as private initiatives reserved for a wealthy clientele. Some local authorities have begun to provide such lodgings for the economically deprived elderly as well. They follow the same formula found in other countries: small apartments with communal nursing, meals, cleaning, and social facilities.

Medicosocial Services

Home Nursing. This service is provided by a national organization of visiting nurses (*Croix Jaune et Blanche*) who attend to all categories of patients at home. Most of their clientele is made up of older persons. A shortage of personnel forces them to provide only basic nursing, preventing the nurses from spending the necessary time with the elderly. In some localities these services are coordinated with home-help services, making their action more complete and satisfactory for the sick old person.

Home Help. In 1972 Belgium had 3,700 home helpers and 1,700 home helpers for the aged (*aide-seniors*). At the same time the Netherlands had 7,000 home helpers and 40,000 home helpers for the aged (*bejaardenhelpsters*). Both countries have the same number of the aged. This gives an indication of the underdevelopment of this type of personnel so essential to the avoidance of unnecessary institutionalization of the frail or isolated elderly.

A misunderstanding about the function of home helpers for the aged has resulted in an emphasis upon heavy domestic duties to the neglect of hygienic and dietetic work for which they have been trained. For this reason and because of the demand for their services in old age homes, a significant number of home helpers have chosen to work in institutions. This has occurred despite the fact that their real and most valuable role is to facilitate the life of the elderly in their own homes.

Conclusions

The nonexistence of an official policy in favor of the aged is one of the main obstacles to the development of an integrated and logical network of

...ures and services for the elderly. Thus, ten years after the creation of geriatric and long-term units, there is still no clear definition of their nature and proper functioning.[1]

Despite many isolated initiatives, several of them private, in general there is a lack of coordination resulting in increased costs and diminished efficiency. Nonetheless, here as elsewhere the acute problems of the elderly now and in the future have begun to permeate the public and private consciousness. Efforts are now being made to find solutions to the problems of the handicapped and the elderly (as well as the problems of their families) without increasing their isolation or segregation from their environment.

GENERAL CONCLUSIONS

The analysis of projects and achievements in favor of the elderly sick in these seven countries makes apparent a number of points in common:

(1) A realization of the extent and degree of the problems of the elderly has been brought about by their increasing numbers.
(2) Social legislation and geriatric projects are all of relatively recent date and are therefore still at an experimental stage.
(3) There is a need to correct mistakes due to a traditional approach.
(4) An obvious disparity exists between estimated needs and the institutions and services available.
(5) Institutionalization is no longer seen as the unique solution to the problems of the elderly.

This analysis also points out a number of dissimilarities:

(1) Not all countries have a coherent health policy for the aged (study of needs, planning, coordination, and control).
(2) The role of the family doctor varies. (Some are state employees, others operate independently, making domiciliary calls or refusing them; some are the pivot of health services; others are not integrated into community organizations.)
(3) The preference for some forms of medicosocial services (hospitals, nursing homes, domiciliary services) varies from country to country.
(4) The reimbursements of health and lodging costs in institutions are very disparate.

From all the dissimilarities and points in common, a number of principles seem to emerge as guidelines for future programs; humanization, prevention, and participation. Humanization involves consideration of the wishes and global needs of the elderly. The first and most obvious result would be maintenance at home. The second would be the limitation of institutions destined to be utilized exclusively by the elderly. This constitutes a general dilemma: if special services and personnel are assigned to the elderly, the segregation of an already marginal group is increased; not to provide them would imply the neglect of specific needs.

Prevention means setting up a variety of facilities to maintain the physical and mental equilibrium of the elderly before an irreversible situation appears. Participation is a right that seems accepted nowadays for most groups. Therefore, the persistence of a paternalistic attitude toward the aged becomes more evident. Projects for them are made in their absence and according to the opinions of planners of another generation. It is not enough to listen to the wishes of the elderly; they must take an active part in all planning commissions concerned with their well being.

The creation of an ideal program that would fulfill these principles and would apply to all situations and in all cultures is not near. Nonetheless, in the light of conditions studied in the various countries, one can put forward a number of guidelines that seem to respond to the expectations of the elderly.

The elderly, like any other group, have health needs (personal and environmental hygiene, food, occasional nursing), economic needs (sufficient income), and psychological and social needs (family and friendly contacts, security, work and leisure activities). Their specific condition is their frailty. This is why help must be above all preventive.

Adequate retirement pension seems to have the highest priority. In the Netherlands the thought prevails that a pension consisting of 3/4 of the salaries is the best policy for the integration of the elderly into society and for the prevention of physical and psychological problems. This is an action to be taken by government authorities.

Other initiatives must originate at the community or municipality level: home help, nursing help, meals, occupations, leisure activities, information, and education. Counseling and service centers as well as domiciliary assistance must exist at the local level in order to avoid institutionalization, a measure so expensive and so repellent to the elderly.

All countries studied are aware of this, but all actions that require a new approach (operating budgets rather than equipment budgets, local responsibility, coordination of existing services, preventive rather than curative measures) are slow in making their appearance. It is at the local level where the elderly can truly participate in decisions concerning themselves. In Canada, the Community Health Centers are actually doing this.

It would be unrealistic to think that all the elderly can remain at home. There will always be cases when only an adequate institution can provide relief in case of sickness. Institutions are necessary, but they should always remain a last recourse. Experience seems to indicate that besides active rehabilitation services there must also be institutions for the heavily handicapped elderly. Most countries have similar versions of the nursing home. Two conditions seem essential: (1) to avoid a "hospital" atmosphere by giving a certain amount of freedom and privacy to patients (freedom to have visitors, to have personal furnishings, individual rooms); and (2) to facilitate the inevitable transfers from the home to institution by having the elderly integrated into residential complexes where they live independently. Denmark seems to have found the ideal solution following this model.

There is a big step from theory to practice. All the ideas put forward in this conclusion have found their application in some of the countries studied. Let Mr. Vig, President of the National Council for the Care of the Aged in Norway, have the last word, "Whether one experience can be of help to others is not for me to say. But I can say this: there is still work and research to be done and there are still new experiences to be gained" (1973).

NOTE

1. These conclusions were arrived at in a comparative study of these units included in the original report but for reasons of space not discussed here.

REFERENCES

SHANOS, E. (1971) "Measuring the home health needs of the aged in five countries". Journal of Gerontology 26: 37-40.
VIG, G. (1973) "Scandinavian experiences in health and social services for older people." Bulletin of the New York Academy of Medicine 49: 1093-1099.

9

ORGANIZATION OF LIFE
The Aged in Poland

ALEKSANDRA OLESZCZYNSKA

The problem of the aged population is now one of the main subjects of social policy in Poland. Compared with other European countries, Poland has a relatively young population. There is, however, a continuing rise in the proportion of aged people, so Poland may soon match other European countries in this matter. Poland has defined the aged or the elderly as those over the usual retirement age, 60 for women and 65 for men.

In 1977, 13.6% of the population in Poland was 60 or over, with 9.9% over 65. There are approximately 4,700,000 elderly people in Poland, and they are fairly well divided between urban and rural areas. As in other countries, there are more women than men in the older population, approximately 20% more females, and the proportion of widows among them is very high. This has important social implications, since research (Piotrowski, 1973) has shown that married couples maintain an independent existence longer than single persons.

Future projections of the aged population show a trend toward an increase in the total proportion of elderly in Polish society (Polish Statistical Yearbook, 1973). There are additional indications that the proportion of people 80 and over will increase particularly rapidly. In this group a considerable number of individuals develop various problems associated with being very old, like incomplete physical and mental efficiency, loneliness, and difficulties in the organization of everyday life.

One of the most important problems confronting the aged is their relationship to the family structure. We know from the research of the Institute of Social Economy (Piotrowski, 1967) that nearly one-half of the aged are married and that most of those (86%) have children; of the whole population of the aged who have children, 67% live with the children, with 76% of those living in rural areas. The family living arrangement does not necessarily mean the elderly member is content. Often the aged living with children who have their own families can be a source of serious domestic conflict.

Family relations between the young and the aged are very well developed, even when they live separately. Only 5% of the aged have no family, and only 5% of those with family do not maintain some form of connection with them. However, loneliness is possible for older people, even if they are living in the same flat with their children's family. Solitude and loneliness are more frequently the problems of women than men, because of a combination of longer life, earlier retirement, and lack of financial resources.

INCOME, PENSIONS, AND OLD AGE

The economic situation of the elderly is usually the single most important factor determining their independence and comfort. The state has established a pension system to insure the economic situation of the elderly. The state pension system covers employees of work establishments, state farms, farmers associated in cooperatives, and, since January 1978, individual farmers.

In selective branches of industry and categories of work, e.g., steel miners industry and teaching, retirement age is 55 for women and 60 for men. For others, the retirement age is 60 for women and 65 for men. The age limit for retirement may be disregarded, which means that in some enterprises people, if willing, may work past the age of retirement. There were over 4.1 million people in retirement in Poland in 1976.

The pensions farmers receive on retirement are calculated on the basis of the amount of land, if any, they pass on to the state or on the amount of farm production they have sold to the state during the years before retirement.

Besides a pension system for farmers and farm workers, there are, as part of the social security system, disability and family pensions. According to the Family Law, persons who have reached retirement age but are not entitled to a pension and have no family member obliged to assist them, receive a monthly social allowance similar to a pension. It amounts to about 80% of the lowest pension.

The elderly, if willing to work part-time, may have an income of up to 2000 zl. a month and keep their entire pension undiminished.

SOCIAL WELFARE POLICIES AND PRINCIPLES

The characteristic principles of Poland's social welfare policies for the elderly can be listed as follows:

- to leave older people in their community as long as possible,
- to move from client-initiated services to active methods of outreach and greater recognition of needs,
- to help families with a moral and/or legal responsibility to care for elderly members.

The following principles serve as a basis for the activities of health protection and social welfare services for the aged in Poland:

- it is the responsibility of the state to organize care for those in need of aid and to provide a proper standard of living for all citizens;
- social services are based on participation of community agencies with stress laid on purposeful initiatives of voluntary organizations;
- there should be uniform management of all health and social welfare services in accordance with the principles of the law and state policy; the state administration is responsible for coordination at each territorial level;
- development of health and welfare activities is based on a plan which forms a part of a more general socioeconomic plan.

The planning system is based on the knowledge of needs, and begins at the level of the individual or family. The general programs are prepared on the central level in cooperation with community agencies and then adapted on the lower level to the specific local needs and according to local initiatives.

HEALTH AND SOCIAL SERVICES FOR THE ELDERLY

The health and social welfare services are organized, controlled, coordinated, and financed by the state. The health protection system covers over 98% of the population of Poland, including the private farmers. The free, or noncontributory, health protection system covers outpatient services, hospitals, rehabilitation services, emergency medical services, and all prescription medicines for retired individuals and 70% of the cost for others.

Basic medical care for all people, including the elderly, is provided by the area doctor. The doctor functions as a "family doctor" for the people living in a given administrative region termed "prophylactic-treatment areas." Each region covers 2,000 to 6,000 persons, with urban areas averaging four thousand people and rural areas averaging five thousand.

The doctors in the regions provide basic health protection for the community. Their principal responsibility is to prevention and detect disease early, as well as to extend care, treatment, and rehabilitation to individuals applying to the dispensaries and to patients confined to their bed at home.

The doctors along with cooperating visiting nurses and social workers make up the basic care team in the community. Other social services are centralized in "Health Integrated Centers."

Health and social welfare services are provided by Health Integrated Centers operating in areas with 30,000 to 200,000 persons. The social service departments, which are part of these centers, employ professional social workers, consultants in law, sociology, psychology, and other areas of specialization. These departments are also responsible for the resident homes and day care centers for the aged. The Health Integrated Centers have a full range of services, including basic care departments, specialized departments, clinics, hospitals, emergency stations, diagnostic facilities, and social service departments. Services not provided by the area doctor or Health Integrated Center can be "Voivodship Integrated Hospitals." Voivodship Integrated Hospitals, which are on the voivodship (province) level, include specialized outpatient clinics and a social-welfare center. They extend consultative assistance in all the specialized fields of medical science and supervise the activity of the Integrated Health Centers. They are also responsible for postgraduate and specialized training for doctors, nurses, and social workers. These Voivodship Integrated Hospitals have gerontological clinics as a part of their specialized outpatient clinics. These gerontological clinics arrange consultations for patients and training for doctors and other medical personnel working with the elderly.

Home-Based Services

A particularly important role in the care of the elderly is played by the various home delivery services (Oleszczynska, 1978). The Polish Red Cross provides care for the sick at home, often enabling patients to remain home when they might otherwise have been hospitalized or institutionalized. In 1976 there were 754 Red Cross stations with 12,765 trained Red Cross Nurses supplying home-base services.

This form of service, home-based, calls for further development, particularly in the countryside. The major constraint is the insufficient number of people working with home-based services. The Polish government is attempting to build up these services and subsidizes the Polish Red Cross in an effort to expand home-based services.

Another important form of home delivery services is the household or homemaker services, which provide old people with assistance in running their households. The homemaker helps with cleaning, cooking, and shopping. This kind of help is provided to people who are physically unable to manage alone. It is organized primarily by the Polish Committee of Social Welfare, as well as by youth and women's organizations. The Polish Committee of Social Welfare employs people for this kind of service, whereas the other organizations have organized the service on a voluntary basis. About 30,000 people avail themselves of these home-based services.

These home delivery services do not cover all the older persons who need them. In many cases it is left up to the family to perform these functions for their elderly members.

Institutional Care

The institutional care for the elderly is covered by social welfare homes, which include:

- resident homes for older people with good health,
- nursing homes,
- nursing homes for people with nervous-system diseases (mainly senile dementia).

Institutional care in these homes is provided for other populations besides the elderly, i.e., invalids over 18 years of age. The basic criterion for admission to a given type of social welfare home is the health condition of the applicant, though additional criteria, including the impossibility of the family to provide sufficient care and the financial situation of the applicant or his/her family, is considered.

Attention has been focused on increasing the efficiency of social welfare homes by extending the scope and forms of their activity. This has been brought about by the organization and development of medical care and rehabilitation management, making available social welfare services to persons living in the vicinity of the social welfare homes. This has changed the role of social welfare homes as they perform the functions of geriatric rehabilitation centers.

The number of places available in social welfare homes is still too small, forcing many older people into other arrangements and long waits.

LEISURE AND FREE TIME ACTIVITIES

For the elderly, like all groups in society, social integration, the ability to be with and in a society, can play an important role in determining the extent of problems facing the elderly. For old people who live alone or whose family members work, day care centers are being organized to provide care, food, and various forms of free and leisure time activities. These daytime social welfare homes constitute a new form of assistance of a semiinstitutional

144   REACHING THE AGED

character. By the end of 1976, there were 41 such day care centers catering to about 1,500 people (Rosner, 1977). There are over 700 clubs for old people in Poland. They are run by various organizations like trade unions, the Polish Union of Pensioners, Old Age Pensioners and Invalids, and the Polish Committee of Social Welfare. These clubs have been organized by the aged and by other organizations for the aged. The clubs, besides planning various kinds of recreation, organize out-of-town trips, conduct groups to special events, and take the elderly to movies and theater shows. Educational activities, including lectures and discussions, have been organized and in some instances institutionalized into "Third Age Universities."

In three cities (Waeszawa, Wroclaw, Opole), Third Age Universities were organized to run educational activities for the elderly. Libraries are open to the general public free of charge, and older people make great use of them. In social welfare homes, recreational and educational activities are carried out on a wide scale, often including the surrounding community.

The trade unions, the Polish Association of Pensioners and the Disabled, and other social organizations run a wide scope of activities. Old people take part in communal life, are active in social organizations, and are especially active in the self-government of their housing development. Every elderly person, if willing, has the possibility of social work in various environments.

CONCLUSION

The developmental trends in social welfare policies for the aged are determined by demographic changes relating the process of aging of the entire population to the broad economic and social changes influencing the needs of this specific group.

In 1971-1973 a plan for the development of health protection and social welfare through the year 2000 was elaborated. This development plan for health services and social welfare was approved by the Polish government in February 1973. The program covers the whole of the problems of health protection and social welfare, and with regard to the latter it is concerned primarily with four basic groups of problems:

— organizing basic scientific research into the needs of the Polish people for social welfare and evaluation of current services,
— developing community-based social services,
— greater investment in institutional social services,
— training of personnel to lay the foundation of professional social services.

Although these programs are not solely for elderly people, their aim is designed to provide comprehensive care for the aged within a total social welfare and health care system for all of Poland's people. Services delivered on the community level will be the basic form of social work intervention. These interventions will include an emphasis on caring for the sick at home with household services, particularly in the country areas, and the continued development of semiinstitutional forms like the day care centers.

Besides the national program many of the voivodships are preparing their own programs for the aged according to their localized situation and needs.

REFERENCES

BRZOZOWSKI, R., O. HOROSZEWICZ, O. KARCZEWSKI, and A. OLESZCZYNSKA (1975) "Social welfare and the lines of its development in the Polish People's Republic." Warsaw.

Cross-Nation Studies of Social Service Systems (1976) Polish Reports. New York: Cross-Nation Studies of Social Service Systems.

OLESZCZYNSKA, A. (1978) Polish Report for European Centre for Social Welfare Training and Research in Vienna. Warsaw. (Xerox copy)

PIOTROWSKI, J. (1973) The Place of Old Persons in the Family and Society. Warsaw.

––– (1967) "The aged in Poland." Warsaw: Institute of Social Economy of the Main School of Planning and Statistics.

ROSNER, J. (1977) Final Report on the Role and Function of Day-Care Homes for the Aged in Poland (Day-Care Centers). Warsaw.

Part IV

COMPARATIVE
PERSPECTIVES

EDITORS' NOTE:

The additional perspectives to be gained from the chapters in this section speak for themselves. This series was created to serve as a vehicle for the comparative analysis of social service delivery systems. The following essays, which focus upon social service delivery to the aged in comparative perspective, enable us to draw on the experiences of many more nations as we seek to understand and improve social welfare systems and their impacts upon a vulnerable and growing segment of our society.

10

FOR THE ELDERLY
An Overview of Services in
Industrially Developed and Developing Countries

VIRGINIA C. LITTLE

STAGES OF DEVELOPMENT

An analysis of levels of development is a useful approach to the examination of social services for the aged. Viewing the modern welfare state as the product of industrial society, we may arrange developing and developed countries along a "residual-institutional" continuum. This spectrum was originally proposed by Wilensky and Lebeaux (1957). Using this method, the following proposed paradigm places the concomitant development of related services for the aged in defined stages (Little, 1974: Table 10.1). The paradigm was applied to industrially developed and developing countries reviewed here.

A clear distinction exists between countries like Afghanistan and Western Samoa, offering "residual" care, and Denmark and Sweden, offering "institutional" care. Interesting transitions are found in countries visibly moving from one stage of development to another in regard to acquiring a range of services and facilities. The city-states of Singapore and Hong Kong are examples of such transitions.

Although advantageous in facilitating categorization, this approach has inherent limitations. First, there exists an underlying assumption that the economic and social changes accompanying development, such as urbanization and the increased participation of women in the labor force, tend to have a similar impact on all societies, regardless of culture and what Ernest Burgess labeled the degree of "societal concern" for older people. Second, this paradigm fails to reflect development as an uneven process. Finally, there is little evidence of "balanced economic and social development" beyond delineation of goals.

Table 10.1:   Specialized Services for the Elderly: Stage of Development Model

---

RESIDUAL: Characterized by:

   (1)   family and mutual aid only; some volunteers;
   (2)   some private homes for the aged;
   (3)   no public funding of facilities for the aged;
   (4)   lack of training programs;
   (5)   lack of home help or other domiciliary services.

EARLY INSTITUTIONAL: Characterized by:

   (1)   organized social services, including volunteer organizations;
   (2)   attempt at supervision/regulation of private homes;
   (3)   some public funding of institutions for the aged;
   (4)   professional training programs with an aging component;
   (5)   demonstration home help domiciliary services.

INSTITUTIONAL: Characterized by:

   (1)   specialized medical facilities, such as geriatric hospitals, chronic care and atten-
       tion homes;
   (2)   licensing and regulation of private homes by a public agency;
   (3)   public funding extended to special housing, community centers, and other
       facilities;
   (4)   substantial development of professional training programs;
   (5)   substantial development of a range of domiciliary services, including home help,
       meals on wheels, laundry, transportation, and the like.

MAXIMUM INSTITUTIONAL: Characterized by:

   (1)   a range of specialized facilities, including day care centers and hospitals, halfway
       houses;
   (2)   participation/leadership in regional/international programs for establishing and
       enforcing standards;
   (3)   active organizations of the aging, political and otherwise;
   (4)   regional centers for research, training and community service in gerontology;
   (5)   a cluster of domiciliary services, coordinated with other health and welfare
       sub-systems.

SOURCE: Little (1974)

VARIANCE IN LEVELS OF EFFORT

A rigorous analysis points to considerable variance in the level of effort. Looking at the 22 richest countries, Wilensky (1975) concluded that age of the system and age of the population must be utilized as controls. He discovered a variance in social security spending as a percent of GNP factor cost from 21.0% for Austria to 7.9% for the United States and 6.2% for Japan.[1] Using the number of home helps per 100,000 population as an indicator of effort, there exists a substantial difference among the seventeen countries for which some data are available from the International Council of Homehelp Services (Little, 1974, 1975). Using a more refined measure, Kamerman's (1976: 529-538) findings for eight countries are similar.

In unique studies of variations in services to the aged, Davies (1971) found sizable differences among local authorities in Great Britain in their provision of services. Utilizing pathway analysis, he was able to identify more than eighty variables which, in their combined effect, would help to explain this variation. He concluded that the essential decision justifying resource allocation is based upon a political assessment of need. Moseley (1968) also found variations in sociomedical services in Britain in the supply of health visitors, home helps, home nurses, welfare officers, and Part III housing. More recent studies (see Hambleton and Scerri, 1974) of the home help effort find similarly situated local authorities providing different levels of services for the aged. Some localities deliver services close to and above the official guidelines of the Department of Health and Social Security. However, some are significantly below guideline requirements.

This variance both among developed states and among local governments in the same state means inequality of access and a lack of equity for older clients because of residential location. However, Svane (1973), who studied five municipalities in Denmark, found an approximation of equality. Whether this would hold for a large heterogeneous society like that of the United States, with a basic shortage of services, is doubtful.

IMITATION AND INNOVATION

Developing countries are not necessarily similar in their provision of social services for vulnerable groups, such as the aged. This is also true of "advanced" welfare states. Western methods are not always or even often followed in non-Western countries. In fact, some attempts to do so have been unsuccessful. Many developing countries are looking for short cuts, hoping to avoid some of the dysfunctional effects of industrialization, such as continuing poverty and unnecessary institutionalization.

Along with diversity we find imitation and continuing interest in learning about and copying services which seem to work well elsewhere.[2] Heclo (1974) views such societal sharing and learning positively. The newsletters of the International Federation on Aging have performed a service in keeping interested persons abreast of developments in many countries. The English publication *Age Concern Today* serves a similar function. The United Nations' *Bulletin on Aging* is a bibliographic, data retrieval effort. All three publications are essentially concerned with calling attention to research findings which may have practical applications communicating information and facilitating societal learning. To what degree the discussion leads to implementation is not readily known.

A few examples of international imitation will suffice. The Japanese have a well-earned reputation for copying other countries. After World War II, they were strongly influenced by American social welfare models and workers. However, when it came to in-home services, they came up with a program based essentially upon the English model, with a few modifications from Sweden. They also use the English term "home help," for which there is no equivalent in the Japanese language. In a more predictable fashion, British Commonwealth countries—in particular New Zealand, and to a lesser extent Australia—have imitated Britain. Canada, attempting a middle course, borrows from Britain and the United States.

When conscious imitation is not present, there are similarities in approach, which often coincide in time. For example, the city of Vienna (Austria) has developed *Pensionistenheime,* similar in concept to what the Swedish call "service houses." Institutions encompassing three levels of care—hospital or skilled nursing, sheltered housing, and community living—are found in such diverse countries as Japan, Israel, and the United States.

When organized social services do not exist, efforts toward service delivery reflect the utilization of traditional helping networks. Examples of such natural systems include the extended family and women's committees. Developed societies tend to view these approaches with nostalgia. Preliminary work in Western Samoa suggests that the concept of the extended family caring for its older members needs further study. This becomes imperative as traditional societies change (Little, 1976a). As Shanas (1965) and others have shown, the family continues to provide the bulk of services in every country. Thus, an innovative service in a developed country may well be to provide back-up services to families.

SPECTRUM OF SERVICES

Services for the aged do not exist in isolation, but are part of a range of institution-based and community-based programs for persons of various ages. As Kahn and Kamerman (1975) have consistently put forth, "Personal social services" require a base of income maintenance, health care, and housing.

Figure 10.1 illustrates this point, suggesting the spectrum of services needed by the young, middle-aged, old, and very old in alternative care settings.

| Afghanistan Indonesia | Western Samoa | Burma | Pakistan | Kenya | Iran India Philippines | Greece | Singapore Hong Kong | | New Zealand Australia | Austria Germany Netherlands | United States | Japan | Israel | Canada | Great Britain | Denmark | Sweden |

Residual   *Early Institutional*   *Institutional*   *Maximum Institutional*

Figure 10.1:   The Residual-Institutional Continuum
of Elderly Services

Issues of need and innovation are addressed in two United Nations' reports with recommendations by an expert group. The first report (1973: 56) reviewed over sixty national plans, and found that one-fifth contained no provision for the aging and that an additional one-fourth provided only social security and insurance schemes of varying coverage. There was no uniform pattern of planning, policy, or programming. The second United Nations' report (1975) was largely repetitive of the first.

An innovative example of modern planning for the aged is Israel's ten-year plan, aimed at developing a regional network of services which are institution-based, but extend to and from the community. Satellite stations are utilized to reach more remote areas.

In general, there is a gap between any plan and its implementation. The following reflects an analysis of service delivery. To achieve this task, we will examine nine headings, once proposed by Hobman (1974) with minor alterations. These include: housing; health (including hospitals); occupation (including retirement); income maintenance; personal social services; nutrition; transport (including escort); family and community. To this list the author adds: information and referral (including outreach). Examples will be given under each heading, suggesting the present level of services and the kinds of innovations found in both developing and developed countries. However, an in-depth examination of each is beyond the scope of the present chapter.

ACCOMMODATION (HOUSING)

Looking at eight developed countries, Kamerman (1976: 535) found no firm data on sheltered housing. The first U.N. Report (1973: 32-33) concluded that, although housing and living arrangements are a major concern, developing countries have given little attention to the special needs of older people. In developed countries the elderly are increasingly becoming isolated and segregated. Housing conditions as reported in the twelve country and three regional surveys were often unsatisfactory, with rents representing a considerable financial burden. However, most aged do not wish to move.

Both developing and developed countries attempt to cope with these problems. In every country the more affluent elderly who choose not to live with their relatives can arrange for living accommodations in a hospital or private setting. In every country one also finds a variety of small private homes which care for older people lacking social supports, often under religious auspices. Such homes are almost invisible in developing countries. Simon Bergman, the noted Israeli gerontologist, reports locating five or six homes for the aged during a brief visit to Fiji. One of the most novel facilities visited by the author was in northern Kenya. This church-sponsored project consists of a semicircle of native thatched roof huts, in each of which lives an otherwise homeless old man with his chickens and his kitchen garden. Such "Mom and Pop" homes have the charm of a happy family, or the under-girding of a religious tradition, but do not offer models for imitation, administrative or otherwise.

The first step in devising a program for service delivery in a developing country involves efforts to ascertain the quantity, nature, and sophistication of existing services and facilities. When the Hong Kong Council of Social Service undertook this task in 1973, they found more than twenty accommodations initiated independently by various religious groups, many ignorant of the others' existence. The Council's Committee on the Elderly sponsored a series of meetings, bringing existing homes into communication, forming subcommittees, and beginning to define acceptable standards (see Ikels, 1975).[3] In Singapore,[4] where a parallel series of events took place, the working committee went a step further in actually closing a substandard home and promoting a new one in an institution formerly used for children (see Little, 1976b). Thus, a movement toward rationalization of existing institutions is often a precursor to greater institutional provision, which generally precedes any provision of community services.

Establishing a model home under government auspices is frequently a second step. The home in Rangoon, Burma, is under Buddhist auspices, but is actually government-encouraged and directed by a former social welfare official. Such publicly supported model homes have been erected in Bangkok, Thailand, and Manila, Philippines. Both have social service units, including students under supervision from the school of social work; both are outside the central city. The Thai home offers alternative living arrangements, including some single rooms and separate small houses on the grounds.

One method of housing the elderly is to segregate them; an alternative is to house them with persons of other ages as part of a broader scheme. In Hong Kong, for example, parts of two floors of the Wah Fu housing estate in Aberdeen have provided sheltered housing for a group of frail elderly, who are supervised by a so-called warden and have the advantage of living in a very large age-integrated community. Two other hostels for the elderly within housing estates have also been developed in Wah Hong and Kwai Fong.

Some developed countries, such as France and Denmark, adhere to a similar approach and attempt to provide elderly housing within a large age-integrated complex. A unique demonstration project at Syracuse University, New York, placed graduate students and older people in the same apartment building, aiming at more intergenerational interaction.

However, it is more usual to provide age-segregated housing of various types which are "purpose built." Every developed country has its old age housing projects and pensioners' flats, depressingly similar high rises of unimaginative design and decor, often with small balconies appended. The institutional character is reduced somewhat by the individual possessions and memorabilia of the inhabitants. A few countries have tried innovative designs aimed toward more humanistic, independent, and aesthetic living. For example, the city of Vienna (Austria) has built a series of Pensionistenheime, where older people live independently as in an apartment hotel, being asked only to appear at breakfast and report their absences. In Sweden new "service houses" for the aged and disabled are replacing former old age homes. Here, too, the residents live independently and arrange through the office for needed social services such as home help.

A crucial issue concerns the degree of protection and surveillance required. Ingenuity has been demonstrated by supplementing the full or part-time presence of supervisory staff with modern electronic devices, such as special telephones, buzzers, alarm and lighting systems. Despite the availability of common rooms and recreation programs, the problem of social isolation continues.

A special problem which some developed countries have faced is that an older person who, at retirement, is well and capable of independent living may later become ill or incapacitated. To meet this need, efforts are made to include various levels of care under one administrative roof. Such services have been termed the "three levels of care" approach. In Japan, for example, the Tokyo Metropolitan Institute of Gerontology provides hospital care, institutional and community living arrangements. Similarly, at the Philadelphia Geriatric Institute, a specially designed hospital and assessment unit is supplemented by separate buildings for supervised residence and a row of nearby houses where other old people live independently with supervision and services available. The rationale for the three levels approach is that an older person may move progressively to different levels of care according to need. For example, after an acute medical episode, an aged person may return to supervised community living without the trauma of relocation.

HEALTH (INCLUDING HOSPITALS)

An overview of the health problems of the elderly is found in a World Health Organization report included in the first U.N. report on aging. The report summarizes present knowledge about the biological processes of aging and past studies of the health status and health needs of the elderly. The report suggests the use of a screening system as an effective means of identifying needs. This technique has been tried in some countries. In Japan every older person is entitled to a free physical examination. In Israel there are model projects, including a clinic on the outskirts of Jerusalem, which attempt to service all older persons in the district via outreach methods. The range of services includes: examination, and medical and social follow-up. There have been demonstration projects in the United States, the best-known being the San Francisco studies by Marjorie Fiske (Lowenthal) and others. The project provides for a well-organized screening program conducted by an interdisciplinary team proving appropriate medical care and social provision. Research findings conclude that, given such care, many elderly who might otherwise be confined in mental hospitals can be successfully maintained within the community (see U.S. Senate Special Committee on Aging, 1971).

Routine health examinations after age forty and six months before the normal retirement or pensionable age are proposed in the World Health Organization report. These may not always be available or affordable in developed countries like the United States. The majority of older persons in developing countries have never had such an examination, and some have never been seen by a physician. Reliance on traditional folk medicine and fears of an intimate examination or of having a blood sample drawn may act as an additional deterrent even when the service is made available.

For this reason developing countries have moved slowly in the direction of Western patterns of health and hospital care. In Western Samoa medical care is primarily assumed by the family, using home remedies. Family efforts may be supplemented by the *fofo*, a massage specialist and sometime counselor. The Women's Committee, serving as the custodian of a small supply of Western medications, has had some orientation to public health and home nursing by the district nurse. A nearby district hospital, with a physician and a few trained nurses, is available to the seriously ill. If the person is admitted as a patient, the family continues to provide most of the care and attention, supplying and laundering bedding and clothing, preparing and serving food, and providing companionship and supervision. An ill person whose medical condition is judged beyond the resources of the district hospital will be flown to the government hospital in the capital city of Apia, which has more physicians and facilities. There is one old age home, started in 1975 by a Roman Catholic order, the Little Sisters of the Poor, where skilled nursing care is available.

In contrast, New Zealand, coping with the range of health problems which confront developed countries, offers a few outstanding services. The Geriatric Unit at Ewart Hospital in Wellington, one example, is run by two young England-trained geriatricians. It offers a wide range of medical and social services, including day care, transportation, and a noon meal to a disabled population of older people. There is a thorough assessment process, which always includes a home visit. The unit maintains a register of older people in need of placement as a first step toward helping them find and obtain the appropriate level of care. Similar pockets of progress are found elsewhere, but are the exception rather than the rule.

In developed countries one looks for specialized geriatric hospitals staffed by physicians trained as geriatricians or, failing that, geriatric wards in general hospitals. In the United States older patients may be shunted to state or county mental hospitals and thence to nursing homes, in the absence of such facilities.

Advanced countries are beginning to have special facilities for death and dying, so-called hospices, pioneered in Britain by Dr. Cicely Saunders at St. Joseph's and presently at St. Christopher's. A similar project has been developed in New Haven, Connecticut, and other locations in the United States. The goal is to establish a special atmosphere of acceptance and caring, in which all staff members participate, permitting a human being to die with dignity.

For those who recuperate, a variety of techniques and facilities are employed for posthospital supervision. Whereas developing societies like Western Samoa may have only a district nurse, who has many other duties, mid-level societies like Hong Kong are building hospital-based programs of community nursing, which also provide preventive care to forestall hospitalization (Carter, 1976). Britain's National Health Service has many facets, including five-day wards for the elderly, floating beds, month-in, month-out hospitalization, geriatric day hospitals, and halfway houses. Thus, there are many steps between the hospital and the community. In addition, there is an organized system of health care visits in some areas; a nurse is assigned to a general practitioner and regularly visits cases in his or her practice. In Australia and New Zealand, as in the United States, hospital-based home care (domiciliary care) is available for a limited number of posthospital cases under medical supervision. However, this service is not routinely available to chronic cases, nor does it function to prevent hospitalization. In the United States a new breed of more highly trained nurse-practitioners is emerging. Such workers assume greater responsibility for health screening, patient assessment, and follow-up care.

An additional question in the area of health care concerns is the provision of necessary equipment, such as crutches, wheel chairs, and commodes. In the United States there is a growing proprietary industry to meet this need for those who can pay. In a few other developed countries, such as Denmark and Germany, equipment is stored in senior centers and may be rented at a modest fee. In some cases rental is free.

Who does eye and ear examinations? Who does dental work? Who cuts toenails and provides foot care? In countries with a national health service, some or all of these services may be provided, although not necessarily cost-free. More comprehensive health screening should serve to spot problems and make appropriate referrals for care. However, a large gap exists between need and utilization. Some ingenuity has been shown in providing foot care. For example, a New Jersey city has a mobile van which travels a regular route, delivering this service. In other cases a unit has been set up in one apartment of a housing project. Such projects minimize the need for travel, thus eliminating a potential utilization limitation.

In all countries the problem of mental health is a neglected area, with few specialized psychogeriatric institutions and fewer trained personnel. In the United States, as Kahn (1975) has pointed out, custodialism is the rule; whereas older persons deemed mentally ill formerly received custodial care in state or county mental hospitals, they are now institutionalized in nursing homes, where they are medicated but seldom receive psychotherapy. Only a small percentage of older persons are seen in a community mental health center. In work with groups the leading technique is that of reality orientation, a variant of milieu therapy. Persons are constantly reminded of the day, the time, the weather, the place, the food, and are stimulated to give other appropriate responses, verbally and socially. This has proved effective with many regressed persons, regardless of disability.

On the positive side of the health picture, the stereotype of aging as an inevitable decline in physical strength and mental capability is being countered by programs of sports and physical exercise. These activities are more organized in both Eastern and Western Europe than in the United States. In the Soviet Union there are so-called "zones of health." In addition to the usual calisthenics, there are other therapies such as music, breathing, and tending plants. European countries like France and Denmark have also developed programs of free or subsidized vacations for the elderly.

OCCUPATION (WORK, RETIREMENT)

The traditional ways ascribed to in developing countries may be more satisfactory in coping with problems of work and occupation than patterns followed in developed countries which mandate retirement at specified ages and then must cope with the consequences.

In Western Samoa men and women continue agricultural and fishing activities as long as they feel able. It is common for a person feeling less mobile to cut down his visits to the plantation to once or twice weekly. In this society curtailment of work activity is gradual. Older men and women have food brought to them by relatives. They busy themselves with weaving, socializing, playing with grandchildren, advising and counseling the young.

In Israel, a very different country, there is also provision for flexible retirement. The work ethic predominates, and some old people work full-time in sheltered workshops and in old age homes. However, aging individuals in the kibbutzim may phase themselves out, gradually diminishing activities or shortening work hours; it is then the responsibility of the group to feed and care for him.

As a country begins to move from residual to institutional concepts of care, it adds social insurances. The first group to be covered is usually government employees, followed by workers employed in industry, with agrarian and self-employed workers among the last. In the social insurance field there is more imitation than innovation, fostered by international associations and publications. According to the U.N. reports (1975: 43) on aging, by 1967 120 countries had created by statute some form of social security programs. Of these, 92 had some sort of old age, invalid, and survivor benefit program.

The implementation of a new program in a developing country is gradual, and coverage may be limited outside the national capital. For example, Indonesia passed a law in 1968 to cover government employees. Not until five years later was a campaign to identify and register government employees launched.

The majority of old people now alive in developing countries have little or no social insurance. The majority in developed countries are covered to a degree and generally receive some sort of old age pension. Problems revolve around the adequacy of benefits, erosion due to inflation, and relative deprivation of the old as compared with younger workers.

Because of the inadequacy of retirement benefits, many older persons try to continue working, or to work part-time. This is made difficult in the United States and other developed countries by restrictions on the overall amount one is permitted to earn without reducing one's benefits. However, during times of societal need, when additional labor force is needed, such as existed in the Soviet Union during the 1960s, such restrictions may be waived or adjusted.

The age of compulsory retirement is also a factor. As a consequence of longevity, an upward adjustment may be necessary. A lump-sum pension payment received from the first employer is insufficient to meet one's needs over a longer expected lifetime. In Japan, for example, "retirement" at age 55 usually means simply switching to another company or to self-employment (Palmore, 1975: 55). Nusberg (1976: 2-3; see also United Nations Report, 1975) cites evidence of innovative programs in European countries which attempt to compensate for these difficulties. Some examples include: efforts to link retirement pensions with increases in national productivity (Germany), provisions for gradual retirement through additional vacation time and part-time work (Norway), providing women with entitlements in their own name (France), and annuities to elderly property owners (United Kingdom).

Behind the apparent rejection of the value of the accumulated wisdom and experience of the aged as well as the rejection of their capacity to continue working lie unresolved issues, such as value conflicts concerning dependence-independence, the importance and functions of leisure time, the need for continuing education and development over the life cycle. Other countries have gone farther than the United States in questioning the stereotype of aging. For example, France provides innovative educational programs, such as Le Troisieme Age.

INCOME MAINTENANCE

A developing country with a beginning social insurance scheme may make other provisions for income maintenance. In most instances, however, such provisions are nonexistent. Hence, the burden falls on the family and on mutual aid. This helps explain the persistence of many-children families, and the reluctance to accept family planning. If one has eight children, four may survive and provide some income security for one's old age. In developing countries with a cultural pattern of reciprocity between the generations, an obligation is also recognized to other relatives of the parents' generation. When there is food, it will also be shared with the "uncles" and "aunts." If there is insufficient food, they may starve.

The gap may be filled in part by publicly operated provident funds, a current fashion in some developing countries. Some funds are essentially a compulsory savings system, with regularly withheld contributions of employees being matched by those of employers and set aside in a special fund. In Western Samoa the system is still voluntary; people are exhorted to save and to take part in the national scheme. More funds are available to older Samoans in the form of remittances from relatives employed abroad in New Zealand and elsewhere, but it is also more difficult for the government to tap such resources.

Developed countries have more highly developed economies and more affluence; however, inequalities of income distribution persist throughout the life cycle. Those who are disadvantaged at younger ages continue to be deprived and may be further handicapped by poor health and loss of spouse in addition to forced retirement and no work. Because social insurance benefits are usually inadequate in amount, in the absence of other resources, most developed countries have found it necessary to augment them by what the British call "supplementary benefits." In the United States this is now termed SSI (supplementary security income for the aged, blind, and disabled). The replacement of state-managed old age assistance by a federalized system which, according to some, establishes entitlement to a guaranteed minimum income may indeed be a step forward. However, it has increased the fragmentation of programs without adding to overall income adequacy. Utilization by eligible senior citizens is low, just as it is with food stamps and other entitlements, which still bear the stigma of welfare.

The welfare stigma is less prevalent in Britain and Western Europe, and there is a basic floor of publicly supported social services which in themselves represent added income. The locus of services and point of access and delivery vary. In Britain, although responsibility is centered in the Seebohm reorganized local social service departments, older people also rely on the post office for check cashing and for a variety of related personal services. There is no comparable service in the United States. With most banks now creating mail-in schemes for checks, rural post offices in the United States may be helpful. However, ill-prepared Social Security offices, traditionally manned by clerks and not responsible for services, have been overwhelmed since the advent of SSI. Studies conducted by the Federal Council on Aging conclude that programs without a locus have resulted in a weak system of income maintenance.

Perhaps the most innovative attempt to augment family income is that undertaken by Japan. Japan is an atypical developed country, with three-fourths of its older citizens living with the oldest married son. This cultural pattern is changing in Tokyo and in the ten largest cities. The Japanese government has tried to maintain this pattern by providing low-interest loans and subsidies to families adding an extra room to their house for older parents. Income tax deductions are also employed to this end.

In most countries there is a group of needy older people not covered or insufficiently covered by social insurance and supplementary benefits, which tend to be at or below a subsistence level. A few countries have tried what the

U.N. reports term "public service programs." In actuality these are a form of demogrant, to use Eveline Burns' term. Payment is made to every inhabitant above a certain age, sometimes to every invalid or surviving widow or orphan. In Hong Kong the first public assistance scheme introduced was an age and infirmity allowance for all persons aged 75 and over. There is now a campaign to lower the age to 65. In the United States, the Prouty amendment to the Social Security Act provides for a similar, although limited and modified, form of financial assistance to persons aged 72 and over. Canada has experimented with such a demogrant, although the benefits available have been somewhat curtailed. Greece grants a monthly allowance to its old people. Since its sum is minute, this act constitutes more of a symbolic gesture than a true attempt at income maintenance.

PERSONAL SOCIAL SERVICES

The two U. N. reports, referred to previously, suggest that both governmental and voluntary sectors are attempting to respond to elderly needs. However, the majority of supportive services do not exist in a comprehensive and coordinated fashion in any one country or community. The core consists of in-home services, making it possible for older people to continue living in the community. Terms coined for this service include: "home help," "Samaritan," "family aid," and "visiting homemaker." In the United States the label "homemaker/home health aide" reflects the willingness of Congress, under Titles XVIII and XIX of the Social Security Act, to reimburse only medically related services. The extent of this reimbursement remains limited. Related in-home services include: meals on wheels, transportation/escort, home repair, chore/handyman, friendly visitor, shopping, and the like. These services require expansion and modernization.

In countries at the residual end of the scale, there are no organized services. In Western Samoa there is no public welfare and only one private charity, the Little Sisters of the Poor old age home. Consequently, services are supplied by the extended family, supplemented by village or church women's committees and occasionally by neighbors.

Some developing countries are trying to build on these natural helping networks to expand services. In Burma, government employed social workers, some trained abroad, conduct brief (one to three months) training courses for women volunteers selected because of their village activity. Upon completion of the course, the trainees return to the village, and in turn train and organize others. Kenya relies on a combination of trained home economists and indigenous untrained community development workers to educate village women, primarily in nutrition and child care. The Kenya pattern is more similar to the home demonstration program of the U.S. Agricultural Extension Service. The trained person makes field visits demonstrating proper methods. Follow-up activities are performed by the local community development person.

In developed countries the provision of a cluster of in-home services has become a major policy issue. In more complicated societal structures more services are required. These services are more expensive, more difficult to fund, and represent complex management problems. The most successful systems, emphasized by Kahn (1975) are those in Scandinavia, Britain, and Western Europe. In these areas the provision of personal social services (or "social care services") is a built-in or institutionalized feature of public welfare. Services are organized and administered by local authorities and made available to all, usually on a sliding scale fee basis. In a few countries, such as Holland, the private sector is organized and subsidized to supply these services.

Japan has imitated the British home help pattern with an additional layer of service extended to employees and their families by a number of Japanese industries. In Japan, as in the United States, there is also a rapidly growing proprietary sector for people who can afford to pay or have insurance coverage.

By and large, old people are served mainly by the public sector, typically by part-time employees who have received only minimal orientation and training for their tasks. An innovative training program has emerged in a few Western European countries whereby young girls, secondary school graduates, are recruited for the "profession" of home help and undergo a one to two year training program. The program combines supervised classroom study and a practicum. They are then employed in the public or subsidized service. Such workers are usually assigned to work with problem families with young children. They seldom render services to the elderly.

If, as in Britain, home help services go largely to the elderly and are continued until death, one problem encountered concerns coverage of a large number of cases with limited manpower. The average person or family is served once or twice weekly for a few hours. Cases requiring 24-hour or weekend help are then served by a different group of part-time helpers. This adds a second layer of service, and provides a slight career ladder for the more experienced workers.

A related problem is that of management or administration. Britain and Sweden rely on "home help organisers," largely untrained persons who perform the task of deploying a largely part-time and fluctuating marginal labor force over a sizable geographic area. They cope with a variety of changing situations and face daily emergencies, including sickness or absence of helpers, which necessitates redeployment. In addition, the organisers do an initial home visit for assessing needs, and subsequent visits to monitor and assess the service plan.

In the Massachusetts statewide home care system, and the demonstration projects imitating it, some of these activities have been identified as "case management" functions. The case manager—a professional social worker in Massachusetts, or a nurse-practitioner in some projects—is responsible for the home visit to assess needs and for team leadership in determining the service plan. Subsequently, the manager connects clients and services by means of purchase-of-service contracts with various providers. Thereafter, service delivery is monitored in relation to client needs. The separation of case management from direct services is viewed as a gain, although in practice case managers do a sizable amount of counseling. The typical case manager works under an administrator, sometimes as part of a team. The role is thus considerably narrower than the overall management and administrative functions of the home help organizer.

The Netherlands has been a recent leader in focusing on administrative and management aspects, experimenting with different patterns. As reported at the April 1975 seminar of the International Council of Homehelp Services in Frankfurt, Germany, these innovations included enlarging organizations on the regional and local level, computerizing, dealing with employers' organizations and workers' unions, and building a network of information and communications. Different patterns of service being tried experimentally include: (1) a so-called "Alpha" service for simple domestic help, (2) service given by a central unit or team, (3) service given during flexible working hours, (4) services by foster families, (5) district care for the aged, (6) first aid or emergency service, and (7) chore services. After evaluation it is hoped that the more effective patterns will become generalized. Another experiment, in Coventry, England, involves doubling the number of home helps in a given district, then studying the impact on other services.

The United States has also developed innovative models for home care. Several have sought to deal with the pervasive problem of health and social services systems which tend to inhabit their own separate worlds, with little communication or coordination. This is dysfunctional for older people, who typically need a package of services and have difficulty in understanding and negotiating the two closed systems. In a little-noticed article in *Social Casework* Simpson and Farrow (1973) described three demonstration projects for coordinated countywide services in the states of Michigan and Minnesota. Each organized itself differently, and each provided a different bundle of services, including health, social, and employment. It was learned that, with political backing and technical expertise, a mixture of funding sources, and active consumer involvement, communication, and coordination can be achieved (Simpson and Farrow, 1973).

In contrast, in a three-county rural area in western Maine, the impetus came from older people, who themselves started Project Independence. Initially it was mostly a transportation service. It later grew to include other social services, and subcontracted with the Androscoggin Home Health Association for health screening clinics as well as home care, helping the association get per capita payments from the towns they served to supplement Title XVIII and Title XIX funds. RSVP, VISTA, and other volunteers provided outreach, nutrition, information, transportation and many miscellaneous services (see Aging, 1975).

Possibly the best-publicized American project has been MAO (Minneapolis Age and Opportunity Centers, Inc.), led by Daphne Krause. She succeeded in putting together a consortium of partners, including the local hospital and the Junior League, as well as service providers and volunteers, to supply a spectrum of services. Less well known, but also worthy of imitation, are two San Francisco-based demonstrations. The On Lok Health Center, serving ethnic groups in Chinatown and encompassing a variety of services, has the unique feature of graduating its improved clients to a senior center social services program where they engage in a variety of group activities. Also unique is a San Francisco project known as "222," which combines day care and home care for a disabled elderly population served out of three hospital bases. Finally, project TRIAGE in central Connecticut, considered a test of national health insurance, is examining the cost-effectiveness of community care by supplying every conceivable and available service to needy elderly on the basis of Medicare and Medicaid waivers. The project follows a team model, led by a nurse practitioner with a large social services component (see Little, 1976).

An American public welfare "innovation," which the National Council on Homemaker/Home Health Aide Services, Inc. deplores, is the reliance on informal helpers, usually relatives or friends of the client, who receive the minimum wage for performing some services not otherwise available. These so-called "self-employed providers" are not supervised or frequently monitored. They testify to the service gap, beginning to be filled by a burgeoning proprietary industry whose rates are lower than those of nonprofit agencies.

Each demonstration project has its own innovations, large and small. Small innovations are legion, but a few may be worth mentioning. Sweden and other European countries have specially fitted vans with heavy cleaning and home repair tools and equipment, making it possible to recruit more male workers. Scheduled and emergency visits to the homes of recipients supplement the work of the home helpers. In Sweden and in Britain the rural postman (or woman) is used to keep in touch with the elderly, shop, do errands, visit, and make regular monthly reports to the social worker. Also,

many countries have added laundry services. Supplying telephones and telephone reassurance services is becoming common.

NUTRITION

In a developing country characterized by intergenerational reciprocity, the
old are fed by the young. In a developed country with an organized in-home
service system, food shopping and meal preparation may be included in the
tasks performed by the helper. However, if the helper visits only once or
twice a week, some supplementation is needed.

Variants of two kinds of programs have been tried in numerous countries:
(1) congregate meal sites; (2) meals on wheels. Each is innovative in concept,
but in practice involves numerous delivery problems.

Congregate meal sites include senior centers, churches, and schools. Eating
a meal with a peer group is generally believed to be advantageous both
nutritionally and socially (in reducing social isolation and promoting peer
interaction). It is also possible to lure meal eaters into other services, such as
health screening. Regulations under the Older Americans Act envisage that up
to 20% of Title VII (nutrition) money may be used for social services; this is
seldom done, since all of the money is usually demanded for nutrition
purposes. This is despite the fact that Title VII is more generously funded
than Title III (services). Although feeding old people has legislative appeal,
congregate meal programs are difficult to administer and experience low
utilization rates in every developed country, including Sweden. Older people
prefer to eat their own choice of foods at home, whether or not their diets
are deemed adequate. Innovative ideas include having older persons themselves plan and prepare the food. Implementation works, but is hard to
sustain. There are numerous technical problems of sanitary standards, high
costs, providing and maintaining kitchen equipment.

Transportation to meal sites is another problem, especially in the United
States, where it may compete with demands for transport for medical
appointments. An innovative program in Sweden transported old people to a
school cafeteria in a school bus to eat the noon meal after the children had
finished. This did not work in Connecticut, where the older people did not
like either the bus or the food, and felt that the fee charged was too high.

Meals on wheels, the second option, is also an idea of universal appeal
which works less well in reality. As a volunteer service in a developing
country, it can add an extra dimension to in-home services. At St. James
Settlement in Hong Kong, active senior participants in the center deliver the
meals to homebound people and do some friendly visiting at the same time;
they also pick up and deliver laundry. This works well within a walking radius

of the center; otherwise, it taxes the one van available for all transportation requirements.

Delivery is becoming a major problem in developed countries like the United States. The volunteer pool is drying up with the increased cost of gasoline and the risks attendant to visiting the inner city. Hence, the meal tends to be dumped on the doorstep by a commercial delivery service, losing the dimension of the personal relationship.

A further largely unacknowledged problem is weekend coverage. In what one study termed a Niskanen effect, a new program begins with considerable elan, but within a year's time settles into system maintenance, giving staff needs and scheduling priority over client needs. The apparent difficulty and added expense of working weekends in a high wage structure country with a normal five-day work week seriously reduces the prestige of the service where it does exist. Such service is severely limited in most parts of the United States.

Having substantially developed their public home help services in the last 10 years, Japanese social welfare authorities are now turning their attention to promoting meals on wheels. Perhaps Japanese ingenuity in packaging and delivering food will achieve a breakthrough. Studies in other countries, such as Austria, are finding a low rate of utilization and a high turnover of clientele.

Problems of financing meals on wheels in countries where food costs are high prevail. Older people on a limited income do not want to pay even partial cost for food they do not like. The success of the SAGA organization in contracting for food service on college campuses suggests that there may be an opening for more efficient, large-scale processing, if the delivery problems can be solved. There has been some experimentation with commercial preparation and freezing, which so far has met with little consumer acceptance.

There has been more success in having food prepared at an institutional facility, such as a hospital, and then packaged and distributed to the nearby community. For example, the kitchen at Philadelphia Geriatric Center prepares kosher meals at a nominal cost. Recipients in the community apparently find meals acceptable and palatable. This kind of facility is also available on a seven day basis, provided the delivery problems to outside customers can be managed.

TRANSPORTATION (INCLUDING ESCORT)

Transportation is a problem in both developing and developed countries. In a less-developed country people walk. As a rule of thumb, an active and mobile adult can reach a hospital within a five-mile radius. An ill or incapacitated older adult would have to be carried, by cart, bus, private auto or whatever means available. It is exciting to see how people respond to the introduction of new forms of transportation and communication, such as the radio or the airplane. For example, in Western Samoa almost every family has a radio; if not, their neighbor in the next fale has one. The radio is used for public service announcements as well as personal messages. For example, the nuns in the old age home broadcast when they need to inform a family that a relative is ill. The availability of air service on the island of Savaii means that sick people can be rapidly transported to the hospital in Apia for medical treatment, rather than attempt a much longer and more difficult journey from island to island by boat or ferry.

By contrast, the United States, at the other end of the continuum, is locked into highway transportation by private motor car, which severely limits the access of older people and others unable to drive themselves. Other developed countries have more expanded public transportation systems—subway or Metro and frequently scheduled buses and trains. It is a common practice to give senior citizens discounts. In some countries, such as Holland, the elderly are exempt from fee charges.

In the absence of reliable public transportation, other means must be devised. Here, too, there has been ingenuity in designing and providing mini-buses, some specially equipped for the infirm and handicapped. Perhaps the most innovative program mounted has been DIAL-A-RIDE, in which the older person calls a dispatcher and arranges to be picked up for a needed trip. In some affluent American communities there are regularly scheduled days and routes, plus special services, such as "dial-a-doctor."

Although growing in numbers and coverage, the present level of services is inadequate and expensive. Since former sources of volunteer transportation, such as the Red Cross of FISH, have tended to evaporate, the net gain is small. While individual towns have engaged in considerable grantsmanship to develop their own services and to acquire vehicles and drivers, a movement toward combining and rationalizing services within an Area Agencies on Aging (AAA) planning area is growing, and is able to tap into urban mass transportation funding.

THE FAMILY AND THE COMMUNITY

Much of what we have covered so far relates to the interface between family and community systems. As we have said, in every country the family system still bears the brunt of the burden of caring for older people. Thus, the rationale for family back-up services, currently more developed in countries like Britain and Sweden than in the United States. Japanese loans and subsidies to families have already been mentioned. European services include in some cases paying family members to provide care; in others, giving relief through temporary hospitalization, days off, vacations, laundry services, and the like. The knowledge that back-up services are available may be of great psychological benefit to families caring for an aged member.

It is now the fashion in the United States to speak of "the aging network," supposedly encompassing every one related to older people, from the President to the Federal Administration on Aging (AoA) to state agencies to municipal agents and older people themselves. This network may be more symbolic than actual.

Older persons are found both in age-integrated and in age-segregated settings. In determining service delivery, it is important to ascertain whether older persons voluntarily seek out the company of their age peers in preference to interacting with persons of different ages and generations. There is considerable variability and individual preference. However, in every country, there has been a greater effort to organize senior centers and clubs. For example, Japan and Israel have large networks (Maeda, 1975). Problems are similar to those encountered in the United States: obtaining funding and attracting the poor and socially isolated who need services the most. In the absence of trained help, centers easily become social clubs, dominated by an activist/in-group who make it difficult for the out-group to participate. Only a few community drop-in centers available to people of all ages have been tried; their success seems to vary from situation to situation.

Senior centers rely heavily on volunteers for services like telephone reassurance and friendly visiting. There is a historic tradition for this kind of volunteering, which is particularly strong in Anglo-Saxon countries. In developing countries one speaks rather of "self help" or "mutual aid." India seems to combine both traditions, with the bulk of community services being performed by unpaid volunteers, who are considered more "pure" and religiously motivated than people who are paid. In developed countries the organization of voluntary efforts has come to be considered a key to providing an array of services for older people which could not otherwise be funded. It is an accepted axiom in the United States that, in order for volunteer activities to be effective, a full-time paid professional is required to organize and supervise.

The larger problem of coordinating the voluntary sector is just beginning to be faced. For example, in Hartford, Connecticut, a Center for Voluntarism has been established, incorporating three previously independent voluntary organizations, including RSVP. This project was promoted by the Community Council and enforced by United Way funding. On a national level the United States has both private and public organizations of volunteers. Perhaps the most innovative in concept have been the Peace Corps for international service and VISTA for domestic service. Both have attracted outstanding senior participants, such as Mrs. Lillian Carter in India and Miss Cordelia Cox (formerly with HEW and CSWE) in Western Samoa. Other older volunteers are doing meaningful work under the Foster Grandparents program, RSVP, SCORE, and Green Thumb, all of which have some interesting approaches.

The publicly funded U.S. volunteer programs, including the aging programs, were administratively combined by former President Nixon under an umbrella called ACTION, within the framework of the Executive Office of the President. Whether this is an administrative model for other countries to follow is dubious. A more instructive community organization experience is that of AGECONCERN in England. This is a private rather than a public organization, and hence more effective as an advocate and spokesman. Remodeled from a loose organization of old people's welfare councils, with volunteers throughout Britain, it has become a center for information, service, and research, and is performing an important leadership role.

INFORMATION AND REFERRAL (INCLUDING OUTREACH)

The development of information and referral systems is significant for the delivery of services to isolated older persons who otherwise might be unable to link up with the community and gain access to needed services. Simpler societies rely on word-of-mouth communication. As more entitlements and services for the aged are created, there is a continuing problem of communicating their availability. This frustration is particularly prevalent in more complex societies. In a heterogeneous society, like the United States, there is special concern in reaching out to minority and ethnic groups. Here the employment of outreach workers, sometimes financed by CETA funds, has been most useful in locating persons previously unknown, with efforts to connect their needs to available services.

An innovative service developed in Connecticut is known as INFOLINE. This is a telephone service, manned by professional social workers who not only answer questions but also act as advocates in securing services. Similar services of help to older people in filling out forms include: applying for public programs, reporting income for tax purposes, and asking for circuit-breaker tax relief. An experimental voluntary service in New Haven, Connecticut, has done a land office business in assisting older people with Medicare and private insurance forms. Other countries, such as Denmark, have developed forms to request a lawyer for legal services. These services are successful to the extent that they establish eligibility and result in satisfactory outcomes.

Will additional information, assistance, outreach and advocacy efforts promote a higher rate of service utilization? Such activities may be helpful;

however, more attention needs to be given to the delivery problems noted throughout our discussion and to the limited success of many innovative and creative approaches to solving them. Perhaps a higher level of participation by older people as planners and decision makers rather than as consumers or recipients will provide a partial solution. However, behind the present lack of services and the ineffectiveness of many programs may be more fundamental issues, such as the persistence of ageism.

NOTES

1. The 1966 figures are quoted as the most recent available data for all 22 of the richest countries.

2. For example, the Massachusetts model of a statewide system of local home care corporations has been imitated in two Connecticut demonstration projects (TRIAGE, Personal Care Project), as well as in Hawaii.

3. Data were gathered by the author in two study trips to Hong Kong in 1973 and 1976.

4. Data were gathered in a study trip to Singapore, 1974. When not otherwise footnoted, observations and data are the author's, based on her study trips abroad.

5. The author is engaged in a cross-national project comparing the impact and effect of homemaker/home help services in the U.S. and Japan. See Little, "In-Home Services for the Aged in Japan: A Preliminary Report." (manuscript).

6. Personal communication, Mag. Anton Amman, University of Vienna, Institute for Sociology.

REFERENCES

Aging (1975) June-July.

CARTER, M. J. (1976) "Community nursing in Hong Kong, 1973-1975." Report on behalf of the Community Nursing Committee. Hong Kong: University of Hong Kong Department of Social Work.

DAVIES, B. et al. (1971) Variations in Services for the Aged: A Causal Analysis. Occasional Papers in Social Administration. London: G. Bell.

HAMBLETON, R. and V. SCERRI (1974) "Three social service plans compared." Research no. 1. Birmingham, England: Clearing House for Local Authority Social Services.

HECLO, H. (1974) Modern Social Policies in Britain and Sweden: From Relief to Income Maintenance. New Haven and London: Yale University Press.

HOBMAN, D. (1974) "Defense through services to the 65-80 and over 80 age groups." Presented at meetings of the International Federation on Ageing, Nairobi, Kenya, July.

"Homehelp-services: where are they and where are they going" (1975) Report of the Second International Homehelp Seminar, Frankfurt, Germany, April.

IKELS, C. (1975) "Old age in Hong Kong." Gerontologist 15: 230-236.

KAHN, R. L. (1975) "The mental health system and the future aged." Gerontologist 15: 24-32.

——— and S. B. KAMERMAN (1975) Not for the Poor Alone: European Social Services. Philadelphia: Temple University Press.

KAMERMAN, S. B. (1976) "Community services for the aged: the view from eight countries." Gerontologist 16: 529-538.

LITTLE, V. C. (1976a) "Aging in Western Samoa." Presented at the Twenty-Ninth Annual Scientific Meeting of the U.S. Gerontological Society, New York City, October 14.

——— (1976b) "Issues and problems in providing home care services for the aging: a cross-cultural perspective." Presented at the annual meeting of the Gerontological Society, New York City, October.

——— (1976c) "Coordinating services for the elderly." Presented at the Hawaii Governor's Bicentennial Conference on Aging, Honolulu, June.

——— (1975) "Factors influencing the provision of in-home services in developing countries." Presented at the Tenth International Congress of Gerontology, Jerusalem, June.

——— (1974) "Social services for the elderly: with special attention to the Asia and West Pacific Region; a preliminary look." Presented at the Twenty-Seventh Annual Scientific Meeting of the Gerontological Society, Portland, Oregon, October 31.

MAEDA, D. (1975) "Growth of old people's clubs in Japan." Gerontologist 15: 254-257.

MOSELEY, L. G. (1968) "Variations in socio-medical services for the aged." Social and Economic Administration (July): 169-183.

NUSBERG, C. (1976) "Foreign trends and innovations in service to the aging." Presented at the Western Gerontological Society meetings.

PALMORE, E. (1975) The Honorable Elders: A Cross-Cultural Analysis of Aging in Japan. Durham, NC: Duke University Press.

SHANAS, E. and G. F. STREIB [eds.] (1965) Social Structure and the Family. Englewood Cliffs, NJ: Prentice-Hall.

SIMPSON, D. F. and F. G. FARROW (1973) "Three community systems of services to the aging." Social Casework (February): 96-104.

SVANE, O. (1973) "Assessment of needs of care for the elderly." Zeitschrift fur Gerontologie. Band 6, Heft 4: 307-315.

United Nations, Department of Economics and Social Affairs (1975) "The aging: trends and policies." ST/ESA/22. New York: UN.

United Nations, Secretary General, General Assembly (1973) "Questions of the elderly and the aged: conditions, needs and services and suggested guidelines for national policies and international action." A/9126 (August 28). New York: UN.

U.S. Senate, Special Committee on Aging (1971) "Mental health care and the elderly: shortcomings in public policy." (November 8)

WILENSKY, H. L. (1975) The Welfare State and Equality: Structural and Ideological Roots of Expenditures. Berkeley and Los Angeles: University of California Press.

——— and C. N. LEBEAUX (1951) Industrial Society and Social Welfare. New York: Russell Sage.

11

AGING IN YUGOSLAVIA

D. NADA SMOLIC-KRKOVIC

The trend toward a larger proportion of the aged in Yugoslavia's population is evident, although the population is still considered a young one compared with that of other European countries (see Table 11.1).

If we take a closer look at our population, we will see that considerable regional differences exist. The populations of Croatia, Slovenia, and Vojvodina show signs of growth in the percentages of those aged 60 and over. The populations of Bosna and Hercegovina, Macedonia, and Kosovo are still in the initial phase of this trend. (See Table 11.2.)

The percentage of the young in the age structure has decreased continuously. This has had an important effect on reproduction, and it will have even greater influence in the future. This shift in the age structure steadily decreases the basis for the further development and enlarging of the popula-

Table 11.1: Proportion of 60+ in the Total Population of Yugoslavia and Specific Republics

| | Census Years | | | | | |
	1921	*1931*	*1948*	*1953*	*1961*	*1971*
Yugoslavia	8.7	8.4	8.7	8.9	10.0	12.2
Aged 60+ in thousands	1,092	1,208	1,374	1,512	1,829	2,496
Bosna & Hercegovina	5.6	5.2	4.9	5.2	6.0	7.7
Montenegro	9.8	9.8	10.6	10.4	10.5	11.0
Croatia	8.8	9.4	10.0	10.2	11.8	14.9
Macedonia	11.1	9.6	8.7	8.2	7.9	8.8
Slovenia	10.4	10.7	10.9	11.1	12.4	14.8
Serbia	8.9	8.1	8.8	9.2	10.4	12.9

SOURCE: Breznik (1972)

Table 11.2:   Long-Term Changes in the Age Structure of
the Population of Yugoslavia in Census Years

Year	Inhabitants in Thousands	Percentage of Proportion			
		Total	0–19	20-59	60+
1921	11,985	100.0	45.5	45.8	8.7
1931	13,934	100.0	43.9	47.9	8.2
1948	15,772	100.0	43.4	47.9	8.7
1953	16,937	100.0	40.8	50.3	8.9
1961	18,549	100.0	38.5	51.5	10.0
1971	20,505	100.0	37.2	50.9	11.9
1981	22,461	100.0*	34.3	54.6	11.0

SOURCES: 1921-1971, Breznik (1972); 1981, long-term projection
*discrepancy due to rounding

tion. Such a change in the age structure has a direct effect on increasing the
death-rate of the population.

There is also an interdependence between the age structure of the population and migration. The regions out of which the greater number of young,
labor-fit populations emigrate are left with a proportionally higher elderly
population. The lack of manpower which arises in more developed areas can
turn the area into a marked immigration zone and thus decrease its proportion of elderly by an increase of young people in the area.

Women in Yugoslavia (with the exception of Kosovo) live longer than
men. About 60% of the women 65 and over are widows, according to the
1961 census, whereas only 34.7% have spouses still living. Widows rarely
remarry. With men, the situation is reversed: only 25.8% are widowers, and
the majority of men (69.3%), have spouses still living.

The age structure of the population of Yugoslavia has changed dramatically in the last 60 years. Much of this change can be attributed to relevant
factors which are active in other countries, but it should be stated that the
age structure has been influenced additionally by the two world wars,
resulting in the formation of chipped generations in some age groups.

Transformations of Family and Social Life

After World War II young people left the villages in great numbers and
moved into the cities to build up industry and become factory workers
instead of farmers. The result was that the elderly were left in villages. They
make up a large portion of the aged who live today in the so-called isolated
"aged households." The process of migration is still strongly felt. Around
50% of all migrants are peasants, and 75.2% belong to the age group from 20

to 39 years (Sentic, 1971). The mechanization of agriculture is a slow process; young people invest their earnings in farming machines and the building of new houses. Even after many years, young people who migrated for industrial employment return to their original homes. They modernize their households, and thus raise the standard of living for the older people who live with them.

The number of so-called "mixed households" is growing. These are households in which the young people work in industry, but live together with their parents and other family in the village.

Studies (e.g. Smolic-Krkovic et al., 1971) show that of the old people living in villages those in the best position are ones who live together with their children or near them. This allows for the continuation of family support systems to aid the elderly family member. Isolated individuals, particularly widowers without children, are in the worst position. Many can no longer work and in some cases can hardly take care of themselves.

An examination of old people of both sexes residing in towns reveals that 62% live either completely alone or with only their spouses. In villages, only 36% fall into this category. Generally speaking, a considerably higher percentage of old persons in Yugoslavia live with their sons and daughters than in Great Britain, Denmark, and the United States (Shanas et al., 1968). In Yugoslavia, 70% of old persons with more than one child live in a household with one of their children.

In most cases when two young people start a family in the city, both work. If they do not have an apartment, they usually live with their parents so they may help each other, especially if a child is born (grandma-service).

In the majority of families, although family relations are different today, the children are the main source of support for the aged in Yugoslavia. If general objection can be made that this care is not sufficient, the reasons may be attributed to the changing life conditions as well as the expectations of life which are different for the children than for the parents. Under the influence of social movements—sudden industrialization and urbanization—the aspirations for a higher standard of living become greater, absorbing the time and effort of the young, especially in cities.

Because of the traditionally formed family relationships, a social consciousness (that somebody else besides the family should care for the elderly) did not exist. As our society makes progress in the direction of more developed countries, we are beginning to recognize the phenomenon which has already clearly occurred elsewhere. The family facing new social conditions can no longer function with traditionally formed relationships. Help from the society for the family is necessary. This trend of development appears tied to the economic and technological development of the society as a whole. The bureaucratic mechanism of the society will determine whether there will be a positive transmission of the wishes and needs of the people or whether barriers will exist, thus preventing the fulfillment of these needs.

INTERVENTIONS FOR THE AGED

Principles and Legal Basis of Social Protection of Older Persons

The principles and legal basis of social protection and help for the aged have been fixed by the constitutions, laws on joint labor, documents from the Association of Communists, Syndicate and socialistic associations, and a number of laws and parliamentary resolutions.

Workers in various organizations of joint labor, self government, and communities, on the basis of solidarity, mutuality and socialist humanism, make their own economic and social security. These goals of social policy are realized by constant improvement and equalizing of living and working conditions.

Working people buy social insurance, on the basis of mutuality and solidarity and rights from past labor, earning for themselves and the members of their family the right for health insurance, pension, protection and other rights in case of disease, lessening of working ability, and old age. To the older persons without money, the society provides social protection.

The constitutional regulations on the liberties, rights, and duties of a person also hold a regulation that children "are obliged to take care of their parents who need help."

According to the law on joint work (ZUR, paragraph 126), "Besides the principle of earning according to work, workers in the basic organization utilize the principles of solidarity, primarily by using mutual funds for partaking in fulfilling certain social and other needs of workers with lower income and the members of their families."

Workers are obliged to regulate by a self government general decree "the rights of workers according to past work" and to "insure the protection of invalids of work and other invalid persons by finding jobs, e.g., tasks which they can work at" (paragraph 189).

The republic and regional laws of social protection (welfare) contain a number of regulations concerning matters of special interest for the social protection of aged persons. These laws explicitly state that aged persons without family care are provided with social protection and social work conveniences and that all-day institutions, homes for the retired and other aged persons, institutions for house care, and other help are to be established.

The Program of the Communist Part (SKJ) emphasizes that the primary tasks of social politics are to care for the working man and the family and to help certain categories of individuals when they are in a bad situation because of old age.

The resolution of the Tenth Congress of the Communist Party (SKJ)— "Tasks in Social Politics"—was in favor of "building hotels and homes for taking care of old people; for their rest and recreation and generally greater social care for the life of old people." And it emphasized the duty of self government interest communities of social protection to "struggle for a more complete satisfaction of necessary needs of aged persons."

The Resolution of the Seventh Congress of the Union of Syndicates of Yugoslavia on improving health protection and health and pension-invalid insurance of workers pointed out that

> the further improvement of the system of pension and invalid insurance should more and more be founded upon the rights of workers according to past work, solidarity, and mutuality . . . , that social conventions and self government contracts [governing] the distribution of income and personal income should contain procedures which will guarantee such a personal income which will strengthen the financial and social security of workers just to be retired, according to their decreased working ability . . . , and that it is necessary that the criteria for the payment of charges of transmission to workers who are retiring be regulated by means of self government contracts and social agreements . . . , [and that] the duty of the organizations of syndicates and basic organizations of joint labor is to further develop adequate forms of communication and expressing careful attention towards retired workers."

Important ideological and programmatic standpoints are contained in parliamentary resolutions and other parliamentary documents, for example, the Resolution of the Assembly of the Socialist Republic of Serbia on the social care of old people in the S.R. of Serbia-Belgrade, May 1971.

RESOLUTION ON THE SOCIAL CARE OF OLD PEOPLE IN THE S.R. OF SERBIA

Social care of old people is part of the general social security policy toward citizens and one of the basic, as well as a lasting, goal, in the field of social policy.

Great social changes have occurred in the past twenty years: industrialization, migration, urbanization, improved social welfare provision, a higher living standard, a prolonged human life, a higher proportion of old people,

and changes in family relationships. These have triggered major social problems regarding elderly citizens.

The age structure of the population in the S.R. of Serbia has been
undergoing a rapid change, especially in the past few years, in favor of older
age groups, although there are considerable regional variations. The number
of persons over 65 in the Autonomous Socialist Province of Vojvodina rose
from 6.4% in 1961 to 8.4% in 1971. The percentage of old people reached
10.0% in the territory of the Republic (which is not part of the Autonomous
Socialist Provinces.) The differences are still more apparent in more restricted
areas and range from under 4% to almost 20%. These changes in age structure
are particularly perceptible in villages, but may also be noticed in larger
urban settlements.

Of the 700,000 persons over 65 years of age in Yugoslavia, about 22%
benefit from a regular source of income, in the form of a pension or regular
social assistance, whereas about 78% of the elderly are without regular
income, the majority of whom are persons working in agriculture. In the
territory of the S.R. of Serbia, there are about 130,000 old aged agricultural
households, which own about 750,000 hectares of arable land (17% of the
total arable land is owned by individual farmers.) According to estimates,
there will be about 230,000 old aged agricultural households by 1975 with
approximately 1,000,000 hectares of land or 24% of all individual farmland.

Until now, social welfare was mainly directed toward socially insecure old
people. Classical forms and methods of social welfare were applied. Little
attention was given to the social position and needs of the population of aged
persons as a whole, and up-to-date forms of social care for old people were
not extensively used. Financial assistance, however, is not the sole means of
helping old people. Health protection is another way. Approximately 77% of
old people in Serbia benefit from health insurance. According to the findings
of previous investigations, it is estimated that about 1% of elderly persons
require hospitalization and at least 1% (in certain settlements this percentage
may be still higher) need to be placed in homes. About 2.5% are bedfast due
to illness or exhaustion (17,000), 96% of whom live in villages; about 15%
have no one to visit them or care for them while they are ill (about 100,000).

The existing homes for old people can admit only about 4% (about 3,000);
and for the most part, there are no services for home care and other aid for
the elderly.

A number of significant results have been achieved in certain areas of
social welfare for old people, including: the health protection act which
provided compulsory measures of health protection; the broadening of the
system of old age and disability pensions; efforts to extend and modernize
the network of old people's homes; important contributions by social and
humanitarian organizations, local authorities, and certain enterprises and

centers for social work. All these achievements provide a solid basis on which a more complete system of social care for the old can be built.

Considering the level of social welfare achieved for the elderly and predictions which are indicative of the growing complexity of their problems, a complete policy of social welfare for old people appears to be essential. In conformity with the real possibilities society can offer, this policy should be based on the following general principles:

(1) Social care of old people is not merely an expression of the humane side of a socialist political system but rather the expression of the basic rights of man, which result from old people's economic contribution to society during their active life, in the form of surplus work, and on which part of the prosperity of the present generation is based. For this reason, social welfare should extend to the population of old persons as a whole. Through an appropriate system and self-management measures, it should be ensured that this part of the population becomes a decisive factor in the policy and practice of social welfare for old people.

(2) The social welfare system concerning the elderly should spring from an adequate moral and ethical attitude of all individuals and factors of society toward old age and old persons. For this reason, the moral and ideological education of old people should be geared toward developing a just and humane attitude toward elderly citizens. (This is one of the vital principles of socialist ethics.) Besides the family, organizations like the school, pioneer and youth organizations, the trade union, the Socialist Alliance, and certain social, humanitarian, and sports organizations, as well as mass media and propaganda, are of a particular importance of achieving this.

(3) The place and role of the family in the social welfare system is of utmost importance. Social measures should, therefore, be aimed at enabling and aiding the family to perform its social welfare function regarding its older members, to the fullest possible extent. Various facilities should be granted to families which include elderly members, e.g., suitable living conditions, certain tax abatements, health and other insurances, legal advice, home aid-nursing in times of illness, help with housework or with work on the farm, and so on. The manufacture of certain devices and other technical facilities is extremely valuable in this respect.

(4) In accordance with the respect of human dignity, social welfare of old people should be based upon a natural and inalienable right to spend their lives in a desired social and family environment—in other words, where they have spent their active lives. Therefore, social welfare of old people should be directed toward creating the conditions for the old person to spend his old age in the most suitable possible manner, in his home, in that of his family or relatives.

(5) Because of pathological health changes which occur in old age, more frequent visits to health services are necessary. This fact causes a great financial strain for the elderly person. Communes and health

insurance agencies should discuss the possibilities of establishing, by means of regulations, a more adequate use of health services and health protection for the elderly. Free medical care should be given to old persons without the necessary means of existence, and the general trend should be toward introducing full health security for the entire population of old people.

(6) Pensions, including additional funds granted in order to maintain the minimum level pension, and other means of financial assistance to old people should be sufficiently high to ensure a minimum standard of living. They should be subject to regular reevaluation so that their real value is guaranteed and in tune with economic trends and the costs of living.

(7) The necessary improvement of the social position and social security concerning old people requires a speedy introduction of pension insurance for farm workers. Funds for this insurance should be derived from the economic potential of extensively cultivated or uncultivated farmland belonging to old aged households.

(8) In urban settlements, social action should be directed toward creating a series of clubs and similar entertainment activities for older persons. Moreover, these institutions could involve them in work, organize their recreation and rest, and grant them reductions in using public transportation, institutions for cultural activities, and entertainment.

(9) In rural areas, action should largely be aimed at granting tax abatements and providing home aid to farm workers who are old, exhausted, and ill, including help with housework and farmwork.

(10) Special homes should be adapted to the needs and means of old people. Therefore, it is necessary to plan the development of a network of "home-type" institutions that are regional and communal, specialized and adjusted to meet the needs of a certain category of users. They must also insure that their number is sufficiently large and their territorial distribution uniform. Institutions of the old people's home type should offer services in harmony with present-day achievements and the human dignity of the user. Users of these institutions should be given the right to exert a direct influence on the organization of life, on the type and standard of services offered, as well as to determine certain expenses in these institutions. Exhausted self-supporting old people from villages should be placed in special apartment buildings in which necessary assistance could be organized and given to a smaller number of old persons, grouped together; and, in some cases, aid should be extended in special homes. Contributions of old persons for housing construction should be used for financing the building of apartments and old people's institutions of the special home type and for constructing and equipping other specialized open institutions such as day care and other various services.

All self-management bodies in society are responsible for social care and activities concerning old people. They include the commune, the local community, enterprises, certain interest communities (these are the main initiators) as well as sociopolitical organizations and citizens' associations such as the Socialist Alliance, the Trade Unions' Confederation, the Red Cross, the Association of Retired Persons, the Invalids of Work, and so on. All of them should define a policy of social care for the old, their own contribution for its implementation, by voting legal acts and concrete measures or by undertaking some other concrete action.

From the point of view of old age insurance and extended social welfare, possibilities should be explored for introducing the right to a special allowance for persons who attend to the needs of old persons in cases where this assistance is essential.

Health insurance funds should cover the costs of home aid and placement of old people in clinics for chronically ill persons which are attached to old people's homes.

Those entrusted with the social welfare of old people must deal with the problem of forming necessary personnel and giving them advanced training to become specialized in work with elderly persons, as well as with improving the qualifications structure of personnel employed in services and institutions for old people.

Those in charge of social care for old people, the commune, local communities, and labor organizations periodically review results and achievements of social care and established welfare policy in regard to old people. Reviews are made on the basis of analysis prepared by expert services and institutions.

Social assistance to old people should be more scientifically based. Therefore, scientific research should be encouraged and developed, and long-term scientific research grants relating to these problems should be established and financed.

In this sense, the Assembly of the S.R. of Serbia expects all social factors, as well as certain interest communities and social-humanitarian and other sociopolitical organizations, to define, with the briefest possible delay, concrete programs of direct and permanent action directed toward the implementation of the principles of the resolution.

Republic bodies, the Institute of Social Policy, and the Republic agency for health welfare are given the duty to develop work programs for achieving the goals set in the resolution, within their jurisdiction and within six months of the adoption of the resolution.

Voluntary organizations

There exist in Yugoslavia several citizen organizations, which act as the representatives of their many members. The most important one is the "Association of the Retired Persons." The tasks of this association are to inform its members of their rights, to help them achieve these rights, and generally to protect their interests. This association has noticeable financial funds for housing projects, apartments, homes for the aged, and the like. In addition, the association develops numerous recreational activities.

The Union of War Veterans is an organization which holds an important position in society. This organization primarily takes care of war participants, army war invalids, and their families. Their rights are regulated by laws and the organization makes propositions for and about these laws. The organization gives much attention to the improvement of health protection and rehabilitation and the engagement of war veterans in social life.

Besides these organizations, the best known of voluntary organizations is the Red Cross, which deals with discovering older persons who need some help and organizing home care for the patients who are immobile or do not have anyone to care for them.

Similar work is organized by some churches, especially the Roman Catholic (*Caritas*).

A very powerful voluntary citizen organization, to which most of the citizens belong, is the Socialistic Association of the Working People of Yugoslavia. This mass organization is supposed to take care of all the needs of the citizens, and therefore can be included as another place the elderly can bring their problems.

Economic and Social Status and Retirement

Self-government socialism and the trade market economy in Yugoslavia function according to the principle: "Earnings depend upon the work done." This means that the economic status depends primarily on the invested work and on the social evaluation of this work. It follows from this that the economic status of individuals differs very much depending upon the profession, the particular job, and so on. However, the greatest differences occur between income during employment and after retirement.

Old age pensions may be drawn at age 60 for men and 55 for women after at least 20 years of contributions, or at ages 65 and 60 after 15 years, but not if the person continues to work. Pensions may be drawn at any age after 40 years' contribution in the case of men and 35 years in the case of women.

Disability pension may be either work-related or not. If the injury is not work-related, full disability pension is available only if the claimant has contributed three-quarters of the time since the age of 20 and if disablement is complete, or if the injury is sustained at an age when there is not the possibility of vocational rehabilitation. If the injury is work-related, there is no required time of contribution. If disablement is partial and/or rehabilitation is possible, other benefit programs are applied, such as temporary or reduced work compensation. Eligibility may be established even if contributions are for less than three-quarters of the time since age 20 if they are concentrated in a way satisfactory to the commune and, especially, if the disabled person is under age 30.

Family pensions are payable to survivors (immediate family) if the deceased was insured for at least five years and if his contributions were concentrated in an order approved by the commune, or if the deceased was qualified for pension after 20 years' work or was otherwise receiving or entitled to old age pension or injury compensation. If the death resulted from work-related injury or illness, no qualifying period is required.

A widow may receive a pension if she is at least 45 years old, or even if she is younger, if she is incapable of working or has dependent children requiring her care. She can retain a permanent pension only if the children become independent after she is 40. Provisions are also made for male survivors. A widower who was dependent on his wife can receive a pension if he is 60 or incapable of work or has dependent children. A child is eligible for a pension until the age of 15, and the deceased's parents are eligible if they are at least 60 (for the father) or at least 45 (for the mother), or are incapable of work.

Pension benefits are calculated on a base of the individual's previous 10 years' average income, revalued to the last 2 years' living cost levels. The maximum amount of old age pension and invalidity pension (for full entitlement) is 85% of the base. Family (survivors) pensions may be up to 100% of the pension entitlement. The minimum (available after 20 years' work) is 55% of the base wage for men and 45% for women. Two percent is added to the 85% for each year's work beyond 35 years.

"Employment," however, does not include individual farmers. Recently, there has been a movement to institute a pension insurance law for the farmers, and this is to be done in each Republic, depending on its resources.

The war veterans pensions are regulated under special law.

According to the sources of income, older persons in Yugoslavia can be classified as:

(1) those who have entirely or partly fulfilled the laws of pension insurance.
(2) family-pensioned persons (bearers of the insurance passed on to them because of the death of the insured).
(3) invalid-pensioned persons (those pensioned before the normal work span because of disease or crippling).
(4) those on war veterans pensions (obtained according to the war veteran laws).
(5) those with pension and part-time job after retirement.
(6) those on social aid (those who have not been employed or have no income sufficient for survival).
(7) those who satisfy their basic needs themselves (farmers and persons who are not qualified for full pension).
(8) those who are taken care of by their families.

The problems concerning employment after retirement are very similar to the ones in other countries. Those persons who are in good health wish to continue with their work, because of the need to retain their previous living standard. They do not want and emotionally cannot stand the loss of their earlier social status which they had while they were actively employed. The generations of older citizens of which we speak were brought up with an ideal that the goal in life is to achieve the greatest ability and acknowledgment in one's profession. Today, they are advised that they should have "hobbies" in order to adjust to retirement more easily. For most of them, their work in their profession was their "hobby," so they await retirement with fear. It is the loss of basic motivation after retirement that makes many retired people lose the meaning of their life.

Health Protection

Health protection is regulated by law in such a way that all employed pay around 9% of their monthly income for health insurance. Those who are not insured in this way must pay for medical help, with those who cannot pay helped by social welfare or other solidarity funds.

All citizens receive medical aid in medical centers and hospitals (there are no nursing homes). Geriatric departments exist only in some hospitals in the larger cities.

Problems connected with the health of the aged are numerous. It is a population which often suffers many illnesses at once. The most frequent are rheumatism and cardiovascular diseases. Medical aid is more accessible to the elderly in the cities than in rural areas. The need for the care of chronically ill and bedfast patients is acute.

Institutionalization and Services

Until recently, the only ones who lived in the homes for the aged were those who did not have any family of their own to take care of them. In the last few years there has been a change in the socioeconomic status of users of these institutions. In 1956 only 573 persons were paying for the entire cost of institutionalization. In 1974 this number grew to 3,939, and the tendency appears to be one of continual growth (See table 11.3.)

The homes for the aged are classified by the service they offer: hotel-type for the residents who are better off and still in good health; homes that include health care and nursing; and special homes for bedfast, chronically ill, and mentally disturbed (senile dementia, chronic alcoholism, and so on).

Table 11.3:   Numbers of Homes for the Aged and Places Available for Pensioners

	1946		1974	
	Homes	*No. of Places*	*Homes*	*No. of Places*
Yugoslavia	158	6,620	124	17,262
Bosna & Hercegovina	9	355	5	740
Crna Gora	3	160	1	165
Hrvatska	33	1,664	42	5,946
Macedonia	6	195	6	394
Slovenia	47	2,500	37	5,664
Serbia	60	1,766	33	4,353
area outside of regions	. . . .		14	1,686
Kosovo	. . . .		2	377
Vojvodina	. . . .		17	1,686

Some of the institutions have day care for other pensioners in the local commune so that they can have their meals in the institution with the residents or they can join a club run by the institution for recreational activities.

Efforts are made in the S.R. Serbia regarding the establishment of diverse institutions that secure placement and other important services to the elderly. A very significant program is the placement of children deprived of parental care and children disturbed because of family conditions into the same institutions as the elderly. This placement provides a number of social, psychological, and educational advantages by allowing closer contacts between children and the aged.

For example, in the home for pensioners at Vozdovac-Beograd, group social work has been utilized for both therapeutic and interest groups. The therapeutic groups are formed according to the criterion of the therapeutic need of the beneficiaries, and they consist of 16 to 28 members. The objective of such group work is the satisfaction of elementary needs of beneficiaries. The interest groups are formed according to the criteria of preference and interest and have 5 to 20 members. The goal of this group work is the organization of cultural entertainment and recreational activities.

In-home services for older citizens are now being organized. More and more of those who receive pensions and can pay for services which they cannot provide for themselves wish to remain in their own apartments. This service is primarily available to the elderly city residents. There is still an urgent need for special services in the rural areas.

The data show that the rural aged, even those living alone and not able to work, do not wish to move into homes for the aged. For them, it is more appropriate to organize necessary help where they live. There are many examples in rural areas where the services for the aged are organized on the basis of mutual neighbor-assistance. The most appropriate is the so-called "village housekeeper" service. Here, village women, specially educated and paid by the center of social work, serve the old people in the village and take care of their needs.

The most needed services for the aged in the cities and in the villages are health services, which include nursing for the bedfast and chronically ill who live with family or are alone in their apartments. At the present time, this service is being provided by the so-called "polyvalent health-social worker."

It is more and more obvious that everything should be done to provide the necessary help to older persons in their homes and not to move them out from their natural surroundings.

Therefore, much emphasis has been given to the "geronto-hostess" service for nursing aged people in their homes and for providing other necessary assistance, including house cleaning, washing the windows and the laundry, shopping and preparing the meals.

Social Work Interventions for the Aged

Community social work is developing at a rapid pace, and, therefore, more and more action is being directed toward the aged population. One of the first tasks was to assess the needs of the elderly. Centers for social work in the local commune were given this responsibility; and on the basis of these data, new programs and proposals for concrete actions have been devised. The clubs or day centers for the aged are prime examples of a program that was initiated through the combined efforts of voluntary and professional organizations, local community groups, and the aged citizens themselves. The clubs involve two-thirds of the neighborhood communities. All the clubs are furnished with kitchens, dining rooms, bars, living rooms, radios, record players, TV sets, newspapers, small libraries, chess sets, dominoes, and other amusement games.

The regular activity of clubs consists of providing hot meals, distributing food in the apartments of the less mobile persons, providing recreational activities in the clubs, supplying books and daily and weekly newspapers and magazines, and organizing work assignments. Besides the regular activities in the clubs, there are from time to time organized one-day excursions, competitions within a club and among the clubs in chess, dominoes, and other games, visits to theaters, cinemas, and other kinds of performances, and excursions outside the town for recovery, rest, and recreation.

The services of the clubs may benefit all those who are members—pensioners, adult persons, the beneficiaries of a regular social financial aid, self-supporting and disabled persons. The clubs have a self-managing organizational structure, which represents the boards of the clubs, commissions, and the councils of the clubs.

These types of clubs are in reality day centers for the elderly. Not all clubs in Yugoslavia have the same program. Most of them are more oriented to leisure activities. This largely depends on the needs and possibilities of the people and the centers for social work itself.

The placement of old people with foster families is also used as a social work method for protection, especially for those who are single and living in rural areas. It is calculated that in S.R. Croatia there are only 600 old people protected in this manner and in Bosna and Hercegovina, in the year 1971, only 293 persons, primarily because it is difficult to find families willing to take care of the aged.

Other Innovations

In the last few years there are more and more aged people who themselves, by contract with other people, give their property and in return receive the necessary protection to the end of their lives.

There are also more and more aged persons who are giving all their property (mostly in rural areas) to the commune, and in return receiving the monthly rent and other necessary support. There is a great interest, especially among aged peasants with no family members, for this type of social protection. In S.R. Croatia alone, approximately 1,200 individuals utilized this form of "Commune" protection.

RESEARCH PROJECTS

The systematic research projects dealing with the problems of the aged in Yugoslavia began in the middle of 1966 with the support of the Department of Health, Education and Welfare of the United States and the Technical Assistance of SFR Yugoslavia. These investigations have been stimulated by the work and personal assistance of Ethel Shanas.

The investigation "Old people in Yugoslavia" (1966-1971) was conducted by the principal investigator Dr. Nedeljkovic and collaborators from the Institute of Social policy in Belgrade. The sample is made on noninstitutionalized persons aged 65 years and over in urban and rural areas in Yugoslavia.

The investigation "Social Protection and Needs of Aged People in the Rural Areas of S.R. Croatia" (1968-1971) and the investigation (the first in Yugoslavia) "Longitudinal Study of the Social-Economical State of Aged People in the Rural Areas of S.R. Croatia" (1972-1976) were conducted by the principal investigator Dr. Nada Smolic-Krkovic and collaborators from the Republic Institute of Social Work of S.R. Croatia.

The same model of investigation has been followed now in other regions of Yugoslavia, and many other research projects have been made to collect data regarding universal characteristics of the aging population. It is enough to say that at the First Gerontological Congress of Yugoslavia, which was held in Belgrade in the year 1977, there were 400 presented papers and 1,000 participants, clearly showing the rapid interest in the growing population of the aged.

REFERENCES

BREZNIK, D. (1972) Demographic Methods and Models. Belgrade.

Information About Social Welfare of the Aged Persons in SR Croatia and Their Cost in 1971 (1972), Zagreb.

Informative Material of the Permanent Conference of the Cities of Yugoslavia (1973) No. 106. Belgrade.

SENTIC, M. (1971) Nos citoyens au travail temporaire a l'etranger, Stanovnistvo (1971) No. 1-2. Belgrade.

SHANAS, E., P. TOWNSEND, D. WEEDERBURN, H. FRIIS, P. MILHOJ, and J. STEHOUVER (1968) Old People in Three Industrial Societies. New York: Atherton.

SMOLIC-KRKOVIC, N., D. MILINKOVIC, and A. VISINSKI (1971) Social Protection and Needs of Aged People in Rural Areas of SR Croatia (1968-1971). Zagreb.

12

SERVICES TO THE AGED IN JAPAN

M I K I O   M O R I

THE SITUATION OF THE AGED IN JAPAN

During the 1960s

The legislation which gave form to Japan's service system for the aged was enacted during the late 1950s and the early 1960s. The National Pension Law was enacted in 1959, the National Medical Insurance Law also appeared in 1959, and the Law for the Welfare for the Aged was enacted in 1963. Japan was experiencing a high rate of economic development. Legislation was enacted with the expectation that a similar high rate of economic development would continue.

In the process of rapid economic development, with mass movements from villages to the cities, people from agricultural sectors moved rapidly to industrial sectors. For a time, traditional forms of family life had continued in the postwar years even though the legal basis of the family system had been changed by amendment of the Civil Law in 1948. Rapid economic development in the 1960s, however, changed the predominant family pattern from that of the extended family to the more industrial compatible nuclear family.

It was changes in society itself, rather than new legislation, which brought changes in the kind of care given to the elderly. It had become difficult under these new social conditions for the younger generation to care for aging parents. These changes had already occurred in Western societies some decades before. In an industrial society, it is not so easy for children to live with an older parent or to send money to an older parent living alone.

During a period of rapid economic development, a government budget is appropriated mainly for economic development. In 1960, the Public Assistance Law in Japan offered a standard of living based on 38% of the purchasing power of an employed person, the lowest in the history of this system. By 1973, this rate had increased to 56%. Until the maturity of the social security system and the advent of more social services, care of the aged is in the hands of the family. Filial piety has been a universal doctrine among the population in general. Most people support the idea that the aged should be cared for by their children. This is still a popular position, especially among the older generation and people in rural areas.

Filial piety is a sense of obligation which all Japanese think of as a natural virtue. Since it is not always so easy for the younger generation to care for their older parents, social services for the aged have come to be thought of as an alternative for the poor elderly who cannot be cared for by their children or by relatives. Often there is bitter estrangement between an aged person and the children in his family. Many people in Western societies are not aware of changes which have taken place and see Japan as a society where old and young live happily together.

According to a government survey in 1969 (Prime Minister's Secretary, 1969) 23% of the population (31% in Tokyo and 18% in rural areas) held the opinion that elderly parents should live by themselves, apart from their children. The survey revealed further that 35% (16% in Tokyo and 48% in rural areas) felt that responsibility for care of the aged was in the hands of their children. In fact, the majority of the aged in Japan do live with their children. Statistics show that 70% to 80% of the elderly in Japan have continued to live with their children over the past 30 years or so, and this picture does not show signs of changing.

In contrast, the percentage of the aged living with their children in Denmark was 14%, in Britain 27%, and in the United States 14%. The percentage of elderly in Japan living with their families is seen as unbelievably high for an industrially advanced country. An American gerontologist has recently written a book about this problem, emphasizing the enviable position of Japan. I believe that a change has already occurred in the Japanese family and that this change is mainly one of the attitude of children toward their elderly parents.

The older generation wants to live with their children. A government survey in 1971 (Prime Minister's Secretary, 1971) showed that 64% of the people 60 or older want to live with their children. Not so many younger people want to live with their old parents. This survey showed that 41% of people in their 20s want to live with their parents, 44% of those in their 30s and 49% of those in their 40s.

Nevertheless, a majority of older parents continue to live with their children. I believe the primary reason for the "living together" of the two generations relates to a shortage of housing, especially in the urban areas. According to a government survey in 1973, 78.9% of people over 60 years of age who are householders own their own homes. The corresponding figure for people younger than 25 is 11.4%. In my opinion, not a few children, against their own will, live with their older parents in a home owned by their parents because of the housing shortage. The house will eventually be transferred from the parents to the children after the death of the parents. Judging from the external appearance, the high percentage of parents and older children living together seems to show filial piety. I am afraid that the sentiment is dependent, rather, on a housing shortage and inheritance expectation. As to the relationship in Japan of parents with their children, it may be more appropriate to speak of "hostility while living together." Living together has come to involve greater distance in feeling between the two generations.

Circumstances are somewhat different in the rural areas. The living together of an eldest son and his elderly parents is a result of their economic condition. Of course, Japan has relatively few instances of dire poverty, but we do experience comparative poverty, especially in rural areas. Many three-generation families live in one house. A government survey in 1976 (Office of the Prime Minister, 1976) showed that the percentage of three-generation families varied from 25% to 33% in rural areas while only 10% of Tokyo and Osaka families were of three-generations. Even a farmer, if he can escape from poor economic circumstances, will live separately from his elderly parents after he has married. Society has changed, feelings have changed, and external appearances are changing. These changes are clearest in the urban areas.

During the 1970s

By the early 1970s, the percentage of the aged living with their children had shown a slight decrease, with parents more frequently living with a son than a daughter. As already indicated (Office of the Prime Minister, 1976), the three-generation family is decreasing. There were 7,728,000 such families in 1954 and only 5,548,000 by 1975. The percentage of all families who were three-generation families was 45% in 1954 and only 17% by 1975. Meanwhile, nuclear families were increasing. There were 8,043,000 nuclear families in 1954 and 19,303,000 by 1975. The percentage of nuclear families was 46% and 59% respectively for 1954 and 1975. A third tendency is an increase in families consisting exclusively of aged persons. There were 431,000 such families in 1953. This number had grown to 1,619,000 by 1975. Only 2.5% of all families were aged families in 1954, but this percentage had increased to

4.9% by 1975. In short, the trend is toward more nuclear families and families consisting exclusively of the aged, accompanied by a decrease in three-generation families.

Care of the aged has changed from a private family problem to a social problem. Even before 1970, the government had become concerned about services for the aged. In 1964, the year after enactment of the Law for the Welfare of the Aged, the government organized a Division for the Welfare of the Aged within the Ministry of Health and Welfare, and in 1968 appointed an Expert on Aging to this division. The writer was the first appointee to this position and served there until retirement in 1976.

From another point of view, by the end of the 1960s, Japan had reached the peak of its economic development and, as a result, had begun to share some parts of the national income in a more generous way to provide social services. Also, an "old power" movement with some political influence had, sprung up among the grass-roots population while progressive parties had gained power in the Diet. As a result, the government party could not afford to ignore the potential political support from the elderly political block. Thus, the Social Security Pension Acts were amended year by year and social services began to see improvement.

SERVICES TO THE AGED

Pension Schemes

Since the enactment of the National Pension Act in 1959, the whole population has been covered by some form of pension scheme. Pension schemes in Japan are divided into eight varieties, with legislation covering each. Large industry is gathered under one system, establishing its own pension plan. Those related to this plan can expect good pension benefits at retirement age. Economically weaker groups have poor pension benefits. The average benefit received under the general Employees' Pension is some six times that of the noncontributory welfare pension plan for elderly with very low incomes. Yearly pension benefits in yen under the eight pension schemes, according to 1976 government statistics, is as follows:

(1) Employee's Pension Insurance   ¥826,312
(2) Seamen's Insurance   ¥873,406
(3) National Pension (Noncontributory)   ¥180,000
(4) National Public Service Mutual Aid Association   ¥1,090,734
(5) Local Public Service Mutual Aid Association   ¥1,132,465
(6) Agricultural, Forestry and Fishery Institutions Staff
     Mutual Aid Association   ¥666,538

(7) Private School Teachers' and Employees' Mutual Aid
     Association   ¥942,069
(8) Public Corporation Staff Mutual Aid Association   ¥1,102,380

The pensionable age is 60 for males and 55 for females under the Employee's Pension program. This age is lower than the comparable age in Western countries and the same as that in developing countries of Asia and Africa. The pensionable age is sixty-five for both sexes under the National Pension Act, which covers the self-employed, and is seventy for the noncontributory welfare pension program.

An aged person receiving benefits under the Employees' Pension program is able to maintain a minimum standard of living, but such is not possible under the National Pension plan for the self-employed. The average salary of an employee was calculated at ¥154,967 a month in 1974 according to a government survey (Ministry of Labour, 1974). The present pension program can be compared to an "invitation to dinner" at which the aged are seated at the table but the meal has yet to be served.

Housing Policy

Yet another "invitation to dinner" is the housing program. On the surface, the number of housing units in Japan appears to be greater than the number of households. A survey (Office of the Prime Minister, 1973) showed that there were at that time 31,059,000 housing units for some 29,651,000 families. The problem is that housing objectives need to be restated in order to show quality as well as quantity. A more realistic goal, for instance, would be one room for each family member rather than one housing unit per family.

Some older people are definitely faced with difficulty in finding housing. In Japan, the housing policy has left the matter of construction primarily to the commércial market. Two-thirds of the newly constructed houses each year are built at the profit-making level. This is not bad in a free enterprise society. Neither is it bad for a laborer who has wage or salary income. It is not good, however, for the low-income classes, which include most of the elderly. Consequently, the government (Ministry of Construction) has subsidized prefectural and municipal governments to build public housing for the low-income classes. The ministry established public housing for aged couples in 1964. The number of units in service totaled some 10,000 houses by 1978.

However, public housing for the aged is inadequate both in number of units available and in the lack of provision at present for single elderly people. Two conditions are apparent. Present housing policy is aimed primarily at supporting the productivity of laborers, with little relevance to the needs of the elderly. Second, residential care for the elderly becomes a kind of compensation housing policy for the aged.

Retirement Age

In general, the compulsory retirement age is 55 in most Japanese industrial and commercial enterprises. This early retirement age makes the problem of the aged more serious. But, this is not so much a problem for the aged as it is a problem for those in older middle age. The retirement age was 50 at the end of the nineteenth century. At that time (1891-1898) life expectancy was 43 years for males and 44 for females. In contrast, today's life expectancy is 72 and 77 years, respectively. Life expectancy at age 55 years of age is now 22 years for males and 25 years for females. Until recently, the elderly could spend their later years under the support of their children. At present, this is no longer always possible. As indicated above, a pension is not always sufficient to meet the needs of daily life. Usually, the elderly person must hunt for a retirement job. Even if he or she finds one and is happy in it, income is almost always smaller than the income from the preretirement job.

Today's older generation also carries a special burden originating in the social circumstances of World War II. The marriage age of older people was, in general, later than today. As a result, not a few people of the older generation are still in their late middle years burdened with the responsibility of bringing up and educating children who in other circumstances might already be of an independent age. Japan is a society with high educational consciousness. Ninety-nine percent of the graduates from middle school enter a high school, and one-third of the graduates from high school enter a college or university. In Japan, children enter primary school at age six. They spend six years in primary school, three years in middle school, three years in high school, and two years in college or four years in university. Students generally graduate and become self-sufficient at twenty-two years of age.

All of this is an expensive financial outlay for parents. Younger persons frequently marry with heavy financial support from their parents. The adult in older middle age also has many financial expenses of his own. For example, there is the matter of a loan for paying for the construction of a home. With all these financial responsibilities, most people are unable to prepare adequately for their later years.

The government's Ministry of Labor has some special programs which relate to these problems. Subsidies to an enterprise which postpones the retirement age and/or employs an elderly person is one such program, and establishment of special administrative sections for the elderly in employment offices and municipal offices is another. These measures have not always been effective, because of the serious and prolonged depression during the past few years. Poor business conditions have especially affected wages of persons in provisional categories of employment.

Homehelp Services

In 1962, the government started subsidizing municipalities which had homehelp services for the aged. As of 1976 (Ministry of Health and Welfare, 1976a), there were 8,821 such homehelpers. The elderly persons who are eligible for these services are limited to the lower-income classes. A member of the lower-income classes is defined as one who, according to government standards, is not required to pay any income tax. Some 30% of all families presently fall into this category. It follows that an aged person who pays taxes or whose children pay taxes cannot receive the public homehelp services. To receive services, they must employ a commercial homehelper. The cost of a commercial homehelper is some ¥10,000 a day, too much for most families to pay.

At the start, the homehelp service program met opposition both from the general public and from government officials. The popular opinion was that care of the elderly is the filial duty of children and relatives. Since responsibility for the general public was thus placed on children and relatives, the object of the homehelp services program was limited to the lower-income classes. In Britain, the number of homehelpers is equivalent to half the number of bedfast elderly, and in the U.S. to one-tenth the number of bedfast elderly, according to the International Council of Homehelp Services in 1976. In Japan there are 350,000 bedfast elderly people. We would have to have 175,000 homehelpers to have the same ratio as Britain or 35,000 homehelpers to have the same ratio as the United States. In spite of their relatively few numbers, homehelpers in Japan have organized the Japan Council of Homehelp Services and are affiliates of the International Council of Homehelp.

By April 1978, the Tokyo Metropolitan Government's special program for homehelp service provided ¥11,500 a month to hire an attendant for a bedfast elderly person. Such allowances for attendants are also popular in Nordic countries. I expect that eventually such a system will be established in Japan at the central government level. There is, however, no consensus yet for introducing this provision. Government still believes that it is the responsibility of children to care for their aged parents.

Health Examination Services

According to the Law for the Welfare of the Aged, the mayor of a municipality will administer a health examination once a year to people 60 and above who live in his jurisdiction. This kind of provision is very rare. I have no knowledge of such a provision in other countries. As a result of this program, many people are found to have conditions requiring medical attention, usually related to highblood pressure and heart disease. Many people, however, are not interested in these health examination services. Only some 20% of those eligible actually have the examination.

Medical Care

The total population of Japan is covered under eight kinds of medical insurance programs. The insured can receive free medical care in some cases and 70% of the medical cost in other cases. Free medical care for those over 70 years of age was begun in 1973. Seventy percent of the medical cost is financed by medical insurance and the rest by the government budget. Free medical care for the aged brought with it a crisis for medical insurance financing. The contribution possible from the National Medical Insurance program is relatively small, but the benefit costs have continued to increase. Every municipality has its own medical insurance program; and so, especially in the rural areas where population ratios of the aged are high, insurance financing has become unbalanced. The government will introduce a Medical Insurance for the Aged Act in the near future. At that time, medical insurance schemes in Japan will be divided into three categories: for employees, for the self-employed, and for the aged.

It is necessary to make reference here to the medical behavior of the aged as a part of the process of receiving free medical care. Before enactment of the medical insurance act some twenty years ago, there had been a long tradition of only members of the upper classes consulting medical doctors. Medical service was a kind of privilege and symbol of the upper classes. For the lower classes, a visit from a doctor came only when an aged person was not expected to recover from an illness. In the poorest cases, people could have no chance to consult a doctor except at the time of being handed a death certificate.

With the enactment of free medical care, the lower classes, especially the aged, rushed to take advantage of this former privilege and symbol of upper class status. It has been noted (Ministry of Health and Welfare, 1955, 1976b) that the number of patients consulting a medical doctor has increased year by year. In 1955 the rate was 3,301 per 100,000 for all age groups, but by 1976 it had increased to 7,186 per 100,000 for a more than twofold increase in 20 years. The increase is even more vivid in the older population. The rate in 1955 was 3,172 per 100,000 for the 65- to 74-year-old age group and 2,304 per 100,000 for the 75-year and above age group. By 1976, the rate had increased to 13,166 in the 65- to 69-year-old group, to 18,934 in the 70- to 74-year-old age group, and stood at 20,326 in the 75- to 79-year-old age group, then dropped slightly to 17,849 in the 80-year-old and above age group, for more than an eight fold increase in 20 years. Meanwhile, the insurance contribution fee was not increasing at the same pace so that an imbalance in the financial situation was to be expected.

Another problem is the lack of a proper nursing home system in Japan. Yet another is that residential care for the elderly continues to be burdened with a stigma something like that related to the poor house systems of the past in Europe and America. Children frequently send their parents not to a social institution but to a general hospital when they need attention in their old age. In Japan we have no system of geriatric hospitals or hospitals for the chronically ill or nursing homes, the facilities to which the elderly are sent in Western societies. Hospital costs are surely higher than the cost of geriatric hospital care or care in a hospital for the chronically ill or in a nursing home. Under these circumstances, we cannot but expect to have financial imbalance.

Policy Regarding Free Time Activity

The biggest problem for the aged is how to use the long free hours and days of retired life. Today's high economic development is the product of the industry and thrift of the Japanese people. The older generation, being industrious and thrifty, have carried today's development on their shoulders. They believe that free time and idleness is unethical. They do not know how to spend the free time of their retirement years. Government surveys showed (Prime Minister's Secretary, 1969; Ministry of Health and Welfare, 1966) that 33% of the people over 60 had no leisure activity in 1966 and that 58% of the people over 70 had no leisure activity in 1969. If TV watching is counted as a leisure activity, many of them answer that this is their leisure activity. They have come to be called the "TV old."

Life expectancy for people at 65 years of age is 14 years for males and 17 years for females. Even if older people are healthy and have no economic problems, are living happily with their children, and are getting a moderate pension, it is still impossible to avoid the matter of what to do with free time. The government has realized the importance of free time activity for the aged and has subsidized municipalities to help organize old people's clubs starting in 1963. These clubs numbered only in the hundreds during the 1950s, but government subsidy has given a strong impulse to the organization of old people's clubs all over the country in recent years. According to the Ministry of Health and Welfare (1976a), by 1976 the number of clubs stood at 111,230 and members totaled 6,763,857. Some half of the population over

60 are now organized into old people's clubs. This, however, should be considered a somewhat conservative rather than a progressive reaction. That only half the population over 60 is so engaged shows the national character of the older generation in this particular era.

There are old people's clubs in Western countries, too, but the character of these clubs is very different. In Japan, old people's clubs are organized by every local area. In Western countries, some are organized on a larger district basis or are based on leisure activity or religious or political interests rather than on geographical division. Another difference is that club organization in Japanese cities is not as active as in rural areas. For example, some 40% of the old people are organized into old people's clubs in the Tokyo metropolitan area whereas some 70% are organized in rural areas. This shows the degree of collapse of gemeinschaft and indicates a modernization formulation.

In the future I expect that the aged will organize their own clubs by interest activity, such as singing, dancing, painting, card playing, or gardening. This tendency is already appearing in the big cities. Club members tend to belong to the lower classes in Western countries but to the middle and lower-upper classes in Japan. In Western countries the middle and upper classes have their own free time activity but lower classes do not and are thus given free time activity in old people's clubs. In Japan, on the other hand, middle and lower-upper class peoples are organized into clubs. The lower classes hesitate to be organized with the higher classes.

Every club received a public subsidy of ¥5,200 a month as of 1978. Other programs include a government subsidy from the Ministry of Education to municipalities to provide a social education room for the aged. There are 4,200 such rooms which had been established as of 1978. Many local governments also organize and subsidize athletic meets and marathon races for the elderly on an annual basis.

Institutions for the Aged

There were 1,695 institutions for the aged in 1976 according to a government survey (Ministry of Health and Welfare, 1976c). The total number of residents in these institutions was 127,201. Of the institutions, 936 were classified as old people's homes and accommodated 15,226 residents. Only 18% of these residents were institutionalized in order to receive care for physical or mental illnesses. The rest were institutionalized for other reasons, primarily lack of adequate housing and economic or family reasons. As mentioned before, the old people's home program can be viewed as being primarily a kind of housing measure. More frankly speaking, it is a kind of poor house policy, or a policy which compensates for the underdevelopment of the pension and housing programs.

We have yet another kind of home for the elderly where bedfast people are accommodated. There were 627 such institutions with a capacity of 21,847 residents according to the Ministry of Health and Welfare in 1976. This kind of institution is not the same as nursing homes in Western societies.

Some 299,000 people over 65 years of age are to be found in hospitals and clinics. This is 27.3% of the total hospital bed space in Japan. In my opinion, these hospital patients must be transferred into institutions for the aged in the near future and services in these institutions must be brought up to the standards of nursing homes in Western societies. These changes will be very difficult because of strong objections from the medical profession. Most geriatricians maintain that the sick, even if not expected to recover, need care in a hospital. I have also referred to the fact that 350,000 old people are bedfast in their own homes without professional attention.

CONCLUSION

Japan has gone through a process of rapid economic development with major shifts in the population from the agricultural to the industrial sectors. These new economic developments have created concomitant changes in the traditional Japanese family structure. Both factors have combined to create the current problems facing the aged in Japan.

In the future it is hoped that the societal responsibility toward the elderly will increase and the national and local government will continue and expand their roles in the delivery of services for the aged. Besides necessary increases in the National Pension Plan and other government grants for the aged, the creation of an adequate system of long-term care facilities for the chronically ill or frail aged will be begun.

The aged should be helped to prepare for retirement. This preparation should include both financial considerations and leisure time activities. The aged should be encouraged to organize their own clubs and associations, especially the urban aged who have been reluctant to join in the past.

REFERENCES

International Council of Homehelp Services (1976) Information Bulletin. Holland.
Ministry of Health and Welfare (1976a) Social Service Report. Japan: Government.
——— (1976b) Patient Survey. Japan: Government.
——— (1976c) Social Institution Survey. Japan: Government.
——— (1966) Basic Survey on the Welfare Services. Japan: Government.

––– (1955) Patient Survey. Japan: Government.
Ministry of Labour (1974) Labour Statistics. Japan: Government.
Office of the Prime Minister (1976) Housing Survey of Japan. Japan: Government.
––– (1973) Housing Survey in Japan. Japan: Government.
Prime Minister's Secretary (1973) Public Opinion Poll of Aging Problems. Japan: Government.
––– (1971) Public Opinion Poll of Aging Problems. Japan: Government.
––– (1969) Public Opinion Poll of Later Life. Japan: Government.

13

THE AGED IN DENMARK
Social Programmes

HENNING FRIIS

Care of the aged has during this century been an area of major public concern in Denmark. Public programmes in the field of income maintenance and services for the aged have been pressed forward by public opinion and have always been met with positive political response both in the Parliament and in the municipal councils.

Although the Parliament, by legislation, sets the overall frame for policies for the aged, the 275 muncipalities and the 16 counties have the operational responsibility for income maintenance programmes and for services (Friis, 1976). In the service area new initiatives have usually emanated at the municipal level. When adopted by many muncipalities, they have been generalized through legislation by the Parliament.

Income maintenance programmes are generally financed through the central government budget. Costs of social and health services are shared between the central government and the municipalities and counties, which levy their own taxes. The total expenditure in Denmark for social security and social services including health amounted in 1975 to 27% of the gross national product against 11% in 1960. The expenditures for the aged for pensions, medical care, and social services increased at the same speed, from approximately 5% of the gross national product in 1960 to approximately 13% in 1975. Half of the amount goes to pensions.[1]

The population 65 years and over was 9.1% of the total population in 1950 and 14% in 1978. Recent forecasts indicate that the proportion of those 65 years and over in the population will only increase to 14.5% by the year 2000. However, the proportion in the age group 80 years and older will increase from 2.5% in 1978 to 3.7% by the year 2000.

The work activity rate for men in the age group 65-74 has, according to surveys of the Danish National Institute of Social Research, declined from

48% in 1962 to 37% in 1977. The corresponding figures for women were 12% and 8%. This rate of decline corresponds with other statistical information.[2]

INCOME MAINTENANCE

Income maintenance legislation in Denmark for the aged has, since the end of the nineteenth century, gradually developed from social assistance for the needy to a national pension system covering the whole aged population and financed through the general government budget (Friis, 1969). Since 1933 the benefits have been adjusted according to the changes in the cost of living index. From 1970 a basic flat rate pension has been awarded to everyone over 67 years irrespective of their private incomes. In addition to the basic pension, a pensioner is entitled to a supplement and a housing allowance, which are reduced when other incomes exceed certain amounts. This system is called the "General Pension" (*Folkepensionen*).

Single women aged 62-66 and incapacitated persons aged 60-66 are entitled to an old age pension consisting of an income-related basic amount and the income-related supplement and housing allowance.

Housing Allowance

Low income pensioners including invalids, widows, and old age pensioners have had for several years the right to a housing allowance. New legislation in this respect was passed in 1978 in order to reduce the housing expenditures of pensioners. This was done to induce the pensioners to stay in their homes and to diminish the differences in housing expenditures among pensioners. Housing costs have increased during recent years because of the greatly increased price of new housing. According to the new law, the general rule is that the pensioners themselves must pay a housing expenditure corresponding to 15% of the taxable income earned by the household members. The housing allowance is paid for the amount exceeding the 15%. However, if pensioners have two rooms more than the number of household members, the rate which they pay themselves is increased to 20%; with three rooms more, to 25%; and so forth. The maximum for the annual housing allowance is in all cases 10,000 DKr. The rules are applicable to homeowners as well as to those living in rented flats. The right to the housing allowance is dependent on certain minimum standards for the dwelling. To houseowner's part of the housing allowance is paid as loans.

The annual pension without housing allowance for single persons of lower incomes in 1979 is 25.00 DKr., which after tax corresponds to approximately

40% of typical earnings for a wage earner after tax. Where both spouses receive a pension, the pension is 47,000 Dkr., corresponding to approximately 60% of typical earnings for one wage earner after tax. Where both spouses have been economically active, the percentage will, of course, be lower. For pensioners receiving the housing allowance, the percentage will be higher. It is estimated that 20% of the pensioners will receive a housing allowance, but the size will vary greatly.

Supplementary and After-Wage Programmes

While the General Pension is the basic level of social pensions, there are two newer additions of some importance.

In 1964 the "Labour Market Supplementary Pension" was introduced by law covering all wage and salary earners, corresponding to two-thirds of the population (Friis, 1969). The maximum Supplementary Pension is 4,000 DKr. after 27 years' membership. The Labour Market Supplementary Pension Scheme deviates in four important respects from Danish traditions. First, it is limited to wage and salary earners. Second, it is financied solely through contributions from employers and employees. Third, these contributions go into an insurance fund. And fourth, the pension is not value secured.

A new scheme in the area of income maintenance for the elderly has recently been introduced by law. This is the so-called "After-Wage" for older members of the unemployment associations, which are the carriers of the Danish unemployment insurance, covering two-thirds of the wage earners. According to this scheme, which started in 1979, unemployed members, 60 to 66 years of age, can during 2 years receive an After-Wage of the same size as their earlier unemployment benefits. The unemployment benefits correspond to 70-90% of their former salary. It is a condition for preserving the right to After-Wage that the member does not work more than 200 hours a year. The intention is that the unemployment benefits be financed by the employers, the members, and the central government. There were two reasons for introducing this new scheme. One was pressures from the trade unions to give the members an option for early retirement at an income level which is higher than the People's Pension. The other reason was to alleviate the labor market of older workers during the recent unemployment crisis in order to make room for younger workers.

It should finally be mentioned that private pension schemes are not widespread in Denmark. They only cover about 10% of the entire population, including 25% of the white-collar workers.

HEALTH SERVICES

Persons of old age, like everybody else in Denmark, are covered by the Public Health Security Act (Friis, 1976). This means that they have access to free medical care in and outside the hospitals. The treatment of illness outside hospitals is centered in the general medical practitioners who are spread evenly throughout the country and who normally are the gatekeepers to medical specialists, home nurses, physiotherapy, and hospitals. For essential medicine a reduction is paid by the health security system.

The health system is of course particularly important for the aged with their declining health. It is estimated that about one-half of the hospital capacity and about one-quarter of the capacity of the general practitioners and the nonhospital medical specialists are used by the populations of 65 years old and over. The expenditure for medical care for the aged corresponds to about half of the expenditure for old age pensions. It is continually under discussion whether it is possible to develop more community nursing and health care which might take some of the load off the hospitals and the institutions for the aged. It is additionally hoped that it could keep the aged as long as possible in their own homes under satisfactory conditions which they much prefer.

HOME CARE FOR THE AGED

The vast majority of the aged live in their own houses or in rented apartments, including municipal housing for the aged. Only 6% of those 65 and over and 33% of those 85 and over live in nursing homes.

According to the Care Law, it is obligatory for each municipality to establish a home help service with trained helpers. The Care Law distinguishes between various types of home help. The type which is particularly pertinent to the aged is permanent home help that assists with the domestic work which cannot be performed by a person with a permanent handicap or who is in frail health or permanently impaired. The work of the home helpers consists of part-time assistance with cleaning, washing, cooking, shopping, mending of clothes, personal hygiene, dressing, and similar services. Actual nursing is done by the home nurse service.

Home help is free for persons with incomes not higher than the General Pension. For others, payment is graduated according to their income. For permanent home help, the maximum payment corresponds to the minimum salary for six hours of home help.

Training of all home helpers was made obligatory in 1976. Home helpers who had no previous training were obliged to apply for a course if they wanted to continue their work. The training programme consists of an introductory course of one week followed, before the end of the first six months' employment, by a four-week (160-hour) basic course, which includes orientation in psychology, gerontology, social welfare, health and care of handicapped persons. The home helpers are later expected to take four supplementary courses. During the courses, the home helpers receive 90% of their salary. The courses are organized in all counties, so they are readily accessible.

There is one fully employed home helper per 30 persons of 70 years and over. About 25% of households with one or more persons of that age receive regular home help. Of the households receiving regular home help, 75% receive 1 to 6 hours help a week, 18% receive 7 to 12 hours weekly, and 7% receive more. According to the development plans of the municipalities, the total number of home helpers will increase 26% from 1978 to 1984. Several municipalities are planning extensions of the home help service to include evening, weekend, and night service.

It is obligatory for all municipalities to provide free home nursing service upon referral from the patient's doctor. The home nurse executes the treatment prescribed by the doctor and provides nursing according to the need of the patient. All home nurses make home visits and have telephone hours. Only a few nurses see the patients at clinics or the nurses' home. The Central Board of Health recommends that the home nurse service be directed by a supervisory home nurse, and such is now the case in half of the municipalities. The home nurse cooperates closely with the general practitioners and the hospitals. They also cooperate with the home helpers and the municipal social welfare office. Some municipalities have or are planning to have coordination of the work of the home nurses and home helpers by a joint executive in charge of both services or through home care centers.

The average number of people 65 years and over per home nurse is about 350, and about 15% in this age group have during the year received home nursing. The municipalities are planning an expansion of 20% in the number of home nurses from 1978 to 1984.

In accordance with the Care Law, municipalities can grant assistance to people suffering from a disability or permanent infirmity due to illness or old age by making technical alterations in their dwellings in order to make them more suited for everyday living. Assistance is granted without regard to the person's economic position, but it is a condition that this assistance must considerably improve the person's ability to remain in his/her own home. Measures in this connection include removal of thresholds and doorsteps, alterations of the kitchen, installation of bannisters, guardrails, and so on.

The municipalities can also provide free technical aids to handicapped people in order to allow their everyday existence to be as normal as possible. Assistance is given toward wheelchairs, artificial limbs, glasses, and hearing aids as well as for specially designed household equipment and for telephones. The public expenditures for the provision of technical aids has increased considerably during the last few years. This is an expression of the growing activity by the municipalities to allow old and handicapped people to remain in their own homes for as long as possible instead of going into institutions.

The municipalities will, according to the Care Law, establish day care homes and day care centers for the elderly. The day care homes are intended for old people who have extensive care needs but who are nevertheless capable of living in their own homes because relatives look after them at certain hours. Transportation is provided to the day care homes. The day care centers are caring for a wider range of old people. They aim at delivering services including chiropody, physiotherapy, and gymnastics, which can best be organized in a center. The day care homes and centers are often established in conjunction with a nursing home.

Among other activities organized by private organizations or municipalities in order to keep the old people in their own homes are home visiting and meals on wheels. These activities are not very much in use in Denmark, probably because of the many other services to old people living in their own homes.

It should be pointed out that the network of home services for the aged has not led to the result that the aged are not assisted by their children. The continuing relationship between children and their aged parents in Denmark was clearly demonstrated by the results of the national survey of a sample of persons 62 years and over in private households carried out by the Danish National Institute of Social Research in 1962 as a part of the cross-national survey on the aged (Shanas et al., 1968). A repeat survey undertaken in 1977 after the expansion of home services gives the same general picture: 11% of those 62 years and over who had a child alive were living with a child; of those living alone or with a spouse, 38% had seen a child at the day of the interview or the day before and 32% had seen a child 2-7 days before; well over half of the aged received various kinds of assistance from their children. It was noted that the aged themselves also assist their children to nearly the same extent.

There is no reason to expect that further expansion of home service will diminish the extent of contact and assistance between children and their parents. The aid from the children will rather be underpinned by the various services. This has become increasingly important as the work participation rate of women has grown considerably in Denmark during the last twenty years.

RECREATIONAL ACTIVITIES

Municipalities and voluntary organizations, including the pensioners' own organizations, have, during the last decades, increasingly organized activities for old people financially supported under the Care Law. The participants generally pay a small part of the expenses.

Clubs for the aged are spreading, and the aged usually take part in the administration of the clubs. More than one-quarter of those seventy years and over participate in club work. In most municipalities various adult education organizations organize special courses for the aged, which are often held in the afternoons. The aged also participate in many adult education activities not particularly intended for this age group.

The Danish Folk High Schools (Adult Education Colleges), which are found all over the country, organize courses for the aged normally over one or two weeks. The Pensioners' Association has organized special Folk High Schools for its members. Grants towards the fees of the Folk High Schools are paid by the municipalities.

In order to increase the possibility for the elderly to get around, reduced fares for public transport have been arranged. The so-called 65-tickets and 67-cards permit all people over 65 or 67 to travel by bus and by train at a reasonable fare at times other than rush hours. In the capital region, everybody from 67 and over can, for instance, buy a season card covering bus and train over a rather wide area for one-fifth of the normal price.

Holiday arrangements for the healthy as well as for the frail aged (abroad as well as within Denmark) are organized by non-profit-making organizations. They make use of unsold seats on airplanes and handle other arrangements with travel agents and holiday resorts.

SPECIAL HOUSING

Local municipalities have since the 1930s built blocks of small apartments for pensioners in the normal housing projects of the non-profit-making building societies. The rent of these apartments is kept relatively low. These apartments, called "pensioners' dwellings," are designed especially for pensioners, but they are essentially normal apartments, and the pensioner living there is expected to be able to care for himself—with home help service if needed.

A compromise between staying at home and going to a nursing home has been introduced through blocks of service apartments built by non-profit-making organizations or by the municipalities. Here, each resident has his own flat, but there is a common restaurant where the residents may take their meals if they do not want to do their own cooking. Most of these blocks have a unit for nursing home patients, and the residents can move from the apartments to this unit if they are no longer able to manage for themselves.

A new departure in housing for the aged is the sheltered dwellings for people who cannot manage on their own but whose condition does not necessitate placement in a nursing home. The sheltered dwellings are specially adapted for people suffering from permanent disability. They serve as ordinary apartments with their own kitchen with the addition of a number of supportive measures, specified in government regulations. They must have a watchroom with personnel who can be summoned to any apartment at any time. They must have personnel who take care of the domestic duties, which usually are performed by home helpers; and they must provide nursing corresponding to that provided by home nurses. They are also obliged to have a common restaurant and sitting rooms.

Sheltered dwellings can be established in independent buildings or as a part of a normal housing structure. They are usually apartments but can also be detached or row houses, as long as the possibilities for use of the collective service are not thereby diminished.

People in sheltered dwellings retain their pensions but pay 25% of their income up to a certain maximum for the accommodation.

According to the development plans of the municipalities, a rapid expansion in the number of sheltered dwellings is expected within the next few years.

NURSING HOMES

So-called "old peoples' homes" were introduced in most Danish municipalities at the turn of the century to take care of old people who could not take care of themselves for social and health reasons. With the development of the "pensioners' dwellings" and other types of special housing for the aged and in particular the spread of the home help service, the "old people's homes" were gradually changed into nursing homes.

According to the Care Law, it is the duty of the municipalities to provide care in a nursing home for persons who because of their health are not able to take care of themselves even with support from the home services or accommodations in sheltered dwellings. Nursing homes can be established by municipalities or counties or as self-governing institutions, with which the municipalities make an agreement. The municipal council has the responsibility of supervising the nursing homes. After the new Care Law, committees representing the residents were, where possible, organized. As yet, only a few resident committees have been established.

Pensioners pay for their residence by their old age pension but receive an amount to cover their personal necessities.

Most nursing home residents live in single rooms. The residents usually bring some of their own furniture with them, but rooms are often small, allowing space for only a hospital bed, a chest of drawers, and an easy chair.

The number of places in nursing homes corresponds to 10% of the population 70 years and over. Approximately 60% of the residents in the nursing homes are 80 years or over. The efforts to limit the intake in nursing homes to those who are so frail that they are in need of intensive treatment (often after treatment in a hospital) has had the effect of concentrating older and more handicapped elderly in the homes. The ratio of staff per resident is, therefore, growing. It was 7 staff to 10 residents in 1975 and is expected to be 8 to 10 in 1984.

CONCLUDING REMARKS

The expenditure of municipal institutions for the aged has, during the last decades, spiraled, partly by an increase in capacity and partly because of improved standards. There has been a strong trend towards expansion of home services and activities for the aged. The aged are eagerly pressing for more services. The municipalities have been faced with a choice between their traditional institutions for the aged and the relatively new idea that old people be enabled to stay in their private homes as long as possible. They have gradually come to understand the need for more of both types, but as yet the balance between expenditures for institutions and expenditures for home care has not changed.

Around 1970, the Danish Institute of Social Research undertook studies to evaluate the needs of the elderly for institutional and home care in five municipalities, including Copenhagen. Four parties assisted in the evaluation of each case: the old themselves, their general practitioners, the municipal social welfare officers, and our own interviewers. The result of the investigation was that approximately 10% of old people aged 70 and over were judged to be in need of institutional placements. Among the people aged 70 and over living in their own homes, it was estimated that about one-fourth needed home help and that about 2% needed home nursing. There were differences between the assessments in the individual cases. The most important result of the analysis was perhaps that whatever the capacity of existing services was, high or low, the assessment showed the same relative degree of need for further services. If this result can be interpreted dynamically, the consequence must be that irrespective of the proportion of help offered, there will still be waiting lists. This means that there is a need for a social-political priority setting as well as for more systematic local visitation and assessment. If such is not undertaken, the services may expand to a degree that is out of proportion with what the municipalities can carry. The municipalities are now obliged to present four-year development plans and are beginning to take this planning seriously. Further, during the 1970s many municipalities have instituted visitation committees, which are deciding upon referrals to home care and institutions for the aged.

The necessity for control and priority setting is not only a matter of public expenditures. It is also a problem of manpower and in particular of qualified staff. Although Denmark has developed staff training for institutions for children and handicapped reasonably well, special training capacity for staff for care of the aged is still rather limited, except in the case of home helpers.

The ideal goal for the programmes I have described is to give the aged the same opportunities for a full life as other groups in the society. It is recognized that not all older people are alike. Some older people wish to continue with gainful work, others want to go into community work, and others want to take up hobbies or studies. Many want to enjoy a life in leisure which they have been looking forward to. It is, however, easier to provide for early retirement based on a "Post Wage" and a pension than to provide new work opportunities, particularly during a period of unemployment such as Denmark is suffering from now. But it is obvious that the new generations of elderly in Denmark will not accept a life in poverty, idleness, or seclusion. They want to keep their contacts with family and friends, and we have found that they actually do so at the same time that they are living independently. They want a standard of life as close as possible to what they have had in their middle years, not only economically but with regard to all the good things of life. They feel that they have earned it after a long life of work. The aged are increasingly influential in society, not because they are old but rather because they are youthful and politically active and politicians know that their proportion in the voting population has been growing.

NOTES

1. A comprehensive comparative report on expenditures and scope of social security and services in Denmark, Finland, Iceland, Norway, and Sweden is published biannually in Scandinavian languages and English under the title *Social Security in the Nordic Countries* (Nordic Statistical Secretariat, Post Box 2550, DK-2100 Copenhagen).

2. For detailed information on the social condition of the aged in Denmark and the services for them compared with those in Britain and the United States around 1962, see Shanas et al. (1968).

REFERENCES

FRIIS, H. (1976) "Denmark: human services in the 'service state,' " pp. 111-127 in D. Thursz and J. Vigilante (eds.) Meeting Human Needs. 2: Additional Perspectives from Thirteen Countries. Beverly Hills: Sage.

——— (1969) "Issues in social security policies in Denmark," pp. 129-150 in S. Jenkins (ed.) Social Security in International Perspective. New York: Columbia University Press.

NOAM, E. (n.d.) Homes for the Aged. Supervision and Standards. Report on the Legal Situation in European Countries. DHEW Publication No. (OHD) 75-20104. Washington, DC: Government Printing Office.

SHANAS, E., P. TOWNSEND, D. WEDDERBURN, H. FRIIS, P. MILHJ, and J. STEHOUWER (1968) Old People in Three Industrial Socieites. New York: Atherton.

14

AGING

An Overview of Programs and Trends in the Federal Republic of Germany

L O U I S L O W Y

THE AGED POPULATION

The total number of elderly inhabitants in West Germany lies just below eight million, with three million men and five million women.[1] The percentage of the older population has risen from about 5% in 1900 to 14% in 1975, bringing Germany into the top group of the industrialized countries. The percentage of older women has always been considerably higher than that of older men: in 1975, 16.6% of all women and 11.4% of all men were beyond the age of 65. The average life expectancy at birth of women has risen to 72 years, that of men to 67; probably no further rise is to be expected for either sex. New diseases arising from environmental or occupational conditions are expected to take their toll. It is expected that the difference in life expectancy between men and women will decrease. One might speculate that changing styles of life, growing participation in the labor force, and resulting stress from work account for these data.

The majority of older women are widowed or divorced (about 60%) compared with only one-fifth of the older men, although the gap widens with increasing age.

Unlike in other countries (Great Britain or the United States), the percentage of the older population is rather stable throughout different parts of the country. There are slightly higher percentages in rural areas, largely as a result of heavy migration of the younger population; the same fact may account for higher percentages in central urban areas with older housing. Mobility among the older population is low. Studies (e.g., Fulgraff, 1978)

indicate that although there is much dissatisfaction among the older population about accommodations and furnishings, especially in rented flats, there is
little inclination to leave familiar neighborhoods.

As in the United States, only about 4-5% of the older population live in
institutions of various kinds.

Most of the aged are women, and most live in large cities, especially West
Berlin and Hamburg. Most men are married (77.4%), and most women are
widowed (53.8%). Ten percent of the aged are in the labor force, usually
self-employed or agricultural workers.

More than twice as many aged as nonaged adults are likely to have low
incomes, and single women are the most likely to be poor. Old age pensions
(social security) are the major source of income for the aged, and most of the
aged are covered.

Almost half of household heads over 65 are single, and 80% of these are
women. Although an objective assessment of living conditions of the aged
described them as inadequate, more than half the aged responded positively
to a survey about living conditions.

Half of the aged have at least one debilitating condition, 80% have at least
one chronic illness (usually heart disease or arthritis), and suicide rates for the
aged are almost twice those for younger adults. Despite these facts, half of
the elderly describe themselves as healthy. About 8-10% are confined to bed,
and about 15% need nursing home care.

The central federal government has legislative responsibility for setting
policy regarding pensions, health insurance, and social assistance; but where
social services are concerned, the Ministry of Youth, Family Affairs, and
Health is responsible only for some research and demonstration programs.
Otherwise, the state (*Lander*) and local governments fund and set policy as
well as administer and operate programs.

Contrary to many assumptions, the voluntary sector plays a major role in
social service planning and delivery, equaling or, in some instances, taking
precedence over the public sector in operating and administering social
welfare services for the aged (Kamerman, 1976). The various voluntary
agencies active at national and state levels are organized into the Federal
Group of the Voluntary Welfare Services. A similar working group operates at
the local level and is particularly important as a planning and coordinating
agency.

The major voluntary agencies include the German Federation for the Care
of the Aged, the most important public education, research, advocacy, planning, and coordinating agency, representing most voluntary agencies in the
field. The Twilight Years Movement, a self-help and advocacy group that also
operates service programs, is a well-known organization, though less important. Some proprietary agencies provide old age and nursing homes; however,

these are minor, representing only about 10% of the total facilities. Some recent abuses in these homes have led to vigorous enforcement of government standards and regulations.

POLICY FOR THE AGED

Policy for the aged has hitherto been considered part of social policy as a whole and, therefore, has benefited from the general shift in objectives from support and aid to prevention and rehabilitation. Objectives of social policy are oriented toward improvement of economic, physical, mental, and social security, recognition, participation, and activity. These are codified in the latest amendments to the Federal Social Welfare Act (*Bundessozialhilfegesetz*) of 1974.

Responsibility for achieving these goals lies primarily with government and private organizations of social welfare (Red Cross, the churches, workers' welfare organizations, and so on), which are, to a large extent, publicly financed. Responsibility extends to guaranteeing sufficient income and providing facilities and services. Participation and activity, however, call for self-responsibility on the part of the aged, for which most of them are not sufficiently prepared or trained.

Income Maintenance Programs

Germany has two types of income-support programs for the aged: a contributory, wage-related pension provided under social insurance legislation and a means-tested social assistance benefit provided under the Federal Social Assistance Act.[2] Eighty-four percent of the aged receive pensions, which are the major source of income for 78% of the aged; 6.4% receive social assistance, but they represent 34% of all those in the FRG receiving social assistance, and this percentage is growing rapidly. Discretionary, means-tested cash benefits and services are also provided under the FSAA legislation.

In addition, there is a special program called Assistance to the Aged which provides supplementary benefits directly or indirectly.

The Federal Republic offers its population several unique benefits through its social security system. Social security is adjusted not only for inflation but for increases in GNP as well so that retirees share in improvements in the general standard of living. Pensions are pegged to general increases in gross wages through annual legislation.

Since 1957 the amount of pensions have increased by over 450%. In 1977, the level of pensions for manual workers and white-collar employees exceeded 74% of average net earnings. After 45 years of employment and training (for which social security credits are also given), manual workers can expect an income of $600 a month and white-collar employees $800 a month—all tax-free. In addition to social security, a family supplement of about $73 a month is provided for each dependent child under 18 and up to age 25 for children obtaining further education or job training.

In the case of divorce and the death of the spouse, the survivors' pension is divided proportionately between the former spouse and the widow or widower according to the length of time of the two marriages.

At the time of divorce, social security credits are split equitably between husband and wife. If, for example, the husband has earned more credits than his wife, the value of the excess entitlement is split equally between the two parties. If only the husband has worked during the marriage and has accumulated credits entitling him to a 60% income replacement rate, each would obtain credits valued at a 30% replacement rate at the time of the divorce. The husband could then make up the lost credits through voluntary contributions.

In 1973 West Germany introduced a flexible retirement age whereby employees may retire any time over a three-year period—i.e., between ages 63 and 65. The pensioner receives a full pension and may continue working, earning up to $480 a month without any loss of pension. After age 65 there is no restriction regarding work-related earnings. Health insurance is also free for pensioners.

Men are retiring at a progressively younger age in Germany. According to the German Institute for Economic Research (*Institut fur Wirtschaftforschung*), the average age of retirement is 60.3; in 1975 it was 61.2 years. The average age of retirement for women has changed little since 1972.

More difficult is the financial situation of widowed women. The West German system of old age security, progressive as it is in many respects, tends to perpetuate existing inequalities of social status and to enlarge them during later years. This at least holds true for the present generation of the elderly, which is still heavily influenced by social and political adversities of the last half century. Social policy for the aged will have to distinguish problems of a transitory nature which need immediate and temporary solutions from those of persisting character which can only be solved by changes in social and individual factors.

Housing

The specific postwar situation of the Federal Republic with a large proportion of housing accommodations being destroyed or requiring basic renovation accounts for the fact that problems or needs of specific groups, for a long time, fell behind the general demand.[5] Nevertheless, the specific concern of the older population was already included in the first home-building act of 1950 and improved upon in subsequent amendments. During the last 20 years over half the housing built in the Federal Republic was constructed with the assistance of public funds. Moreover, a 1967 Rent Allowance Act provided for rent subsidies on a means-tested basis. Both these acts have been of substantial aid to the aged, yet housing is still described as inadequate. In addition, the Federal Social Assistance Act guarantees the aged assistance in locating housing as well as in adapting and maintaining housing. Most of the aged population in West Germany (96%) live in "normal" homes whereas only 4% (with regional variances between 2 and 8%) inhabit special units such as old age homes or nursing homes. The older population is severely disadvantaged compared with other age groups. They live significantly more often in the older, ill-equipped homes, predominantly in the cities. Nevertheless, only a few of them are inclined to move into more modern accommodations.

Sheltered housing constructed with federal and state support is beginning to be available to the aged. Sheltered housing includes the following types: buildings containing housing only for the elderly; single apartment units distributed throughout ordinary housing; special quarters in one-family housing (often discouraged as being too isolated). The major objective is to provide some help for the aged, yet support them in living in housing and communities where ordinary families live, close enough together to permit easy and economic provision of support services.

The federal government (Ministry for Urban Development and Housing) sets policy and regulates location, construction, and design of this housing. For example, no large segregated clusters of housing for the aged can be built, and sheltered housing must be near shopping facilities, transportation, families. Actual implementation and operation of this housing are at the state level; however, state support for housing varies widely among the individual states but is mandatory in order to obtain federal participation (usually about 15%). Private funding is also required. Unfortunately, although rentals for the aged are subsidized, such subsidies may still be inadequate; rentals are often higher in these specially designed facilities than they are in ordinary housing, creating difficulty for the aged.

Eligibility is by means and need tests. Coverage is about 1%, and availability is different in different states and localities.

Major alternative solutions to housing problems are oriented to maintaining and improving independent living arrangements in unplanned settings which are the norm for older persons and correspond with the majority of needs. The alternative program of congregate arrangements, though of growing interest, will probably remain of secondary importance.

Health Program

Health insurance is provided for all aged (in addition to almost all others) as a contributory benefit and covers 90% of the population under a National Health Insurance Program. Medical and dental care, hospitalization, appliances, and prescription drugs are all included. An additional means-tested program of medical assistance, covering the same benefits, is provided for those who are not covered by the National Health Insurance Scheme (Flamm, 1974: 48).

Preventive Medical Assistance concentrates its efforts on helping children and young persons, mothers, and old people to recuperate and to convalesce. Various aid organizations have for many decades been carrying out extensive programs specifically for the recuperation of children, young people, mothers, and more recently also for the aged. There is a considerable network of suitable recuperation establishments, mostly run by voluntary associations and supported and furthered by *Bund* and *Laender* as well as by National Organizations, such as the German Mothers' Convalescence and Recuperation Scheme (*Deutsches Muttergenesungswerk*) and the *Kuratorim "Deutsche Altershilfe."* Social Assistance avails itself of the use of all these institutions when sending people away for recuperation or convalescence and, if need be, covers the costs in individual cases.

Apart from helping in individual cases, it is also the task of Social Assistance to cooperate in insuring examinations and the early diagnosis of disease. Individual aid for preventive medical care is also given within the framework of payments made by the Social Insurance agencies.

Long-Term Care Facilities

About 5% of the aged are in institutional facilities: 1% in nursing homes and 4% in old-age homes. Coverage is considered quantitatively inadequate even though current emphasis is on expanding community support services so that the aged can remain in their own homes as long as possible. For the future, coverage is projected at about 2% for nursing homes, with the hope that greatly expanded sheltered housing will eliminate the need for traditional old age homes. At present, over 60% of these institutional facilities are supported by government agencies, 20% by public agencies, and 20% by proprietary agencies. Publicity about abuses in proprietary facilities led to new legislation in 1975 mandating licensing, regulation of fees, and more frequent and regular inspections. In addition, residents are now expected to participate in shaping nursing home policy and in management.

Home Care

Some of the elderly are so helpless, because of sickness or infirmity, that they need continual nursing and care at home. Many of the people in need of nursing care want to remain as long as possible in their accustomed surroundings; therefore, domiciliary nursing care by family members, close friends, or neighbors is encouraged. If nursing personnel is required, a nursing allowance is paid within the framework of the statutory incomes limit, which amounts presently to DM 150 a month, but which can be higher in individual cases. If it is not possible to arrange nursing care through the help of volunteers, the costs of employing regular family or domiciliary nursing staff may be met by Social Assistance Programs. In view of the growing need for nursing care, recruitment of a sufficient number of nursing personnel remains a special concern. Assistance is given not only for personel nursing but also for household chore services.

There are many chronically ill in special nursing homes that are in many cases linked with old age homes. In cases of nursing home care, Social Assistance covers the nursing charges to the amount of the cost-adjusted maintenance rates. While the number of frail elderly (chronically sick and infirm) over 75 is growing, the existing homes have long since been unable to meet the demand for residential nursing. Planning for more nursing homes, an increase in the available number of beds, and particularly the recruitment of more nursing staff have become a serious concern of Social Assistance. In this respect, it has become apparent that even within a well-developed social security system it is not possible to satisfy social needs by money benefits alone.

While Assistance to Aged Persons is primarily concerned with keeping the old people in the community, it is, nevertheless, the indispensable task of Social Assistance to look after older people who need nursing care in residential homes. In view of the growing geriatric needs, the number of beds in nursing homes is in no way sufficient. Communes are endeavoring to take account of this need by giving financial support to the establishment of more places in residential homes. However, since illnesses in the later years are more chronic and less acute, hospitals have moved toward the establishment of geriatric wards. The tasks of Assistance to Aged Persons are supplemented by self-help organizations of the elderly, voluntary welfare organizations, and special aid schemes. The Federal Ministry for Youth, Family Affairs and Health and the Ministry of Labor and Social Affairs have each set up an advisory committee for problems concerning the elderly.

INNOVATIVE SERVICES FOR THE AGED

Social Services in the Community

Homemaker and home-health services include personal care services as well.[4] These services are funded by a combination of state and local authorities, voluntary agency contributions, and individual fees. Voluntary agencies provide most services, although a few public agencies, proprietary agencies, and religious organizations provide some. Funding is primarily through recipient fees, but these are partially reimbursed through social insurance or social assistance. In addition, government subsidies contribute directly about 17%, and social insurance programs, about fourteen percent. Fees are graduated, and eligibility is based on need. Coverage is largely inadequate, and availability is limited mainly to urban and industrial areas. Regulation is insufficient; personnel are inadequate and now available only at a ratio of about 1:6,000.

At present, in addition to the specialized agencies providing these services, comprehensive social service centers are being set up to provide a range of community services for the aged. Staff includes nurses and social workers, who are primarily from voluntary agencies. The major objective is to improve service delivery, training, and professionalization by establishing a single organization to integrate supportive social and health services at the local delivery level for a population of about 20,000 aged.

Meal services (congregate and home delivered) are available to about 1% of the aged, although demand is estimated at about 5%. Where programs exist, service can usually be obtained five days a week and is provided under the auspices of voluntary agencies. Eligibility is based on need; fees are graduated; costs are covered primarily by recipient fees (75-80%), private philanthropy (15%), and local social welfare agencies (5-10%).

Most meal services are provided through social centers or clubs, which also provide personal care, leisure activities, and counseling. Multifunction centers incorporating these out-of-home services, in-home services, and housing are considered social stations. These social stations are located primarily in urban areas and are used by about 3% of the aged. Three-quarters of the users are female, single, poor or working class, with limited education. A typical center serves 350 people daily and is funded as follows: federal government, 17%; state government, 23%; local government and welfare agencies, 35%; and voluntary sector (agencies and private philanthropy), 25%.

Since 1975, the city of Bonn has operated seven such "social stations." They are run by nonprofit organizations and funded mainly by the local government. Individuals can obtain a variety of health and social services at these centers from the six to twelve trained persons assigned to the centers on a full-time basis. When demands make additional staff necessary, part-time personnel are moved in. A central depository stores equipment such as health aids—e.g., walkers—which can be transferred to centers for loans to individuals in need. Most of the services provided can be reimbursed by the nation's social security system; for those not so covered, a fee is charged according to ability to pay.

The experience to date has been that the existence of "social stations" has decreased the need for institutionalization and made people feel more secure in the knowledge that they can receive help immediately. At the present time, there are, in fact, spaces available in institutional homes.

Bonn spends 1.2 million DM ($600,000) a year in providing the seven "social stations." That amount, 1.2 million DM, would provide a mere 66 places a year in institutional homes. The assumption is that more than 66 individuals are being kept out of institutions through the existence of "social stations."

Information, advice, and counseling (including legal counseling) are available free for all aged. There are, however, no firm data regarding coverage—in part, because there is no precise definition of what a counseling service is or criteria for determining either demand or need for this service. These services are available either at fixed locations or at mobile centers. Home visiting is stressed. Over 90% of these programs are under voluntary auspices. The staff is composed of doctors, nurses, pension advisers, lawyers, and social workers.

Other service programs include: telephone provision, radio and TV provision, or elimination of the tax on radio and TV—all available as means-tested benefits. There are telephone reassurance services by volunteers that are free to all who need the service and vacations as part of the preventive health service. Present coverage is about 2% and varies among states. The demand, in contrast, is now equal to about 15%. Users are predominantly female and low-income, often from among the senior center participants. Chore services and mobile handyman services are becoming increasingly popular.

The use of public servants in assisting the elderly is growing. For example, mailmen have been given an intensive two-day course at a geriatrics center. The chief function of their role will be to transmit the wishes and needs of older people along their route to the proper authorities. They will also report anything amiss, such as unemptied mailboxes or broken windows, and they will provide their older clients with coupons permitting them to request a geriatric nurse, emergency food rations, or counseling on entitlements to public benefits.

More active participation by the elderly in shaping policies has become a salient feature in the last few years. A Senior Council (*Seniorenrat*) composed of retired union members, in existence for two years now in the city of

Kassel, has proven very popular with both retired and active union members. More than 1,000 individuals participate in at least one major event presented by the Seniorenrat each year, and 300 members meet twice a year in full assembly. The Seniorenrat came into being in order to assure retired workers an opportunity to exercise a voice in the union's decision-making process, to share information of concern to retired union members, and to make available to the union and the community the skills and knowledge acquired over many years by retired persons.

In its two years of operation, the Seniorenrat has convinced the Kassel Federation of Trade Unions (DGB) that preretirement education is necessary for older workers and that a continuing dialogue between older workers and retired persons is a great asset in preretirement education. The social minister of Hesse undertook several model preretirement projects in 1977 for which educational leave was provided to participants.

The Seniorenrat plays an influential decision-making role on the board of the district council. The seniorenrat is now engaged in drawing up a plan for the aging for the city of Kassel and has submitted a proposal to national union headquarters requesting that it incorporate in its charter the idea of collaboration with retired members.

Continuing Education

Hamburg and a number of other cities will take part in an experiment in continuing education for older adults, funded by the Federal Ministry for Education and Science and organized under the direction of the German Center on Aging Concerns (*Deutsches Zentrum fur Altersfragen*).[5] The purposes of this project are to (1) learn what publicity efforts are most successful in attracting older people to continuing education; (2) determine how continuing education can be used to overcome isolation and loss of identity among older persons and, at the same time (3) strengthen their self-confidence so that they become more assertive about expressing their needs; (4) stimulate educational institutions to do more to reach out to the elderly and (5) develop teaching techniques best suited to the older learner.

Hamburg will focus on reaching out to retired laborers, older housewives, and other retirees with little formal education; these are the people who are most neglected by the current educational establishment. After an initial test run this year, the program will operate from June to December 1979 in Hamburg and other cities and will be evaluated in early 1980. The experiment is also scheduled to reach people in housing projects for the elderly, old age homes, and nursing homes.

Bildungsarbeit mit alten Menschen (educational efforts with older persons) is fast becoming a major arena of activity. Numerous cities (e.g. Cologne, Nuremberg, Munich, Hannover) are designing special courses and programs to enrich the learning potentials of the elderly. Increasing numbers are taking advantage of these offerings, and a recent publication by Petzold and Bubolz has had significant impact on the thinking and practices of such programs.

SOME MAJOR TRENDS

I would like to address three major trends here: (1) preparation for retirement; (2) self-help efforts by the elderly; and (3) improving the relationships of young and old.

Preparation for Retirement

This has become a major concern of industry and labor. Several private organizations in the field of aging here have assumed a major role, vis à vis industry and labor, to help aging people to cope with impending retirement. Recently, the Federal Ministry of Youth, Family and Health has become quite involved in this enterprise. In 1977, a team of scientists, social workers, adult educators, journalists, and gerontologists developed a paper setting forth a major declaration of principles (Kuratorium Deutsche Altershilfe, 1977). This paper points out that we are confronted in all parts and in all phases of life with a number of problems that have to be dealt with; in order to cope with such situations, it is necessary to learn to do so as early as possible and preparation for the later years should begin early and continue as a life long process so that people are not surprised when they face the tasks confronting them as they grow older. However, most people do not anticipate this period, do not deal with it, and, therefore, they suffer the imminence and suddenness of aging. This is particularly true when mandatory retirement forces people to look for new purposes in life as they try to occupy themselves in their suddenly increased leisure time.

A number of service agencies have developed education and training programs for employees of industry and for labor union members. The courses take place during working hours and on weekends. Paid leaves of absence for people to participate in such projects are provided. As an illustration, a major industrial concern in Ludwigshafen started with a discussion group on "Is aging a problem for you?" All employees were invited to participate. In the beginning there were few takers, but eventually, more and more participated until they designed a whole series of seminars with topics ranging from the social-psychological aspects of aging, pensions, and social security to nutrition and opportunities for leisure. Other institutes and seminars dealt with self-assessment and medical and mental health problems. The participants took a closer look at themselves and examined how they felt about getting old. The members indicated that they had found these sessions stimulating, and participation increased over time. As of the present, these programs are part and parcel of this particular industry, and other employers follow this model. Tews (1971), Blume (1968), Thomas and Lehr (1968) have evaluated and analyzed these experiences and found them worthy of emulation. Through the *Deutsche Gewerkschaftsbund,* several labor unions began to conduct similar discussion groups with union members. They also offered their membership opportunities to try out new work career experiences at the cost of the unions. They found that older people presently are less inclined to choose new careers and more attuned to build upon the interests that they have acquired over a lifetime and to engage in activities quite different from those in which they were involved during their regular working years.

Self-Help Efforts

In Hannover, the senior council movement has become a way of life. It is an attempt to organize elderly, and to build upon their own self-interest. "Reactivation through self-help" has become as timely a slogan in Germany today as "Remain fit" or "Continue to be counted." Senior centers and golden age clubs have mushroomed in the last few years, pretty much on the model of those in England and the United States. In the past, these clubs have been created *for* older people rather than *by* older people.

Recently, in Hannover, the seniors acted on their own behalf and organized their own council. They negotiated with the city fathers and prevailed upon them to invite the existing thirteen golden age centers to elect delegates for such a council. This new organization developed a legislative and executive body, and has been designated to speak for all the elderly in the city of Hannover. The seniors are involved in planning and monitoring tasks such as housing, continuing education, information, and referral programs, mail delivery, and reduction of costs for public transportation. They also help in raising the consciousness level of the elderly, and the active involvement of the elderly themselves has created a new vital force for the city as a whole. To what extent this model, which began in 1976, will become a trend is by no means clear yet, but several other cities in West Germany—Berlin, Hamburg, Dusseldorf, and Cologne—have examined this model.

Improving the Relationship of Young and Old

In 1976, the Kuratorium Deutsche Alterhilfe was instrumental in organizing a painting competition under the motto, "Youth Sees Old Age." Seventy thousand children from 6 to 15 years of age were involved. More 9-11 year old children had sent in pictures than children of all other age groups. A sample of 3,500 pictures was evaluated. The paintings were sorted according to sixteen themes such as "old age homes," "the active old person," "the old person in the family," "old people and animals," loneliness," "dependency," "church, religion, and funeral services," "grandmother and grandfather," "street and transportation," "symbolic aging," "vacation traveling," and "from birth to death."

The younger children had portrayed "old" age more positively than older children, although many stereotypes and myths were exhibited even by the younger children. In this respect, they are as prejudiced in Germany as in many other parts of the world. Other children showed prejudices to a great extent and presented a feeling of uneasiness and even fear about old age. As a consequence, many schools, kindergartens, and continuing education and parent education programs have become engaged in trying to change such images. In various schools (including ones on the secondary and tertiary level), several projects are now under way to acquaint students with the needs of the aging and to look at old age not just as a problem to be dealt with but as a normal stage of human development.

In Cologne, for example, teachers and professors are involved in creating projects and exhibits dealing with the conditions of older people. Moreover, they infuse the curriculum with topics related to aging. Schools of social work, medicine, and nursing are slowly beginning to include in their curriculum material about the elderly, even for students who do not necessarily expect to work with older clients or patients. We do see new beginnings, and the recognition that the elderly are an important and growing segment of our population has become more widespread than ever before in the history of the Western World. At the same time, there are deficiencies in bridging the gap of the generations. The mass media have a large role to play in overcoming some of these difficulties. The finding of the Harris Study in the United States that the elderly themselves have negative images of themselves could also be confirmed in West Germany. There is no doubt, however, that a decent social security program providing adequate income, housing, and health measures is a vital underpinning toward creating a new consciousness in the young that they themselves will become old and, therefore, that old age is not a stage to be avoided or dreaded, but something that is part and parcel of the total life cycle. West Germany, with an increasing aging population, faces a problem confronting many societies, namely, how to support this increasing aging population through the increased productivity of the younger segment of its people.

The World Assembly on Aging that was voted in by the United Nations, to be held in 1982, will have to address this question and propose alternatives, since this question is a crucial one for all societies in the years to come.

NOTES

1. Demographic and general statistics are based on data by Fulgraff (1978).
2. Data presented in this section are based on the work of Flamm (1974: 95).
3. Data presented in this section are based on the work of Flamm (1974: 98).
4. Data presented in this section are based on the work of Flamm (1974: 48).
5. Data based on information from *Aging International* (1978).

REFERENCES

Aging International (1978) 5, 2 and 3.
BLUME, O. (1968) Moglichkeiten und Grenzen der Allenhilfe. Germany: Bubingen.
FLAMM, F. (1974) Social Services and Social Work in the Federal German Republic. Frankfurt: Eigenuerlag des Deutschen.
FULGRAFF, B. (1978) "Social gerontology in West Germany: a review of recent and current research." Gerontologist 18, 1.
KAMERMAN, S. B. (1976) "Community services for the aged: the view from eight countries." Gerontologist 16, 6.
Kuratorium Deutsche Altershilfe (1976) "Declaration of Principles." Koln, Germany: KDA.
TEWS, H. P. (1971) Soziologie des Altern, I and II. Heidelberg: Auelle and Meyer.
THOMAS, H. and U. LEHR (1968) Altern: Probleme und Tatsachen. Frankfurt: Verlegsgesellscheft.

15

SERVICES FOR THE AGED
IN SOUTH AFRICA

LESLIE MARTINE

A recent publication of the International Federation on Aging entitled *Toward Planning for the Aging in Local Communities* (Dunham et al., 1978) clearly indicates that in most countries there is a vital need to give attention to dealing with problems of the aged. Demographic statistics show that the world's population is aging. "For both the developed and developing regions of the world the rate of increase in the population over sixty years of age will be considerably greater than for the population at large" (Dunham et al., 1978). Population figures for South Africa confirm this trend. The total population in South Africa increased from 5,175,000 in 1904 to 21,794,000 in 1970 (the last census). The estimated figure for 1976 is 26,129,000. This last figure includes the estimated figure for the Transkei, which became independent in 1976 and has an estimated de facto population of 2,096,000 persons. A breakdown of the four population groups—Blacks, Coloureds,

Table 15.1:   Breakdown for Population Groups

	1904	1970
Blacks	3,490,000	15,340,000
Coloureds	446,000	2,051,000
Indians	122,000	630,000
Whites	1,117,000	3,773,000
	5,175,000	21,794,000

AUTHOR'S NOTE: *I wish to acknowledge the contribution made by Robert Carew, formerly of the University of Natal and presently of the University of Queensland, whose enthusiasm originally prompted the writing of the chapter. I am also most appreciative of the help given by many colleagues both in the acquisition of data and in discussion of the material.*

Indians, and Whites—according to the census figures for 1904 and 1974 is shown in Table 15.1.

It is quite likely that the picture in 1904 may indicate a higher proportion of Whites to the non-White population than in 1970 because of under-enumeration of the latter in 1904.

Interesting population projections have been made by Professor J. L. Sadie (1973) of the University of Stellenbosch, South Africa. The figures for years 1980 and 2000 are given in Table 15.2.

Naturally, with an increasing population, expansion is needed in every sphere of life. A breakdown of the age structure of the population is relevant in looking at services for the aged. The White population of South Africa has the most aged proportionally. This is clearly indicated in the Official Year Book of the Republic of South Africa (1977: 32).

In 1904 only 1.87% of the White population were 65 and over; in 1921 the percentage has risen to 3.52%, and in to 1970 to 7%. Actual figures show that White persons aged 65 and over numbered 30,600 in 1911 and that the figure had risen to 249,221 by 1970. The figures for those aged 65 and over for the total population for 1970 are shown in Table 15.3.

Sadie's (1973) figures indicating the percentage age distribution of the South African population in 1975 are shown in Table 15.4.

Figures given for the expected increase of the aged relative to the general population are most interesting and indicate an increase in the proportion of those 60 years and over in comparison with the total population, the Whites still being the older group (see Table 15.5).

Table 15.2:   Population Projections by Groups

	1980	2000
Blacks	20,639,000	37,293,000
Coloureds	2,818,000	4,890,000
Indians	825,000	1,215,000
Whites	4,433,000	5,726,000
	28,715,000	49,124,000

Table 15.3:   Population Aged 65 and Over by Groups

Blacks	552,747
Coloureds	63,083
Indians	11,278
Whites	249,221
	876,329

Table 15.4:   Age Distribution of Population
in 1975 (in percentages)

	0–14 yrs.	15–64 yrs.	65+ yrs.
Blacks	44	52	4
Coloureds	45	52	3
Indians	38	59	3
Whites	31	62	7

Table 15.5:   Expected Increase of the Aged Relative to
the General Population (in percentages)

Year	Blacks	Coloureds	Indians	Whites
1970	4.4%	4.4%	3.2%	10.3%
1980	4.9%	4.6%	3.9%	11.6%
2000	5.6%	5.3%	5.8%	12.7%

It is interesting to compare these figures with world figures given by the United Nations in 1975.

From the United Nations projected 1980 figures and the 1975 South African figures, it can be seen that the figure for Whites (7%) lies above that of the world total (5.8%), the figure for Blacks (4%) is above that of the figure for Africa (2.8%), the figure for Coloured (3%) is also slightly above that for Africa, and the figure for the Indians (3%) is slightly below that for South Asia (3.6%). In respect to expectation of life, Coloureds have the lowest figure—52 years in 1970—while Blacks follow at 55 years, Indians at 61 years, and the Whites at 68 years.

The age structure in this country is one reason that initial developments in the field of aging have been largely for the White group. Traditionally the Black aged have been cared for by their families, and it is estimated that 90% of the Indian aged still live with their families, or in assisted housing schemes in close proximity to their children.

In 1960, 67.7% Whites over 65 were living independently, 5.4% in homes for the aged and 21.6% with their children. Today approximately 72% of White aged live independently, 20% live with their children, and 8% in old age homes. Generally speaking, there is an ever-increasing dependency on living in flats and smaller houses because of the high cost of building, and, consequently, it becomes more and more difficult to accommodate the extended family.

It seems, then, that the indications are that more provisions will be needed for the elderly. Also, figures show that the number of persons in the 75 and over, or old-old, group are increasing, indicating a need for a range of supportive health and social services.

ANALYSIS OF SERVICES FOR THE AGED

Dunham et al. (1978) suggest a nine-point guide in order to analyse programs and services for the aged. The following areas are included: physical health, mental health, housing, work and income security, aids in daily living, transportation, education, recreation and leisure, and volunteer services.

Services for the aged in South Africa covers a wide spectrum, and facilities in all the above areas are found. Unfortunately, these services do not reach all the old people, and there are many gaps in services to be filled.

In South Africa some of our earliest institutions and organizations provided accommodation and care for the elderly. For instance, the first congregation of the Dutch Reformed Church at the Cape instituted a poor relief service for the needy in 1665 and specifically mentioned the aged. Developments have often been the responsibility of private initiative, which has taken a lead in inaugurating services to complement government resources.

In South Africa the Department of Social Welfare and Pensions (which in its early stages served all race groups) maintains in one of its reports (1966: 2) that it

> renders its welfare services in the closest co-operation with private initiative. It is a matter of policy and conviction that welfare work ought to be the responsibility of the state, the church and society. This tradition has proved itself over the years and will remain the foundation for future development.

Taking the country as a whole, there has been a very uneven development, probably accounted for by this policy, which has meant that services have arisen not necessarily where the greatest need has been but where resources have been available.

Care of the aged in South Africa can be found in nine different areas:

(1) Department of Social Welfare and Pensions,
(2) Department of Coloured Affairs,
(3) Department of Indian Affairs,
(4) Department of Plural Relations and Development (formerly Department of Bantu Administration and Management),
(5) Department of Community Development,
(6) Department of Health,
(7) provincial administrations,
(8) local authorities,
(9) various homeland governments, namely, Bophuthatswana, Ciskei, Gazankulau, Kangwane (Swazi), Kwa Zulu, Lebowa, Qwa qwa (Basotho), Transkei, and Venda.

These homeland governments are in various stages of taking over their own responsibilities assisted by the South African government. They will not be covered in this paper.

Today with South Africa's policy of separate development, functions that were originally carried out by the Department of Social Welfare and Pensions are now shared by three newer departments, namely, the Departments of Coloured Affairs, Indian Affairs, and Plural Relations. These departments take the responsibility for developing or subsidizing homes, as well as service centres for the aged. They are also responsible for the administration of the noncontributory old age and war veterans' pension schemes (social pensions) which are means-tested. Within the Department of Social Welfare and Pensions, there is a separate subdivision for the care of the aged, which was established in 1968 with the following functions:

(1) to keep abreast of developments in the field of welfare work with the aged,
(2) to give advice on policy matters,
(3) to plan services for the aged, and
(4) to assist with information and guidance in regard to new services.

The Department of Community Development serves the aged in the field of housing. The Department of Health speaks for itself, but health functions also fall under the provincial administrations and the local authorities.

Further discussion of the work of these departments will be included under the relevant headings.

Health

The first Public Health Act in South Africa was passed in 1919 and was repealed only with the passing of the recent Health Act No. 63 of 1977. Under the original act there were three clear divisions with the state department of health taking responsibility for mental hospitals as well as tuberculosis and leper hospitals, curative services falling under provincial hospitals and preventive care, e.g., well-baby clinics, and in a few instances geriatric clinics, resting with the local authorities. This arrangement, as can be imagined, produced a rather fragmented service. The new Health Act, according to Gordon et al., (1978) lays emphasis "on the promotion of good health, true preventative rather than curative action and the better co-ordination of central, provincial and local bodies involved in providing health services." This act also provides for the establishment of a National Health Policy Council to assist in such coordination.

Social pensioners are entitled to free medical attention for curative and specialized services at the provincial hospitals. The state department of health provides services for those who are house bound either in private homes or old age homes. The state—through the district surgeons—also provides services for those who live in areas where there are no provincial services. Persons needing hospital services are required to go to the nearest provincial hospital. Social workers are employed by many of the provincial hospitals. The position regarding Blacks is slightly different. Gradually the homeland governments have taken over the control and financing of health services to the homelands, and comprehensive health services are being developed through both hospitals and clinics. Clinics are available in the homelands, and these may be found in urban areas as well. Patients are screened and if necessary are referred to hospitals for treatment. In addition to hospitals in the homelands, there are still provincial (general) hospitals which serve the Blacks.

Many pensioners are faced with transportation difficulties in getting to hospitals, since their homes are often situated great distances away. Sometimes people are required to catch as many as three buses to get to a hospital, thus incurring considerable expense. To overcome this problem, some areas provide ambulance services—through either the province or local authorities. There are also volunteer ambulance services as well as voluntary workers who provide transportation to and from hospital. District nurses of the Provincial Administrations visit, among others, aged persons who have been discharged from the hospitals. Generally speaking, such services are not adequate to meet the needs.

In the Cape Peninsula area, day hospitals have been developed especially in the Coloured areas. This has brought medical care within easier access for many, but certainly not all, of the old people.

In Durban the State Health Department operates four district geriatric clinics, giving weekly or bimonthly sessions. A fifth clinic is in the planning stage. These are staffed by public health and other registered nurses, and the district surgeon attends for specific periods. A chiropody service is included. At present these clinics serve only Whites and Indians.

In some areas the local health commissions, provincial bodies which act as local authorities, provide medical clinics which serve, among others, the aged.

Certain local authorities have geriatric services. The first geriatric assessment clinic was started in Germiston, Transvaal, in 1968, and Germiston's Geriatric service is now well-established. The Germiston City Council provides the premises for a Service Centre for the Aged. Here part-time chiropody and physiotherapy services are financed by the city council. The Germiston Preventive Geriatric Clinic provides a screening service with examination of eyes, hearing, teeth, feet, blood pressure, and the like. The patients are referred to the appropriate medical services for treatment when necessary. Geriatric public health nurses visit the aged in their homes. Germiston extended their services to Blacks in 1975 and to Asians and Coloureds in 1976.

The Johannesburg municipality has geriatric clinics in five areas, and in most instances these run on a weekly basis. At these clinics patients are screened and referred to the district surgeon or to hospitals for medical attention when necessary. Chiropody services are also available by appointment, and a fee is charged for such attention. These clinics operate in conjunction with the Johnnesburg Council for the Care of the Aged so that social work services are also available.

The Cape Town City Council runs two assessment clinics for the Coloured aged. These work in close cooperation with the Cape Provincial Administration Day Hospitals.

Other health care is provided by the Cape Town After-Care Hospital and Convalescent Home. This is unique in South Africa at present in that it is attached to a teaching hospital. This facility is effective in reducing unnecessary occupation of acute hospital beds and thus reduces the cost of caring for elderly patients.

In Queensburgh and Kingsburgh (local authority areas in Natal), community health nurses provide services to the aged and work in close liaison with the District Surgeon.

In Natal, the Hill Crest Hospital, which is administered by the province, caters to long-term or chronically sick patients. Often the patients are transferred from Durban or Pietermaritzburg hospitals. However, to many it does seem "far from home." It is not easy for relatives to visit unless they can travel by car, so it has not proved popular.

A psychogeriatric assessment clinic was started at the Valkenberg Hospital (for mental patients) in the Cape in 1977. Patients are hospitalized for short observation periods, and the aim is to return them to their former or improved accommodation within the community, where they can remain and receive medication and regular supervision where necessary.

Addington Hospital, Durban, is to start a similar unit beginning this year. It is interesting to note that this is a provincial (general) hospital whereas Valkenburg falls under the central government, thus indicating the development of integrated services.

At least one mobile occupational therapy service operates in the country. It is in the Witwatersrand area, and this is of great value to old people.

At the Oral and Dental Hospital, attached to the Witwatersrand University in Johannesburg, reduced fees are in operation for social pensioners both for dental treatment and for dentures. A mobile dentistry clinic is also planned for the Witwatersrand area and this will be of great value to old people, particularly those in institutions who will be given priority. The anticipated charge is $.50 per treatment and R10 for a set of artificial dentures (less than 10% of the normal fee).

In the private sphere some general practitioners attend to old age pensioners free of charge or for a nominal sum. There are many private nursing homes which provide accommodation and nursing services at economical rates. The Red Cross Society in Johannesburg runs a geriatric clinic but provides a purely advisory service. Such items as wheel chairs and home nursing equipment are available on loan in many areas from such organizations as the Red Cross Society and St. John's Ambulance Association. Otherwise, applications for medical aids such as wheel chairs, dentures, and spectacles can be made directly to the relevant government departments concerned with welfare. In such instances these aids are given free.

Housing

Housing needs are met in various ways and the state local authorities, welfare organizations, and the private sector all play a role in the provision of accommodation.

In the early nineteenth century, institutions such as the Zeemans Hospital in Cape Town cared for the chronic sick, for female lepers, and for the feeble minded. The aged were included in these categories where appropriate. The idea of separate homes for the aged developed in the last quarter of the nineteenth century, when several homes were initiated by private charitable organizations and individuals. The Dorcas Home for Aged women was opened in the Cape in 1883, and a home for men was founded in Cape Town in 1896. In Natal, Nazareth House was established in Durban in 1898 and provided accommodation for children and the aged of both sexes. Homes of this order were also established in other parts of the country.

By 1920, as far as can be ascertained, there were about 17 homes for the aged in the Union of South Africa, accommodating approximately 400 residents. After Union in 1920, provincial authorities made grants available to some of these homes.

With the formation of the Department of Social Welfare in 1937, the subsidy scheme for homes for the aged was developed. This covered furniture and a per capita grant which, in principle, still exists today and will be described later. At this stage the Department of Social Welfare served all race groups, but today there are four separate departments, as mentioned earlier, serving the four main race groups in the country.

Departmental policy is to promote the appointment of trained nursing staff in homes which cater to the infirm and aged. Capitation grants to homes are paid on a differential scale according to the classification of the aged person, i.e., normal, infirm, frail, and very frail. Classification is made according to the number of nursing personnel required. The subsidies for Whites in all the classifications are higher than for the other race groups.

The Department of Plural Relations (for the Black race) recognizes two categories of aged persons, i.e., the normal aged and the chronic incapacitated, including the frail aged. However, grants are assessed according to the needs of the specific homes. Grants are either paid directly to the homes by the Department of Plural Relations or administered by the relevant Administration Boards (local authority).

Subsidies to build homes for all race groups are provided through the Department of Community Development. The relevant department concerned with welfare must approve the ground plan; then application is made to the Department of Community Development for a building loan, which is normally granted on a long-term basis of 30 to 40 years at a subeconomic interest rate of 1%. The building must satisfy minimum standards according to the Housing Act of 1966. The subdivision of the Welfare of the Aged of the Department of Social Welfare and Pensions is prepared to give advice to architects, welfare organizations, and other interested bodies. This department also lays down a method of screening applicants for homes. There must be a selection committee including a professional officer from the Department of Social Welfare and Pensions or there is liaison with the other relevant departments.

In May 1968, the Department of Community Development established a standing committee entitled the Committee on Standards for Welfare Housing. The membership of this committee includes representatives from the Department of Community Development, the National Housing Committee, and the Department of Social Welfare and Pensions. The committee is responsible for liaison with these bodies in order to set up effective standards for institutional care and suitably adapted housing for the aged, as well as the provision of loans for such housing from the National Housing Fund. Money provided by the Department of Community Development for Housing is often administered by local authorities who in some cases build houses for the aged.

The Pretoria municipality provides "loans" to old age pensioners to alter their houses where necessary to make accommodations more suitable or to do necessary renovations. The pensioners are not asked to repay the loans during their lifetime but are asked to bequeath their houses to the local authority. On the whole, the state has preferred to assist organizations to establish homes for the aged rather than to provide such services itself.

At the end of 1975, the Minister for Social Welfare and Pensions stated that there were 259 subsidized homes for the aged providing accommodation for 14,560 White persons, including 7,420 infirm persons on a subeconomic basis and 2,345 on an economic basis. The figures given in Parliament in 1977 were that a total of 361 homes provided accommodation for 21,828 White persons. The subsidies are paid on a per capita basis and also cover furniture and interest losses. In addition to the 361 subsidized homes, another 65 homes were registered in 1975, providing accommodation for 2,237 White persons. There are four state homes for White aged.

The Department of Social Welfare and Pensions also has four settlements to accommodate indigent White people, including a number of old people. Settlements were started by the government during times of economic distress in order to help people rehabilitate. The first settlement for the aged was started by the Department of Labour in 1931 and was later taken over by the Department of Social Welfare in 1938 soon after the latter's formation.

The Department of Coloured Affairs subsidizes 16 homes, providing accommodation for 1,266 residents. Fourteen of these homes are in the Cape, one in Natal, and one in the Transvaal. This department has one state home, de Novo at Kraaifontein in the Cape, which accommodates 300 men and women, including indigent aged and the chronically infirm.

The Department of Indian Affairs does not have any state home, although it does subsidize two homes for Indian aged, both in Natal: the Aryan Benevolent Homes in Durban and in Pietermaritzburg. It is interesting to note that the home in Durban, now known as the Clayton Gardens Home for the Aged, originated from the Benevolent Home for the Aged and Destitute in Durban established in 1916 by the organization Arya Yuvuk Sabha formed by the Indian Community. In 1924, the Home was awarded an annual grant of R100 from the Indian Immigration Department and in 1925 the province of Natal made a grant of R200. In 1946 added facilities enabled the Institution to provide separate buildings for the aged and the children, who had been accommodated first in 1926. In 1965 the aged section moved to its present quarters, a group of cottages formerly housing White aged persons even though it is in an Indian proclaimed area. Today this home has 31 cottages for dependent aged, 19 cottages for independent couples, a 28-bed hospital, and a physiotherapy clinic. A fulltime social worker is employed, and in the day centre there is provision for group work activities and occupational therapy.

The Department of Plural Relations and Development subsidizes four homes in White areas, and in certain housing schemes some of the accommodations have been set aside for aged person. There are at least 25 homes in the various Homelands. Figures given in Parliament during 1977 revealed that the 250 homes accommodated 2,682 persons. Approximately half of the accommodation is for frail aged.

Housing in the Private Sector

An interesting project has been undertaken in Claremont, a Black township near Durban. A Black Women's Group under the aegis of the Young Women's

Christian Association has launched a scheme to build an old age home. The members of the group canvased the people of the area to ascertain whether an old age home was needed, and today they have a waiting list for the prospective home. In addition to its own fund-raising efforts, the group has been assisted by a Rotary club as well as the Urban Foundation, an organization particularly interested in the improvement of the quality of life, mainly in the urban African townships of South Africa.

There are a wide variety of schemes instituted by the private sector. Special groups—such as Women's Institutes, Memorable Order of the Tin Hat, Sons of England, Red Cross Society, South African Nurses' Trust Fund, many church groups and service organisations—have been responsible for the development of homes for the aged. Also, many groups have been formed specifically for such a purpose. The majority of these homes serve White persons, although there are several for the other race groups. Some complexes are very large, housing as many as 800 residents. In many cases different types of accommodation are included in the same complex.

Organizations have been encouraged, particularly by the South Africa National Council for the Aged and by the government through subsidies, to include accommodation for frail aged in their homes. This has been found to be an ever-increasing need. Generally speaking, these accommodations include provision for independent or semiindependent living through self-contained cottages or bed-sitters, with some cooking facilities as well as communal living. There are also arrangements which provide for approximately 6 to 8 persons. An example of this is the complex a Natal business woman built. To her own home she added four adjoining fully furnished flats, which she offered to pensioners at a nominal rental. She also gave the residents access to a fruit and vegetable farm for their daily requirements as well as a swimming pool.

At one home in Natal, persons are given the opportunity to sponsor a cottage. To be eligible, a man must be 65 years and a woman 60 years. Sponsors may live in the cottages for their lifetime; thereafter cottages revert to the organization. The present capital outlay for a cottage varies from R5,000 to R14,500.

A home at Pinelands in the Cape Peninsula has a donorship scheme which will ensure rent free accommodation for the rest of the donor's lifespan. Donors also have preference over other applicants. Accommodation in this scheme consists of self-contained flats of various sizes.

Some homes are confined only to social pensioners; some homes have an income limit but do not confine themselves to social pensioners. Charges may be at a flat rate or on a pro rata basis. Some homes require residential or other qualifications.

One organization which has concerned itself with low-cost housing for the aged is the Association for the Aged (TAFTA) in Durban. In addition to special homes that have been built, this organization has bought several accommodation blocks in order to retain flats and rooms occupied by old people and avoid the selling of the buildings for other purposes. At the present time TAFTA is considering buying a hotel which has gone into liquidation. This hotel has just over 100 rooms, most of which have private bathrooms. If the conversion to an old age home takes place, accommodations should be of a relatively high standard. Many old people find accommodations in private nursing homes which cater to both normal and frail aged.

Services at old age homes include physiotherapy, occupational therapy, chiropody, and hairdressing. Various types of recreation are provided, such as bingo, bridge, whist, carpet bowls, and croquet. Typical facilities are a post office, a tuck shop, a sewing room, a provincial library, and a chapel. There are many volunteers who assist by providing transportation for residents, taking them shopping, showing films, or taking people on outings. At one home, volunteers have formed a duty roster to assist in times of staff shortages.

Finally, it is worth noting that the Witwatersrand Training College for Advanced Technical Education runs a two-year correspondence course for the training of personnel of old age homes. This course has played its part in the raising of standards in the care of the aged.

Private Welfare Organizations and Other Services

A great variety of services are offered to the aged through family welfare organizations, specialized welfare organizations, service centres, church groups, service organizations, and other private endeavors. Coordinating the private welfare organizations' efforts to assist the aged is the South African National Council for the Aged, which was founded in 1956. Many, but certainly not all, organizations working for the aged are affiliated with this body. The formation of this council was stimulated by the interest generated at the first National Conference on the Welfare of the Aged, which was convened by the Department of Social Welfare in 1950. At this time there was increasing realization of the special needs of the aged. Specific attention was being paid to the aged in the United States, Great Britain, and other countries. This prompted welfare agencies in South Africa to request the conference. The formation of the council has been an important coordinating force in work with the aged in South Africa.

The council is a member of the International Federation on Aging. Stated briefly, the aims of the council are:

(1) to promote the interests and well-being of the aged,
(2) to coordinate activities of all welfare services among the aged,

(3) to acquire and distribute information concerning the needs of the aged,
(4) to serve as a channel for member organizations to negotiate with government authorities, including matters of legislation,
(5) to encourage and extend welfare work among the aged,
(6) to cooperate with National and International organizations (the Council is a member of the International Federation on Aging).

The Council appoints subcommittees for special purposes. For example, a medical subcommittee has recently given its attention to health services. This committee paid particular interest to the passing of the new Health Act. It is at present interested in the establishment of a chair of geriatrics at the University of Cape Town. Toward this end, it is working in conjunction with the Faculty of Medicine at the University of Cape Town and the Cape Peninsula Welfare Organization for the Aged. A chair of geriatrics is also planned for the University of the Witwatersrand. Such developments should help to highlight the problems of the elderly in South Africa.

One feature of the work of this national council was the institution of the Honour our Aged Week in 1962. Agencies throughout the country have been encouraged to draw the attention of their communities to its aged members during one particular week of the year. Programs for the week vary from place to place and time to time. The National Council also has two publications, *Senior News*, a quarterly publication mainly for the benefit of organizations, i.e., to keep them up-to-date with new developments, and *Seratus*, a bimonthly newspaper published for senior citizens themselves.

The National Council for the Aged has also undertaken minor research projects through funds made available from the Zerilda Steyn Memorial Trust and Sunday Times National Charity Fund. The following inquiries have been conducted: the health needs of geriatric patients discharged from hospital, rehabilitation of patients with cerebrovascular accidents, a study of Zulu women past the age of childbearing in Kwa Zulu (with reference to the role of the elderly women in Zulu Society), research in conjunction with the geriatric assessment unit attached to Valenberg Psychiatric Hospital in the Cape. In addition, this council is undertaking direct research in connection with service centres throughout the Republic with a view to advice and guidance concerning the establishment and functioning of such centres.

Qualified social workers are employed in many of the organizations, and the relevant government departments offer subsidies for such posts. In the past, the basis of the subsidies laid emphasis on the casework method, but the policy is changing and agencies are finding it easier to develop group work and community services. Social work services offered by such agencies include supportive help, material help, counseling services in relation to family problems, personality difficulties, bereavement, accommodation, and pensions. In some instances administration of pensions is undertaken and general rehabilitative services are rendered. Group work is undertaken by some agencies with persons who are living in private accommodation and also with those living in homes for the aged.

Following again the policy of separate development, organizations for specific race groups are developing. In Durban, for instance, the Association for the Aged (TAFTA) works closely with the Durban Association for the Indian Aged, which was founded in 1970. TAFTA also assisted in the formation of the Durban Association for Coloured Aged in 1977.

There is a large network of clubs and service centres throughout the country. They do exist for all racial groups, although those for Coloureds, Indians, and Blacks have developed more recently and many more are needed. Service centres exist in many of the larger cities and towns, for example, Johannesburg (which also has a centre for Blacks), Cape Town (where there are 3 centres, including one for Coloureds), Durban, Pietermaritzburg, Port Elizabeth, and Pretoria. The Beehive Centre for Blacks in Johannesburg has 700 members, a social worker, a clinic, including a chiropody service, a library, a second-hand clothing shop, and a sheltered workshop. In addition, a good three course meal is served at cost. This centre was started by the Johannesburg Council for the Care of the Aged. More centres are being planned.

The Department of Community Development makes loans available for the building service centres, usually at a subeconomic interest rate of 1% per annum. Since April 1975, subsidies have been paid for service centres by the Department of Social Welfare and Pensions. Service centres receiving subsidies must maintain a minimum standard of services established by the Department of Social Welfare and Pensions. During 1975 five service centres were subsidized.

Several organizations run laundry services for Whites, Coloureds, and Indians; and one, for Blacks, in Soweto. In Pietermaritzburg members pay their electricity accounts at the Centre for the Aged, which transfers the payments to the municipal office thus minimizing traveling problems for the members.

Recently the focus has been on retirement. The inaugural conference of the National Institute for Retirement (Nira) was held in Pretoria in February 1976. At this stage retirement councils were already in existence, e.g., the Witwatersrand Retirement Council, which was established in 1967 with its head office in Johannesburg, and the Western Cape Retirement Council started in Cape Town in 1969. The Durban Retirement Council was started in 1976. It is the intention of Nira to assist in the establishment of retirement councils in other areas.

The objectives of these councils, stated generally, are to enrich and enhance the lives of all retired persons. The target group is those aged 45 years and over so that adequate preparation for retirement is made. Representatives from industry and commerce, as well as those concerned with social work services for the aged, have been involved in the development of such councils. Certain employment bureaus as well as the retirement councils assist retired persons to seek reemployment. Within the Department of Social Welfare and Pensions, an interdepartmental committee was appointed to consider "Planning for Retirement." Its report is expected in 1979. The committee's terms of reference included the organization, structure, and financial position of existing organizations offering courses in preparation for retirement, as well as the desire and need for a national program for preparation for retirement. This committee was asked to consider how such a program should be run and which department of state should be responsible.

There are many private arrangements in caring for the aged. There are some persons who invite aged persons to tea in their homes on a regular basis, members of service clubs and other organizations often take old people on outings or arrange for them to attend dress rehearsals of play productions and other shows, free of charge. One of the Rotary Clubs in Johannesburg has started a Sports and Recreation Club for Older People. Outdoor activities, including formal sports and informal games, are provided, as well as exercise classes and indoor activities for rainy days. This club has also produced a brochure entitled "Looking for a Worthwhile Project" to stimulate similar interest among other service clubs. The Mercy Aid Society of Durban provides free tea and cakes to aged persons once a month, at which time it also distributes food parcels and monthly food vouchers. At Christmas and Easter, gift vouchers and hampers are distributed. Pensioners benefit in many instances from concessions in bus travel and also at some supermarkets, dry cleaners, and hairdressers.

INCOME MAINTENANCE

Social Pensions—Noncontributory

The first form of pension in South Africa was introduced in 1837 for field cornets. In 1882 the Zuid-Afrikaanse Republiek established a pension fund under the administration of the Master of the Supreme Court when money was received from various countries during or after the war of 1880-1881. These funds were used for the support of the wounded, widows, and orphans. Monthly allowances were paid out at least until the end of the century.

In 1916 the Jeppe Commission conducted an inquiry, inter alia, into methods of assisting the indigent aged. The decision reached was that children should be responsible for supporting parents no longer able to help themselves.

During the Depression years not only were many persons without families but for some the family members were too poor to help. The Pienaar Commission of 1926 investigated the possibilities of the introduction of old age pensions and disability grants and also considered the viability of a comprehensive social security scheme.

The government of the time decided against a contributory pension scheme; and with the passing of the Old Age Pensions Act of 1928, a means-tested old age pension was introduced for Whites and for Coloureds. Men over 65 years and women over 60 years were eligible.

War Veterans' Pensions were introduced with the passing of Act No. 45 of 1941. This, in the main, corresponded to the Old Age Pensions Act but provided an additional monetary allowance. Another advantage of this act is that men may apply for the pension at the age of 60 years, the same as women, and in special circumstances they may receive a pension before reaching the age of 60 years. In 1944 old age pensions were extended to Blacks and to Indians. Legislation for the aged is consolidated in two acts: the Aged Persons Act No. 81 of 1967, which provides measures for the protection of the aged, the establishment of institutions for the aged and accommodation standards for them; and the Social Pensions Act No. 37 of 1973, which legislates for the various noncontributory pensions, including the Old Age pensions and the War Veterans' Pensions.

As mentioned earlier, State Old Age Pensions are based on a means test. The qualifying age is 65 years for men and 60 years for women. There are certain residential qualifications. The applicant must be a resident in the Republic at the time of application and either be a South African citizen or have been resident in the Republic for a period of five years immediately preceding the date of such application. However, in the latter case he must be allowed, by terms of the Aliens Act, to take up permanent residence or be exempt from such a provision for an unspecified period. Under certain conditions old age pensions may be awarded to persons who enter the Republic from other countries.

There are various regulations regarding the means test. A certain amount of "free income" is allowed which does not affect the amount of pension that is awarded. Thereafter, pensions are assessed on an individual basis according to the nature and amounts of the pensioner's income.

All persons over the age of 85 years are entitled to an attendant's allowance. This allowance was introduced in 1962, and amounts have not changed since then. Those under the age of 85 years who, because of their

Table 15.6:   Distribution of Pensions in 1976

Pension	Whites	Coloureds	Indians	Chinese	Blacks
Old Age	135,953	78,154	14,267	108	176,880
War Veterans'	14,620	6,823	211		183
Total	150,573	84,977	14,478	108	177,063

physical or mental condition, need the assistance of another person may apply for an attendant's allowance, provided the pensioner is not living in a subsidized old age home.

Anyone who defers the application of the pension is entitled to additional benefits based on the length of deferment. This additional benefit is added to the monthly pension; e.g., if a White woman first applies for a pension when she is 63 years old, she will receive, on the basis of R88 basic pension, a monthly pension of R97. For males over 70 years and females over 65 years of age, salaries or wages are disregarded for purposes of the means test but other income is taken into consideration and the pension is assessed individually. Anyone over 100 years of age may receive a pension regardless of his income.

War Veterans' Pensions are also means-tested and paid on similar conditions to the old age pensions. However, the qualifying age is, as stated earlier, normally at 60 years for both men and women. There are certain conditions of military, naval, or air service; and the pensioner is also eligible for supplementary or attendant's allowance as with the old age pension.

Figures for 1976 showing the distribution of pensions are given in Table 15.6. Old age pensions are also paid by the various Homeland Governments. In the Transkei, for example, the present old age pension is fixed at a uniform rate of R22.50 a month. It should be noted that all pensions, allowances, and so on have different payments depending on race, with Whites having the highest payments, then Coloured and Indian, and then Blacks.

Civil Pensions

At the time of the promulgation of the South Africa Act 1909, the four colonies administered their own pension laws covering retirement pensions for civil servants, members of the police force, and so forth. After Union, the Pensions Section of the Treasury was created. In 1912 the Public Service and Pensions Act was passed. The Military Pensions Board was created in 1920, and in 1923 widows pensions were granted under the new Public Service and Pensions Act. In this year also, a separate Pensions Office was established which became a separate department in 1949 and 9 years later, in 1958, amalgamated with the Department of Social Welfare to form the Department of Social Welfare and Pensions.

The Pension Funds Act passed in 1956 provides for the registration, incorporation, and dissolution of pension funds and matters relevant to these aspects. A report by the Department of Social Welfare and Pensions (1966) states that "as far as could be ascertained at the time when this legislation was considered, South Africa was the first country to pass legislation making specific provision for the registration and control of pension funds."

The Department of Social Welfare and Pensions controls the following pension and provident funds:

(1) Government Service Pension Fund, which incorporates pensions for public servants, permanent force personnel, members of the South African police and prison forces, provincial and the Territory Service staff, and pensions for widows of government servants.
(2) Government Employees Provident Fund.
(3) Associated Institutions Provident and Pension Fund, which covers persons in the employ of universities and technical colleges.
(4) Joint Pre-Union Pension Fund.
(5) Cape Widows' Pension Fund.
(6) Pension Fund for Government Non-White Employees.
(7) Authorities' Service Pension and Provident Funds.

Some of the more important pension schemes administered by the department with benefits being paid directly from state revenue are:

(1) for members of Parliament, administrators, certain persons employed in the diplomatic service, and commissioners general.
(2) for judges and their widows.
(3) for persons serving as members of statutory bodies.
(4) for employees at the Simonstown Naval Base.

At the present time a National Contributory Pension Scheme is under consideration, although it has caused considerable controversy. The idea of a contributory pension scheme has been widely supported, but, according to Gordon et al. (1978), the "proposed contribution rate of 7.9% of earnings" has been criticized particularly by existing pension funds as being "unrealistically low compared to the benefits offered." The Minister of Social Welfare and Pensions has said that it is likely to be some time before any such scheme reaches completion.

Pensions and provident funds exist in the private sector. Figures given for 1975 show that there were 104,484 pensioners and 2,845,364 members in a total of 9,535 funds. Regretfully, membership of these funds has often been confined to White employees. But, in recent years particular attention has been paid to incorporating Black employees.

Old age pensioners are not entitled to supplementary government benefits. Persons who are awaiting old age pensions may be given financial assistance through one of the relevant government departments. But this is not automatic; indeed, special application must be made for such relief. Relief to aged pensioners is given through various benevolent or welfare societies that exist throughout the country. This is often in the form of food parcels.

Consideration of the Policy of Differential Welfare Benefits

Services for the aged are fairly comprehensive but by no means universal. It is quite clear that although provisions for the aged are basically the same for all race groups, in reality marked differences do exist. Most of the problem regarding low pensions, particularly to the Blacks, Coloured, and Indians, is related to the fact that South Africa's social security system operates on a noncontributory basis and funds are more limited than they would be with a contributory scheme. Some effort has been made to overcome the disparities in the pension and subsidy schemes, but there are still substantial differences.

The justification for unequal welfare benefits appears to be based upon two interrelated factors. The first is closely linked to the historical developments of welfare in this country; the second is related to the idea that Coloured, Indian, and Black population groups enjoy a lower cost of living than that of the Whites.

Historical Justification

As mentioned in the beginning of this paper, much of the development of welfare services has been initiated by the private sector. Hare and McKendrick (1976) support this view and refer to the activities of the various church groups and other voluntary welfare organizations in the development of social welfare services in the early twentieth century. With the industrialization and urbanization that followed the discovery of diamonds and gold, many social problems arose. The Carnegie Corporation of New York financed a Commission of Investigation into the Poor White problem. One of the major consequences of the report was the National Conference on the Poor White Problem held in Kimberley in 1934. This led to the formation of the Department of Social Welfare in 1937, a government body which at that stage served all races. This department took over existing government welfare services and supported established voluntary (private) welfare organizations, the majority of which served Whites mainly. Coloureds at that time enjoyed closer liaison with the White group. The needs of the Blacks and Indians, on the other hand, were, and to some extent still are, expected to be met by the extended family system.

Initially, Blacks were essentially a rural community, and official government policy, accentuated by the group areas legislation, has been to treat them only as temporary residents of urban areas. Homeland areas now exist in close proximity to the cities so that Blacks are considered temporary residents of White urban areas with their true citizenship in the Homelands.

Traditionally in the rural areas men and women who had reached old age were considered to be an asset to the community, and they performed a number of important functions. For example, in preliterate societies they passed on the traditions and folklores of that society. Their accumulated wisdom entitled them to esteem; consequently, they were consulted on many day-to-day matters, ranging from the most appropriate time to plant and harvest crops to the customs related to the arrangement of marriages. Grandmothers and other elderly female kin provided a useful child-minding service, which released younger women for work in the fields. They were also the source of reference as far as child-rearing practices were concerned.

Under such circumstances, the onset of old age was not viewed by the individuals concerned with fear or regret, since this period of one's life was, to some extent, welcomed because of the prestige accorded the aged by the rest of the members of society.

The mores evolved that the children and other members of the family considered it their duty to care for the elderly.

For such a system to function adequately, it was necessary for the society to be closely knit and well-integrated to allow the mores related to the care of the aged to operate successfully. It was also necessary for the extended family to be self-supporting as far as food and other necessities were concerned.

The majority of the group officially classified as Indian consists of people who originally were brought from India in the nineteenth century to work in the cane fields in Natal. Again, traditionally the needs of the individual were met through the extended family system. An important aspect of life on the sugar estates was the fact that families were able to live together or at least in close proximity to one another. This system of closely knit families persisted with the drift to the towns, provided houses were large enough to accommodate the extended family. Today the Indian group is not viewed as a rural one and many of the Indian (and Coloured) families have been moved to new housing schemes where the unit is more suitable to the nuclear family.

With the emphasis on the extended family meeting the needs of the community, there has been an underdevelopment of resources by both government and private agencies to support the aged.

The Cost-of-Living Justification

Whites, it is argued, experience a significantly higher cost of living than other ethnic groups for two primary reasons. First, the cost of renting accommodation is much lower for other race groups because rents are subsidized by the government to a far greater extent than in the case of White housing. Second, food preferences differ. The realities of such an argument for differential old age pensions and other welfare benefits will now be considered.

There is little doubt that on the average Whites pay higher rents than other race groups. However, the concept of choice is extremely important as far as the renting or purchasing of housing is concerned.

Members of the White group appear to have many more opportunities to choose the area in which they wish to live, the type of dwelling they wish to rent or purchase, and the amount they are willing to spend on accommodation. There are limited opportunities for the non-White groups to purchase houses and land. The availability of these are far outweighed by the demand for them.

It can therefore be argued that with so little choice there is a justification for the charging of low rentals. Doubtless if all had a greater say about where they wished to live and the type of dwelling they desired, many would be quite willing to pay a higher proportion of their salaries toward accommodation. Differential pay scales between groups do still exist, although in several instances they have been overcome.

If one traces the evolution of food preferences in South Africa, there is little doubt that Blacks enjoy maize and it is very much part of their diet, as is rice among the Indian group. In the past in the Black rural areas there was an abundance of game to supplement this diet. Black families' wealth was indicated by the number of cattle the family owned. This tradition of measuring wealth was based on pragmatic reasoning: cattle provide milk, meat, and hides. Thus, the family could balance its diet of maize with meat and milk. They could barter these for other foodstuffs they required.

A look at any South African Indian cook book clearly illustrates that rice is supplemented wherever possible by other food in order to obtain a balanced diet.

The Black, Indian, or Coloured family whose main diet consists of maize or rice is doing so not through preference but through necessity; the family cannot afford anything else. There is ample evidence indicating that tuberculosis through malnutrition is the greatest health hazard experienced in the rural areas and homelands.

The costs of other items in a family budget such as clothing, transport, cleansing materials, medicines, schooling, heating, lighting, and so on are the same for all race groups. Schooling is in fact more expensive for the Black group since Black secondary schooling is not subsidized by the government.

It appears, therefore, that one cannot justify the payment of unequal old age pensions and other benefits through the argument that certain groups enjoy a lower cost of living.

CONCLUSION

In describing services to the aged in South Africa, certain differences have been noted. There is an awareness of these, and it is hoped sincerely that equality will come. With the development of the separation of welfare functions within the four main governments for the relevant race groups, there seems to have been a slowing down while these departments become established. But, needs in the area have perhaps been highlighted, since comparisons can be made more easily. Furthermore, the separate departments have opened up more direct channels of communication; and as the groups have been given opportunities, new services have arisen. They continue to do so, although progress is often slow. Some of the recent changes in South Africa have been improvements in some of the differential salary structures. With equal pay comes a more equal distribution of money provided by each racial group through taxation. A consequence of this should be equal distribution of social security and other welfare benefits. Other changes have occurred in legislation to make home ownership easier for the Blacks, which has been extremely difficult in the urban areas in the past. It is hoped that the necessary amendments will also be made in the welfare structure, particularly in relation to differential pensions. A move to a contributory scheme, at least in part, may well be the answer.

REFERENCES

Aging International (1975) Bulletin of the International Federation on Aging 2.

DUNHAM, A., C. NUSBERG, and S. B. SENGUPTA (1978) Toward Planning in Local Communities: An International Perspective. Washington, DC: International Federation on Aging.

GORDON, L., S. BLIGNAUT, S. MORONEY, and C. COOPER (1978) "A survey of race relations in South Africa—1977." South African National Council for the Aged. (unpublished)

HARE, I. and B. McKENDRICK (1976) "South Africa: racial divisions in social services," pp. 71-96 in Meeting Human Needs. 2: Additional Perspectives from Thirteen Countries. Beverly Hills: Sage.

SADIE, J. L. (1973) Projections of the South African population, 1970-2020. South Africa: Industrial Development Corporation of South Africa.

South Africa, Department of Information (1977) Official Year Book of the Republic of South Africa. South Africa: Government.

South Africa, Department of Social Welfare and Pensions (1966) Report of the Department of Social Welfare and Pensions, 1964-1966. South Africa: Government.

EPILOGUE
Highlights, Implications, and Summary

MORTON I. TEICHER

The basic similarity among people all over the world, regardless of culture, color, or class, is reflected in the fact that all people grow older and that this process of aging is inevitably accompanied by fraility and feebleness. Those who are offended by discussions of the problems of aging deny an eternal and universal biological fact. The process of aging is universally irreversible, universally inevitable, and universally unpreventable. Flowing ineluctably from this given fact of life is the need for collective consideration of support services. This consideration must rest on the recognition that all human beings—regardless of age—have dependency needs. These needs vary in intensity throughout the life cycle and are probably greatest in the beginning and ending phases of that cycle.

To meet these pervasive needs, a great range and variety of services are required. For aging persons, these services need to be both institutionally and community based. The choice between caring for aging persons in the community or in institutions is an artificial one. Both sets of services are essential. Similarly, both medical and social services are mandatory. To force a choice between them is as artificial as the choice between institutions and community services. Arguments between social and health authorities regarding territorial jurisdiction only result in losing the aging persons in the interstices between the disputants.

Increased interest in the care of the aging is perhaps the most important development in recent years. Forced upon us by the sheer increase in numbers of aged persons, this focus of interest should compel us to provide better services to this growing segment of the world's population. The services which are required need to be comprehensive, coordinated, caring, and concerned. The services have to express our commitment to the aging and to their families. This commitment has to be translated into well-financed services along a broad continuum which recognizes diversity of need and the changing nature of need as aging persons move through a lengthening life cycle.

Our review of services to the aging has taken us to many countries. Among the revelations of this review is that we still have a long way to go. No single country has yet solved the problem of meeting the needs of aging persons.

While it may well be that the problem is ultimately insoluble, it is clear that some countries are closer to solutions than others. We still have much to learn.

NOTES ON THE CONTRIBUTORS

M. M. DESAI received her Master of Science in Social Work at Columbia University in 1950 and returned to her native India, where she has participated in a variety of important social work efforts, including the development of industrial social work units in several industries in Bombay. She was on the faculty of the Delhi School of Social Work and then joined Tata Institute of Social Sciences in Bombay, where she serves today as Professor and Head of the Department of Family and Child Welfare. She has held important posts with the governments of India and Ceylon and was a United Nations advisor.

YECHIEL ERAN is a Community Services Coordinator for the Association for the Planning and Development of Services for the Aged in Israel. He is also a lecturer at the Tel Aviv University School of Social Work, and he served previously as a lecturer at the Paul Baerwald School of Social Work of the Hebrew University in Jerusalem. He holds an M.S.W. from the University of California at Berkeley as well as a Bachelor of Arts degree in social work from the Hebrew University. He has held important posts in social planning and community organization in Iran and Israel.

AURELIA FLOREA was born in Roumania and was educated in Italy, where she received a degree in political science as well as a diploma of social work from the University of Rome. A prolific writer, Aurelia Florea is director of the Instituto Superiore per gli Studi sui Servizi Sociali in Rome and the editor of the magazine *La Rivista di Servizio Sociale*. She has conducted a number of major studies in the field of social welfare focused on gerontology.

HENNING FRIIS is the Director of the Danish National Institute of Social Research in Copenhagen, Denmark. Following completion of graduate studies in economics at the University of Copenhagen, he served as Social Science Advisor to the Danish Ministries of Social Affairs and Labor and as a member of a number of governmental committees on various aspects of social welfare. He served as Chairman of the Social Science Committee of the International Gerontological Association and a member of the Executive Committee of the International Sociological Association. A consultant for the United Nations, he has conducted studies in Egypt, Ireland, and India. He was also a consultant for DANIDA and the Ford Foundation in the Philippines and Bangladesh.

CELESTINE FULCHON is consultant for the Natural Supports Program of the Older Persons Service of the Community Service Society of New York. She completed her doctoral studies in social psychology at New York University, where she served as a graduate assistant in the Human Relations and Social Policy Program.

ADRIENE GOMMERS is a doctor of medicine and a geriatrician. She is head of the Unit of Gerontology and Director of the Graduate Program in Health Services Administration at the School of Public Health of the University of Louvain in Belgium. Her principal work has been in the area of biological parameters of aging, in which she has published numerous articles and research reports.

BERNADETTE HANKENNE is a Registered Nurse with a Master of Arts in Health Services Administration. She has organized domiciliary health care services and has done research on the hospitalization of the aged in Belgium. At present she is conducting an investigation of the role of nursing personnel in old age institutions.

ELSIE HELLER is Specialist in Geriatric Services of the Community Mental Health Services of Westchester County. Prior to her present post, she was on the faculty of the Graduate School of Social Work of New York University. She has served as supervisor of the program of intercountry adoption for International Social Service.

FRED D. HIRT is Executive Director of the Miami Jewish Home and Hospital for the Aged. He is also on the faculty of Florida International University. Mr. Hirt serves as chairman of the Nursing Home Ombudsman Committee. Active in several national welfare organizations, he has appeared on several national television programs to discuss the problems of aging. He holds a Master's degree in Hospital Administration from Wagner College Polyclinic Medical School.

IRIS ELLEN HUDIS is Group Services Coordinator for the Natural Supports Program of the Community Service Society of New York. She received her Master of Social Work degree from Columbia University and has a Post-Master's Certificate in Gerontology from the Brookdale Center on Aging of Hunter College. She taught statistics for the behavioral sciences in the Department of Psychology at the University of Miami.

M. D. KHETANI has been involved in social work research in India since 1974. Her last post was with the Tata Institute of Social Sciences. She is currently a doctoral candidate in social work at Washington University in St. Louis. A member of the Indian Association of Trained Social Workers, she was educated in Bombay and holds a Master of Arts in Social Work as well as a Certificate in Social Research from the Tata Institute of Social Sciences, Deonar, Bombay.

SUSAN K. KINOY is Associate Executive Director for Program Services of the Community Council of Greater New York. She is the professional adviser to its Citizen's Committee on Aging. Formerly the Director of the Kingsbridge Neighborhood Project on Aging, in Bronx, New York, and creator with Jack Ossofsky of "Project Find," she is Instructor of Social Policy and Aging at Adelphi Brookdale Post-Graduate Gerontology Center and at Columbia University School of Social Work Continuing Education Program.

VIRGINIA C. LITTLE holds a doctorate in International Relations from Yale University and a Master's degree in social work from Smith College. She is presently Professor at the University of Connecticut School of Social Work, where she has been a faculty member since 1967. She is also a Fellow of the U.S. Gerontological Society. Her special interest in social service delivery systems for the aging has involved study trips to more than twenty countries in the last five years. She serves as home care consultant for the State of Connecticut and the Capital Region Community Council. She is the principal American investigator in a cross-national research project with Japan and the first U.S. associate of *Age Concern-England*.

LOUIS LOWY is Professor of Social Work and Associate Dean of Boston University School of Social Work. He also serves as an associate member of the Department of Sociology at the same university. Born in Prague, Czechoslovakia, he studied philosophy at Charles University before his arrival in the United States, where he continued his studies for a professional degree at Boston University and a doctorate at Harvard University. Dr. Lowy has had extensive experience in professional social work in the field of group work. In 1961 he was asked to become director of training programs for